Factories for learning

Manchester University Press

Praise for *Factories for learning*

Kulz's brilliant and chilling ethnography of Dreamfields Academy shows that students no longer merely learn to labour, as Paul Willis once put it, but rather education itself becomes a factory. Schools do not foster critical intelligence but rather make, shape and discipline young people in the doctrine and dream world of neoliberal capitalism. The book reveals the cruel hopes and authoritarian aspects of a modern urban academy schooling. It left me with a sense of outrage because these black, white and Asian working-class students, and every student for that matter, deserve so much more from education than this. This book outlines with sociological precision and keen attentiveness the shape of that educational betrayal.

Professor Les Back, Goldsmiths, University of London

This book is a 'must read' for all, particularly for teachers and parents. Christy Kulz's ethnographic study unmasks how education practice within an urban academy school is raced, classed and gendered. This timely and exceptional book reveals how inequity is sedimented within the academies policy. It reveals a complex picture of how this academy is led and managed; how the relentless pursuit of better outcomes drives the ambitious aspirations of the headteacher and how the ethos of 'structure liberates' reflects the zealous drive to educate and civilise 'urban' children to become units of economic productivity to attain social mobility. The headteacher's evangelistic zeal is realised through disciplinary and regimented processes which subjugate teachers and pupils.

Christy Kulz shows how inequality is perpetuated in the school through the panoptic architecture of the school buildings, the stark surveillance of pupils and the enforcement of draconian rules which re-inscribe gender, race and class stereotypes within a regimen that serves to 'normalise' or whiten pupils' identities. She shows how this results in symbolic violence on black and minority ethnic bodies and how, for some pupils, the promise of social mobility remained an unrealised aspiration given the insurmountable structural inequalities they encountered every day.

This book will be a seminal text documenting the effects of the academies policy on schools, teachers and a generation of young people.

Professor Vini Lander, Edge Hill University

Christy Kulz has produced an incendiary and detailed account of the reality of life in an academy school. Kulz's ethnographic research, using a single school case study to explore wider issues of education reform, control and the creation of inequity, is in the best traditions of British sociology of education. The book is essential reading for anyone interested in the grim reality of education on the conveyor belt that lies behind the shiny deceitful rhetoric of aspirations and social mobility.

Professor David Gillborn, University of Birmingham

Factories for learning

Making race, class and inequality in the neoliberal academy

Christy Kulz

New Ethnographies

Series editor
Alexander Thomas T. Smith

Manchester University Press

Published by Manchester University Press
Altrincham Street, Manchester M1 7JA

www.manchesteruniversitypress.co.uk

British Library Cataloguing-in-Publication Data
A catalogue record for this book is available from the British Library

ISBN   978 1 5261 1617 8   hardback
ISBN   978 1 5261 1619 2   paperback

First published 2017

Typeset in Minion by
Servis Filmsetting Ltd, Stockport, Cheshire
Printed in Great Britain by
TJ International Ltd, Padstow, Cornwall

Contents

Figures

Foreword

Ask any parent, guardian or carer what they want for their child – they will tell you 'a good education and a happy life'. For us education is the golden key that opens the door to the 'good life'. If you are lucky enough to walk through its gilded portals (and 130 million girls in the Global South can't), you will enter the hallowed halls of 'the meritocracy'. In the mesmerising world of meritocracy you are offered the dream of social mobility. It holds out the promise that if you have high aspirations and are naturally gifted with intelligence and talent, you can break free of the chains of your birth and climb the ladder to ultimate success. In our so-called post-equality, colour-blind world where race and gender are off the political agenda, the shiny promise of 'happy-ever-after' futures lies at the end of the meritocratic rainbow for everyone, whatever their background – or so the seductive fairy-tale of neoliberal success goes. Our twenty-first century political leaders, Blair, Obama, Cameron and Trump, have all euphorically espoused the 'audacious power of hope' and the benefits of 'living in an aspiration nation', in which 'anyone can make it to the top'. It is ironic that in this neoliberal age, marked by the unfettered free-market economic self-interests of a small but powerful plutocratic ruling political elite, their enthusiastic commitment to meritocracy as a means to 'uplift' the 'poor and huddled masses' has been far from realised. The proof of the 'equality' pudding is in the eating, and despite the plutocracy's unshakable faith in meritocracy, the inequality gap between the rich and poor in Britain, as in the USA, is entrenched and growing. In fact, recent OECD figures show Britain is among the lowest in the developed world for social mobility, with class differences stagnant since the 1970s and our earnings more likely to reflect our fathers' than in any of the other OECD countries.

How we achieve this meritocratic dream of social mobility in a fundamentally inequitable society, deeply riven with the historic fissures of racist, classist and sexist divisions, is the question that lies at the heart of our heated debates on the relationship between educational inequality and social mobility. In Britain the political battle lines for achieving educational mobility are drawn, not on redressing the inevitable dead-end 'destiny' of structural inequalities of race, class and sex 'ascribed' at birth, but rather in the ideological sand of which type of schools can best 'engineer' the cracks in the walls of these seemingly insurmountable structural social inequalities. In a tug of war over our children's education, the political elite on both the 'left' and 'right' cannot agree on the way forward and, as a result, we have evolved a chaotic hotchpotch of educational provision to confuse even the most clued-up, 'opportunity-seeking' middle-class parent. In our British two-tier educational class system, state initiatives sit alongside well-established fee paying private schools. The independent and public school systems are designed exclusively for the small but influential wealthy elite. In the patchwork of state institutions we have faith schools and selective grammar schools, the traditional engines of meritocracy, which divisively 'cream off' the chosen few. Many comprehensive schools on the 'sink estates' where the bulk of the working class residuum reside have now become academies. Under the umbrella of these centrally funded 'aspirational', deregulated, free-market schools are separatist initiatives such as 'free' schools, designed to cater to the neoliberal sentiment of 'consumption' through 'choice' for the 'just about managing classes'. Last but not least are the academies' 'poor relative', the vocational city technology colleges, which mop up the human casualties of the academic meritocratic dream. It is not an education system that seems to be serving the poor and disadvantaged working classes very well. As the Government's 2016 Social Mobility Commission's report, *State of the Nation,* shockingly shows, just five per cent of children eligible for free school meals gain five A*-A grades at GCSE.

Christy Kulz's important and timely book is about the inner workings of the academy school system. In what she so aptly calls *Factories for learning* she reveals exactly how, in both overt and imperceptible ways, the meritocratic ethos of neoliberal aspirations is woven into the fabric of our educational establishments. Andrew Adonis, one of the early 'masterminds' of academies, proclaimed the aim of these schools is to, 'break the cycle of underachievement in areas of social and economic deprivation … by establishing a culture of ambition to replace the poverty of aspiration'. This causal vision firmly locates systemic educational failure at the unaspirational feet of the feckless black and white working class communities who live in 'disadvantaged' areas. Funded directly by central government and free from local authority control, academies invited business sponsorship into their free-market solution to balance the books of social disadvantage. Academies have been systematically rolled out at a pace since their heady inception. Now almost two in three secondary schools are academies, extending their reach to one in every four pupils. They grew from a nascent stream of a few experimental schools under New Labour in the early 2000s to a veritable flood of glistening Coalition and Conservative flagship institutions with 'state-of-the-art' buildings and highly paid superheads. These are the lucky ones. The not-so-lucky, less celebrated schools in the more deprived cities and regions of Britain have to make do with the traumatic process of restructuring so they can 'rise like a phoenix', rebranded as an academy. However, despite the unabated enthusiastic political commitment to academies, the evidence from respected independent sources such as Ofsted and the Sutton Trust shows academies are clearly not working to raise the attainment of the most disadvantaged pupils. Moreover, beneath the high profile media stories of academy success, glitz and glamour, some have been found to engage in the 'dark arts' of disappearing failing children, who threaten their ranking on the all-important, 'live or die' league tables. With little scrutiny and accountability of academy governing bodies, financial scandals abound in which those entrusted with our children's education are stealing the 'food' out of our babes' mouths.

Looking back at the genealogy of the academy school system I realise, with a sense of shameful culpability, that I was there when the idea of the academy school system was first 'birthed' as a solution to the malaise of poor standards and failing schools in Britain. It was twenty years ago, in 1997, when New Labour under Tony Blair swept to power after years of being kept out in the cold by the Conservative regime. The modern Cool Britannia, 'can-do', neoliberal British society was born in a euphoric blaze of hope and glory. The Prime Minister Tony Blair's mantra was *'education, education, education'* and within weeks of his election I was invited by David Blunkett, the Secretary of State for Education and Employment, to be member of the Schools Standards Task Force. It was a select meeting of the great and good in education, arts and entrepreneurship, and we set about with great gusto with talk of 'turning around' failing schools and 'raising standards' through literacy and numeracy – and who wouldn't want that! I often wondered why I was there. I was from the 'ivory tower' of academia, not an educational practitioner, and the only woman of colour in the room, but it soon became clear. My research on the radical work of the black Caribbean supplementary school movement appealed to the 'progressive' left. The struggle of the post-war Caribbean migrant 'Windrush generation' to set up their own black-run schools outside and in opposition to the hostile racist state education system, stuck a chord with the beating heart of the New Labour's neoliberal ideology and its turn to marketising education. Little did I realise at the time that what I saw as transformative grassroots radical action through commitment to education would be turned on its head and embraced as the true embodiment of 'aspirational meritocracy' – a prime example of disadvantaged communities 'doing it for themselves.' Before I knew it the energy and resilience of the black women who ran the supplementary schools was being harnessed as a model for 'out of school provision', especially for the excluded black kids! The market prevailed – just as it does with academy schools.

In Christy Kulz's seminal book we can find many answers as to why academies are failing their pupils. Kulz's spellbinding ethnography of Dreamfields Academy, a fictional name for a real school, focuses on the everyday detail of school life. This case study of one urban school offers a refreshing insight into a dimension of school life, illuminating the seductive grasp of market-driven neoliberalism and its effect on the lives of working-class pupils in contemporary educational spaces. Kulz describes her personal dilemma of being a former employee now embedded as a researcher, in what often seemed like a war zone. In the year and a half she spent at the coal face at Dreamfields she documented the subtle institutional disciplinary regimes that reproduce racialised, class and gender inequalities. From her vivid descriptions of the charismatic headteacher, to the overworked teachers, to the multiracial pupils who were schooled to be like 'robots', and their anxious, aspirational parents, Kulz reveals the complexity of the ascendant market-driven neoliberal discourse framing twenty-first century British education. Deploying the metaphor of the 'conveyer belt', Kulz deconstructs the journey the pupils take from innocence and freedom to fear and compliance. The panoptical surveillance afforded by the glass buildings and the spirit-breaking, military disciplinary regime ensured the chaotic 'difference and diversity' of the urban residuum was erased and replaced by an 'inspirational' middle-class subjectivity and work ethic. White middle-class values and ideals of 'good behaviour' defined success and those that failed to comply were relegated to the darkness of the penal confines of the dreaded LSU (Learning Support Unit), or exiled beyond – excluded from school and cast out into a medieval-like oblivion.

At the core of Dreamfields Academy is Mr Culford, the Headteacher whose mantra, 'structure liberates', is grounded in his firm belief that working-class urban children are 'unhappy', coming as they do from chaotic and unstructured backgrounds. As he argues, his school's 'structure' liberates them to do better. Kulz's elegant prose powerfully captures the frustrations, terror and comedy of abject situations in which this 'structure' unfolds. There are the bizarre assemblies where Mr Culford espouses contemporary morality tales of good and evil and rags to riches to inspire the young people into the culture of 'aspiration'. Then there is the madness of the frenetic after-school 'chicken shop run' where security guards drive around in a Mercedes Benz policing the pupils' penchant for unhealthy deep-fried 'working-class snacks'. While some pupils are 'knowing subjects' and perform symbolic resistance through feigning submission and dissent, most learn to play the 'game' as it is a futile endeavour to resist the neoliberal promise of happiness!

Christy Kulz's *Factories for learning* is a worthy twenty-first-century addition to the classic canon of school ethnographies written in the 1970s, 1980s and 1990s. Lacey's *Hightown grammar* (1970), Stephen Ball's *Beachside comprehensive* (1981), Máirtín Mac an Ghaill's *Young, Gifted and Black* (1988), and my own *Young, Female and Black* (1992) drew on the long-established sociological tradition of 'identity' studies. Focusing on youth subcultures and teacher-pupil relations, we sought to expose the 'inside story' of how schools reproduce social inequalities through 'cultures of reproduction'. When I first read Kulz's book I immediately thought of Paul Willis's ground-breaking study *Learning to labour* (1970). While Willis's white working-class 'lads' performed their elaborate anti-work cultures of resistance in the post-industrial age, forty years on Kulz's sophisticated intersectional study reveals the complex nature of the seductive neoliberal turn. Far from rebelling, most young black, white and Asian working-class students in Dreamfields work hard to remake themselves into 'good workers' in order to access the bounties of the happy neoliberal 'good life'.

I hope you enjoy reading this beautifully crafted book as much as I did. It is an insightful, critical and perceptive tale of life in a modern urban school, which powerfully lifts the lid on the cruel and pervasive 'myth of meritocracy', so we can honestly begin to answer the crucial but elusive question, 'why is there still so little social mobility in Britain?'

Heidi Safia Mirza

Acknowledgements

First I would like to thank the students, teachers and parents at Dreamfields Academy who generously offered their stories, time and help. I would also like to thank the Economic and Social Research Council for providing the funding that made this research possible, as well as those at Manchester University Press for their help preparing this manuscript. Special thanks goes to Heidi Mirza for her continual encouragement and generosity of spirit and to Beverley Skeggs and Kirsten Campbell for their superlative guidance. The NYLON new scholars' network and the Race, Ethnicity and Postcolonial Studies group both provided stimulating spaces for sharing ideas; many thanks to my colleagues who read drafts and offered valuable feedback. I also enjoyed the much-needed camaraderie of Margarita Aragon, Anna Bull, Miranda Iossifidis, Malcolm James, Hannah Jones, Joshua Paul, Carolina Ramirez, Naaz Rashid and Philippa Thomas along the way. Thanks to my parents for their support and to Kerry Holden, Sarah Howard, Charlie Revell and Lucy Wells for friendship and fruitful discussions. Finally, my appreciation goes to Jake Painter for his patient care and to Vita 'Pop' for her continual sunshine.

Abbreviations

ASBO	Anti-Social Behaviour Order
CTC	City Technology College
DfE	Department for Education
ERA	Education Reform Act
GCSE	General Certificate of Secondary Education
HOY	head of year
IRP	independent review panel
LEA	Local Education Authority
LSU	Learning Support Unit
MAT	multi-academy trust
PE	physical education
PTA	Parent Teacher Association
SATs	Standard Attainment Tests
SIMS	School Information Management System
SLT	Standard Attainment Tests
SMT	Senior Management Team

Series editor's foreword

When the *New Ethnographies* series was launched in 2011, its aim was to publish the best new ethnographic monographs that promoted interdisciplinary debate and methodological innovation in the qualitative social sciences. Manchester University Press was the logical home for such a series, given the historical role it played in securing the ethnographic legacy of the famous 'Manchester School' of anthropological and interdisciplinary ethnographic research, pioneered by Max Gluckman in the years following the Second World War.

New Ethnographies has now established an enviable critical and commercial reputation. We have published titles on a wide variety of ethnographic subjects, including English football fans, Scottish Conservatives, Chagos islanders, international seafarers, African migrants in Ireland, post-civil war Sri Lanka, Iraqi women in Denmark and the British in rural France, among others. Our list of forthcoming titles, which continues to grow, reflects some of the best scholarship based on fresh ethnographic research carried out all around the world. Our authors are both established and emerging scholars, including some of the most exciting and innovative up-and-coming ethnographers of the next generation.

New Ethnographies continues to provide a platform for social scientists and others engaging with ethnographic methods in new and imaginative ways. We also publish the work of those grappling with the 'new' ethnographic objects to which globalisation, geopolitical instability, transnational migration and the growth of neoliberal markets have given rise in the twenty-first century. We will continue to promote interdisciplinary debate about ethnographic methods as the series grows. Most importantly, we will continue to champion ethnography as a valuable tool for apprehending a world in flux.

Alexander Thomas T. Smith
Department of Sociology, University of Warwick

Building new narratives: academies, aspiration and the education market

Children who come from unstructured backgrounds, as many of our children do, and often very unhappy ones, should be given more structure in their lives. So it means that the school in many ways becomes a sort of surrogate parent to the child and the child will only succeed if the philosophy of the school is that we will in many ways substitute and take over where necessary ... Therefore we want staff who commit themselves to that ethos. It's not a nine-to-five ethos; it's an ethos which says the only way that these children will achieve is if we go the extra mile for them. (Mr Culford, Principal of Dreamfields Academy)

This research focuses on Dreamfields Academy,[1] a celebrated secondary academy based in the borough of Urbanderry, which is located within the large urban conurbation of Goldport, England. Dreamfields' 'structure liberates' ethos claims to free children from a culture of poverty through discipline and routine. Since Dreamfields opened in 2004, it has become popular with parents, politicians and the media and is continually referenced as proof of the academy programme's effectiveness. The New Labour government opened over 200 academies between 1997 and 2010. The subsequent Conservative–Liberal Democrat coalition government and Conservative governments rapidly expanded and reformulated the programme so that by 1 July 2016, 5,302 schools were academies while 1,061 were on the way to becoming one (DfE, 2016). Academies were originally created by New Labour to 'break the cycle of underachievement in areas of social and economic deprivation' by 'establishing a culture of ambition to replace the poverty of aspiration' (DCFS, 2009; Adonis, 2008). Former Minister of State for Education Lord Adonis described how these schools would build aspirational cultures and act as 'engines of social mobility and social justice' at the 'vanguard of meritocracy' (Adonis, 2008). Poverty is not framed as a structural problem, but born out of 'cultures of low aspiration'. Academies have faced opposition for their lack of democratic accountability as they can set their own labour conditions, deviate from the national curriculum and operate outside local authority control.

Urbanderry is a socially and economically mixed borough where poverty and gentrification coexist. Forty per cent of Dreamfields students receive free school meals, while over eighty per cent of students come from ethnic-minority backgrounds with black African, black Caribbean, Turkish, Bangladeshi and Indian students comprising the largest groups. These statistics, indicating Urbanderry's poverty and ethnic diversity, are frequently juxtaposed with Dreamfields' outstanding test scores, which have consistently exceeded the national average in terms of the number of students achieving five A-star to C grades at General Certificate of Secondary Education (GCSE) level. This capacity to generate results has continued throughout the sixth form, with numerous students receiving offers from elite universities.

Dreamfields has dazzled politicians with its results and received a revolving door of visitors keen to replicate its magic recipe. I watched Dreamfields steadily garner public acclaim while I worked at the school; its accumulation of accolades against the odds was the stuff of Hollywood films. The 'structure liberates' ethos certainly 'worked' in terms of producing good grades, but what else did this ethos do, and how did it do it? There was clearly more going on than the straightforward achievement of test scores, as an economically deprived and ethnically diverse student population was allegedly culturally transformed. These 'goings-on' within the school connected to points beyond its iron gates, both locally and globally. My personal troubles at carrying out the ethos began to relate to wider public issues and a sociological project came into being as I sought to apply my life experiences to my intellectual work (Mills, 2000: 8–10). Surveying the largely proud student body, I could not help but feel pleased to see children who might have endured a crumbling school with substandard provision experience a sense of achievement and potentially gain access to a slice of the 'good life'. But this uplifting tale seemed to ignore the more complicated stories underlying its glossy veneer of success. Les Back writes about trusting your interest as a researcher and pursuing niggling feelings of uncertainty while others seem certain (2007: 173). Dreamfields' road to a brighter future is paved with the soaring rhetoric of the self-made citizen; however, this road and the demands made along it are rarely questioned, but positioned as an unexamined social and cultural good. This chapter begins by mapping the key questions framing the research and begins to explore the Dreamfields ethos, before examining how the birth and development of the academies programme embeds and extends a vision of marketised education originating in the 1980s. This connects to a wider turn towards authoritarian methods in education.

Mapping the questions

This book examines how raced, classed and gendered subjects are (re)produced in urban space through the discursive practices of the market-driven neoliberal school. It examines how hierarchies are being reformulated, as race and class are lived in and through one another in complex ways. At a Specialist Schools and Academies Trust annual conference Tony Blair pronounced that 'education is the most precious gift a society can bestow on its children' as he called for more academies (Blair, 2006). This research interrogates the social and cultural dimensions of this gift that seeks to graft more 'suitable' forms of capital onto its students. I will focus on the conditions underlying this gift's exchange with children, parents and teachers, remaining conscious of how value is generated from the power, perspective and relationships that create the initial conditions of possibility for exchange (Skeggs, 2004).

Dreamfields' 'structure liberates' ethos does not govern from a standpoint of neutrality, but through the daily imposition of norms. Principal Culford's interview extract at the start of this chapter signals how his interpretations of Urbanderry and its residents are presented as 'common-sense' truths; this is further explored below and in Chapter 2. Although Dreamfields' public discourse clearly states what the school is attempting to do and implements a policy with which to do it, my questions are concerned with what the discourses deployed by Dreamfields *actually do* and how they are translated into everyday practices of the self (Foucault, 2001). It explores how individual pupils, teachers and parents come to act on themselves and others in relation to Dreamfields' discourses.

The research examines how Dreamfields fits within a wider trajectory of education policy and local governance. The academy's discourses draw on historical representations rooted in empire, industrial capitalism and the development of classificatory mechanisms which constitute raced and classed forms of personhood. I interrogate how Dreamfields governs through a range of disciplinary practices before asking how students, parents and teachers interpret and receive these practices from a variety of situated positions. The research builds a complex, yet incomplete picture illuminating how neoliberal modes of governance play out in daily practice. This action occurs against the backdrop of the evangelical promotion of social mobility and meritocracy, despite increasing poverty and the continued dismantlement of the post-war settlement. I set out to provide a contextualised study of the education market in action by showing the implications neoliberal reforms and a result-driven focus have on the shaping of subjectivities. The book approaches these questions by putting Dreamfields' institutional discourses in conversation with the narratives of students, teachers and parents in order to place the macro, micro and shades in between in relation to one another. As discussed in Chapter 2, the research draws on ethnographic, interview and participatory methods to examine the research questions. Now I will use ethnographic fieldnotes to introduce and reflect on the Dreamfields ethos.

Building aspirational spaces and futures[2]

It was a late July morning in 2011 and my last day of fieldwork at Dreamfields. It was also the end-of-year assembly when over 900 pupils from Years 7 to 11 are brought together in the sports hall for speeches and awards. Fitting all these bodies into one room was a meticulously executed operation and the school was abuzz with hushed excitement. The sounds of the school band filled the room until head-teacher Culford took the podium. The room fell silent as he asked students to spend a couple of moments reflecting on the year and what they had or had not achieved. The heavy silence of hundreds of bodies shifting in plastic chairs was finally broken by Culford saying that students should never take these years for granted because the past year was a year they would never have again. He reiterated this point with such sombre conviction that I started to reflect on the previous year with newfound regret – I could have, I should have done more. Culford also urged students not to take Dreamfields for granted, pointing out the numerous advantages they had, how lucky they were and how good Dreamfields was compared to other schools. He repeated the frequently referenced Ofsted (Office for Standards in Education, Children's Services and Skills) report which described it as outstanding. Besides the amazing extracurricular activities and lessons, Culford pointed out what a wonderful building they had to learn in. He described how many schools he had visited across England were depressing places to spend the day, while Dreamfields was light, airy and open. Culford confessed that he had never given much thought to buildings before working with architects on Dreamfields' building, but he was now very aware of design.

Large images of familiar skyscrapers and prestigious buildings in central Goldport were projected onto the wall. Culford said he found these iconic buildings and centres of global finance important because they showed man's power to effect change. Regarding these towering beacons of capital, Culford pronounced that the world does not impact upon us, but we have the power to impact on the world and effect change through bold ambition. He qualified this claim with a quick under-the-breath aside that sometimes the world did affect us, but forged onwards, adding that he wanted Dreamfields students to be ambitious. Culford used the example of ancient cave paintings to demonstrate how 'man' had chosen to impact on the world by showing human ingenuity. And because of Dreamfields' no-excuses culture, it meant that it did not matter what background you were from – you could and would achieve here.

Culford then showed a picture of Larchmont Grove, the comprehensive school that Dreamfields had replaced. An image of a decrepit pre-fab building mottled with graffiti was placed beside an image of Dreamfields' gleaming new structure, juxtaposing the failure of the past with the success of the present. Finally, Culford announced that there were currently 12 million Somalians starving. In response we should appreciate what we have and give money to worthy causes, as this was all we could do to help. After this curt conclusion to a complex geopolitical disaster, he asked students to close their eyes, bow their heads and think about people who were sick, dead, or in trouble. A grave silence followed until Culford raised his head and left the podium. Gradually the mood lightened as the band launched into the feel-good hit 'Forget You' by CeeLo Green.

The message of Culford's assembly speech was similar to those preceding it: aspirational subjects can transcend structural inequalities through sheer determination. 'Structure' liberates students from their positioning, making poverty or racial inequality irrelevant. Culford has described Dreamfields Academy as an 'oasis in the desert' of Urbanderry, positioning the borough as culturally deficient while also justifying the use of disciplinarian approaches. Meanwhile, monuments to capital in wealthier districts of Goldport represent success and a wonderland of infinite possibility accessible to newly mobile subjects. Like the smaller weekly assemblies that conclude with students bowing their heads in self-reflection, the self and its achievements are continuously scrutinised and act as the focal point for intervention. Culford works hard to instigate a belief that mobility dreams can come true, reiterating the advantages held by Dreamfields students. Larchmont Grove's crumbling remains are employed to signify the supposed failure of comprehensive education to provide these opportunities. Dreamfields marks a break with this failure by asserting that students can write their own biographies (Beck, Giddens and Lash, 1994).

Approaching the site

Urbanderry is an ethnically diverse borough. In addition to residents from white British and other white backgrounds, there are substantial black British Caribbean and black British African populations, as well as Turkish, Indian, Chinese, Vietnamese, Bangladeshi and Pakistani residents. Crime rates are falling, but remain higher than the Goldport average, while significant amounts of residents receive benefits and live in social housing. Housing in the borough is disproportionately costly and gentrification has long been under way, making Urbanderry a popular destination for middle-class professionals. A mixture of estates and increasingly expensive Victorian properties surrounds Dreamfields. Growing inequalities are often brought into sharp relief through the geographic proximity of rich and poor residents (Dorling, 2014). To the north-east of Dreamfields several speciality shops stand adjacent to a block of council housing. Further north is a street lined with cafés and boutiques where patrons tinker on iPads and eat expensive sandwiches. These residents coexist with other residents like the Urbanderry Boys, a local gang. One café's sign announces that pavement seating is for customers only, while the one or two chicken and kebab shops left on the street and a small collection of public benches host a very different audience. These classed and racialised divisions in urban space are rendered highly visible due to their intense proximity, highlighting how a social mix does not infer mixing or subsequent social parity, as cleavages run across social and material space (see Benson and Jackson, 2012; Butler and Robson, 2003; Byrne, 2006; Hollingworth and Mansaray, 2012). Flattening out these glaring disparities is a key feature of Dreamfields' aspirational narrative, yet what signifies gritty appeal for some is actual danger for others.

As previously mentioned, I became acquainted with Dreamfields through my employment at the school. I had never intended to work in a school – an establishment I had few fond memories of – yet the contradictory complexities of this space brought together a number of my previous interests in unanticipated ways. Shortly after moving to Goldport with my partner, we discovered that his relative had taken a post at a new academy adjacent to our flat. While I was in need of some part-time work to supplement my work as a writer and performer, Dreamfields needed extra hands to move boxes and furniture into classrooms in frantic preparation for its September opening. A few days' heavy lifting became a long-term, part-time job, first teaching drama and later working as a learning mentor. Initially I was bewildered by Dreamfields' dynamic, disciplinarian environment. While it was undeniably positive to watch pupils receive excellent grades, the securitised, authoritarian atmosphere felt uncomfortably draconian. Yet it was repeatedly stressed in staff briefings that structure was good for students – it allowed teachers to teach and students to learn. It appeared to work, so I placed my reservations aside and tried to perform my role with conviction. Many of my subsequent interviews with teachers mentioned similar qualms and feelings of surveillance that I did not actively articulate at the time but certainly felt. As Les Back describes, by seeking out the alternative stories that are seldom the obvious feature of dominant narratives we can read against the grain and locate the bumps littering the smooth terrain of success (2007: 9).

Dreamfields has been evidenced as proof of the academy programme's effectiveness and its ethos used a blueprint for numerous urban schools and academy chains. While I am not claiming that all academies mirror Dreamfields, it is a valuable site for examining how aspirational academy rhetoric plays out in practice. This book seeks to shed light on some of the less dominant stories weaving their way in, around and through celebratory portraits of a smiling, multicultural student body unproblematically headed towards success. Now I will examine how the roots of the academy model stretch back to the education reforms of the 1980s.

Education comes to the market

Dreamfields Academy is not an anomaly, but descends from a long trajectory of educational reforms. Thatcher's 1988 Education Reform Act (ERA) dismantled the post-war education settlement through pivotal changes that shifted power towards central government while decreasing the power of Local Education Authorities (LEAs). The ERA introduced parental choice and open enrolment, monitored school performance through regular testing and the publication of results and established the national curriculum. It also evolved budgets to individual schools and instated routine inspections. Open enrolment prevented LEAs from balancing intakes across schools, allowing some schools to become oversubscribed while others withered. Linking intake to funding meant each child recruited added to a school's coffers, while losing students meant losing resources and an accelerated decline. The steady decline of Dreamfields' predecessor, Larchmont Grove, from the late 1980s until its closure in the mid-1990s can be partly attributed to these reforms.

These alterations reconfigured parents as consumers and schools as small businesses competing for survival in a local market. This focus on raising standards through competition has left behind any ideals of equitable provision for all as 'market rights' replaced 'welfare rights' and public values were effectively privatised (Ball, 1990: 6, 8). 'Choice' acts as a disciplinary mechanism, not a promoter of equality, within a market that 'rewards positioning rather than principles and encourages commercial rather than educational decision-making' (Gewirtz, 2002: 71). Middle-class cultural capital is privileged and outcomes are not meritocratic, but reflect the unfair advantages and disadvantages held by those entering this market (Reay, 1998). The national curriculum was 'steeped in a neoconservative glow' and prescriptive ideas of national culture, while the activities of progressive local authorities attempting to address issues of race, class and gender were curtailed (see Gill, Mayor and Blair, 1992: vii). Meanwhile the GCSE pass rate, the dominant way of measuring success or failure, has 'created an *A-to-C economy* in schools where "the bottom line" is judged in relation to how many higher passes are achieved' (Gillborn and Youdell, 2000: 43; emphasis added). Dreamfields' colour-blind approach and strict focus on producing the 'bottom line' efficiently caters to market demands.

The Conservatives' City Technology Colleges (CTCs) were the prototype for New Labour's academies programme. CTCs were inspired by US magnet schools implemented in urban areas in the 1970s with the intention of promoting racially and socially mixed schools through increased parental choice and competition. Although results improved, these schools were criticised for promoting inequality. Geoffrey Walford describes how the appeal of CTCs rested on breaking the influence of leftist LEAs by attracting selected pupils into a private sector while claiming to provide opportunities for inner-city youth (1991). New Labour's academies were a reincarnation of CTCs using public–private finance and were initially established in urban deprived areas. A private sponsor would contribute £2 million in exchange for shaping the school's ethos and providing inspirational leadership, while the government footed the remaining bill.[3] While private investment was highlighted, the state stumped up over £20 million to build Dreamfields compared to the sponsor's £3 million contribution.

Lord Adonis (2012: 7) proclaims that academies reinvent the inner-city comprehensive; however, academies are working from a fundamentally different premise. Funding was progressively shifted towards some disadvantaged areas of England to give New Labour's programme a social justice angle, yet the discursive shift from welfarism to a new managerialism remained intact (Gerwirtz, 2002: 46). The initial academies were 'a *condensate* of state competition policy with all its tensions and contradictions in microcosm', concerned with flexibility, entrepreneurism and the participation of 'heroes of enterprise' (Ball, 2007: 160; emphasis added). Academies signified *'a "break" from roles and structures and relationships of accountability of a state education system.* They replace democratic processes of local authority control over schools with technical or market solutions' (Ball, 2007: 177; emphasis added). Although some individuals may have gained access to money, jobs and status, marketisation fundamentally altered how the education system works.

Narratives of failure and 'loony-left' problems

The spirit of the Swann Report (1985) and its aim of 'education for all' where schooling addresses racism and promotes an understanding of multiculture are past-tense concerns in the era of academisation. In fact, these concerns are frequently associated with educational failure. Instead of the negative perceptions and unfortunate condition of some Urbanderry schools from the late 1980s throughout the 1990s being directly related to the ERA's market-led reforms, they came to be associated with anti-racist education or the goal of a comprehensive system. A significantly more complex terrain often underpinned dominant narratives portraying schools like Larchmont Grove as irredeemable sites of failure. In many urban areas in England, racial and gender-based discrimination were being fought out against a backdrop of entrenched poverty, shrinking central government investment, the implementation of school-choice policies and council mismanagement. Within the Conservatives' standards agenda, testing and inspection regimes became equated with progress. A failure–success binary became the bedrock of debates, without recognition of how the ERA structured this binary, by plunging many urban schools into daily crises that left little time for strategic management and subsequently fostered low standards and poor teaching quality (Mirza, 2009: 26).

These changes intersected with the widely publicised ridicule of some local councils as bastions of 'loony-left' policies by New Right Conservative politicians and the popular press. The New Right used numerous fictitious tales targeting white anxiety to attack anti-racist education, presenting it as the cause of British cultural decline (see Gordon, 1990). Concerns over local anti-racist movements were crafted 'into popular "chains of meaning"', providing an 'ideological smokescreen and hence popular support for the Thatcherite onslaught on town hall democracy' (Butcher et al., 1990: 116). Outlandish tales of political correctness gone awry blurred the lines of causality, with New Right organisations tying left-wing extremists and slumping educational standards to the development of anti-racist education (Tomlinson, 1993: 25–6). Many local authorities adopted less robust approaches to race equality towards the late 1980s owing to negative publicity, while the Labour Party avoided directly identifying with radical urban left authorities. Sally Tomlinson (2008) describes how there was far more commentary on anti-racist, multicultural education than action within schools. Yet the political climate of the late 1980s veered towards framing anti-racists, rather than racist attitudes, as the problem (Ball and Solomos, 1990: 12).

'Loony-left' labels discounted racial discrimination and promoted division, while concealing legitimate struggles within urban areas where radical councils were hardly equitable utopias, but also struggling with discriminatory practices (Ball and Solomos, 1990). Some ten years later, the academy programme offered a route of securing long overdue investment for Urbanderry's schools. Academies were presented as an 'apolitical' means of remaking Urbanderry while diminishing the power of LEAs. The rise in investment and attainment in urban areas like Goldport has coincided with more middle-class families migrating back to urban centres and sending their children to state schools (Butler and Robson, 2003; Hollingworth, 2015).

A progressive 'crisis'

Movement away from a comprehensive system can be traced to developments in the late 1960s and 1970s as the New Right skilfully mobilised and manipulated populist narratives to generate moral panics about falling educational standards prompted by progressive methods. The Black Papers, an influential series of pamphlets, epitomise this critique of the comprehensive system. The Black Papers were released shortly after Anthony Crosland's Labour Government requested LEAs to start converting all schools into comprehensives. Written by various authors, these polemics offered 'common-sense' home truths and claimed to speak both for and to a 'silent majority' of 'ordinary' parents who feared for their children's future. Comprehensives were framed as harmful to intelligent working-class children while eugenicists were referenced to conclude that intelligence was hereditary and made class differences inevitable (Cox and Dyson, 1969: 20). Contradictory ideas were amalgamated and framed as complementary, while the abstract figure of the 'ordinary' parent acted as a unifying concept where anxieties could be projected and differences glossed over. The Right drew on justifiable insecurities in the face of an economic downturn, placing marginalised groups in competition with one another while appealing to the individual's perceived powers to exercise choice. The Black Papers found a receptive media audience, while Labour lacked a cohesive rebuttal or coherent package of progressive policies, and Crosland's circular was revoked in 1970 by Edward Heath's Conservative government (CCCS, 1981: 163–5).

Dreamfields' focus on discipline, results and respect for authority descends from this New Right focus. The now familiar-sounding solutions to alleged violence and anarchy in schools included stricter standards for students and teachers, as well as parental vouchers promoting school choice. While the right claimed to crusade against unfair taxation and state oppression, paradoxically it enabled the creation of a more authoritarian, less visible state (CCCS, 1981: 250–1). This dynamic has been further accelerated by academies' centralisation of power and the hollowing-out of local participation in education. In the late 1970s Stuart Hall described how calls for heightened classroom discipline and an 'assault' on progressive methods were authoritarian state practices imposed in the face of an ideologically constructed crisis (1978: 34). Similar calls for discipline were made in the wake of the 2008 financial crisis and the welfare state has been steadily eroded through the imposition of austerity policies. In 1981 the text *Unpopular Education* concluded that Labour needed a more imaginative vision for education; they did not possess original ideals, interrogate its contents, or unsettle assumptions that it should cater to industry (CCCS, 1981: 265). Over thirty years later, Labour's new vision has struggled to arrive. Lord Adonis (2012) defended the Conservatives' development of free schools[4] in a *New Statesman* article entitled 'Labour should support free schools — it invented them'. Differences have become a matter of packaging and terminology, not principle. Labour's election of Jeremy Corbyn as leader in 2015 and his re-election in 2016 with an even larger mandate could signal a shift away from academisation in the future; however, the party is divided and its future direction uncertain (Mansell, 2015).

Non-democratic solutions

Technocratic settlements offered common-sense solutions in the face of difficult negotiations within urban spaces like Urbanderry. The absence of a coherent, broad programme of opposition compounded by the long-term underfunding of schools and low expectations faced by many students made academies an often welcome development. Several parents described how Urbanderry deserved Dreamfields (see Chapter 4). Overhauling 'failure' creates an opening for radical agenda-resetting, yet this settlement disregards battles over inequality while curtailing civic participation. Rather than addressing these issues, Dreamfields attempts to transcend contentious terrain through the erasure and denial of inequality. 'There is no room for voice, only for choice' as parent–school relations become a commodified matter of exchange value (Ball, 1990: 10). Schools and teachers must reconceptualise themselves as businesses, where workers produce test results via the students. Power is centralised, as the Secretary of State individually contracts each academy, and accountability to an elected local body disappears (Clayton, 2012). David Wolfe, QC, at Matrix barristers' chambers, explains how parents and pupils at academies have few direct legal rights compared to their counterparts at maintained schools, as they are no longer party to these contracts (Wolfe, 2015).

Finance capital's participation in education has also grown through academies' focus on entrepreneurialism. Take Arpad Busson, the founder of the Absolute Return for Kids (ARK) academies chain and global education corporation, who was also a founder of EIM, a hedge fund-management company.[5] These networks extend into new territory, but Ball points out how they exclude certain actors – particularly 'problematic' entities like trade unions. Membership to this network requires being on the same ideological page (2007: 133). Changes to education's administration and governance are not just technical alterations in management, but part of what Ball calls a 'broader social dislocation':

> It changes who we are and our relation to what we do, entering into all aspects of our everyday practices and thinking – into the ways that we think about ourselves and our relations to others, even our most intimate social relations. It is changing the framework of possibilities within which we act. This is not just a process of reform; it is a process of social transformation. (2007: 186–7)

This social transformation highlights how the discourses, policies and practices of neoliberalism have been planned and funded by actors who stand to profit from the deregulation of labour and resulting capital flows (Davies and Bansel, 2007: 48; see Saul, 2009). As the neoliberal state hands power to global finance and recasts people as strategic producers of their life narratives, education functions as a key site for remaking and reshaping the field of human action in ways that benefit the powerful. The financial benefits being realised by academy chains or multi-academy trusts (MATs) have resulted in numerous scandals as public funds are being paid into the private businesses of MAT trustees and executives as the private sector accesses public coffers (see Adams, 2016; Boffey, 2013; Boffey and Mansell, 2015, 2016). While global capital attempts to morally legitimate itself through running public services like education, the state validates itself through the market by allowing our public institutions to be remade as private enterprises.

Through this process, spaces of negotiation formerly provided by local authorities are forced out of existence as power is transferred to central government and its various partners in business, finance and beyond. Although often flawed, local authorities did provide a route for democratic participation. Residents were positioned as citizens and potential contributors rather than consumers. Impenetrable to the local citizen and removed from public scrutiny, these new structures do not provide any mechanism for public intervention. Instead parents, teachers and students act as passive respondents to customer satisfaction surveys. Ball describes how this new 'architecture of regulation' involving complex, intertwined relationships based both in and beyond the state is accompanied by a subsequent 'opacity' in policy which renders boundaries between the public and private ambiguously blurry (2007: 131). Actors can occupy various roles simultaneously within business, the state, philanthropy or non-governmental organisations as it becomes less obvious how, why and where decisions are being made. Opacity and 'questionable practices' were highlighted by a recent report showing that conflicts of interest were common in academy trusts, while the auditing of trusts was weak and many boards were not adhering to guidance (Greany and Scott, 2014). MATs have come to preside over numerous schools, acting as a privatised replacement for local authorities without being subject to the same level of accountability. The faceless control of unaccountable structures guiding education without a public brake to temper its motion signals the need for robust, local democratic structures.

Academies remade

Teachers' and parents' capacity to shape educational provision has been further eroded under the Coalition and Conservative governments. The Conservative–Liberal Democrat coalition oversaw a rapid expansion of academies and free schools that further detached education from structures of local accountability and embedded the academy model as the norm. The Academies Act 2010 invited all schools to apply for academy status and was rushed through Parliament using a compressed process usually reserved for the passage of emergency legislation. Widespread critiques were made as the tabling of amendments by MPs after its second reading was restricted to 30 minutes compared to the usual period of days or weeks (Vaughan and Marley, 2010). Its quick passage at the end of the summer session allowed outstanding schools to be fast-tracked into academy status by September.

Although schools deemed to be 'underperforming' still required a sponsor to convert, this was no longer necessary for adequately performing schools. For many schools, conversion was more about the hope that their budget would increase rather than the pursuit of freedom (Abrams, 2012). In January 2011 all local authorities suffered a top slice off their allocated grant to help fund the programme – regardless of the number of academies in their area; the 2011–12 slice was £148 million, rising to £265 million in 2012–13 (Benn, 2011: 29). Councils had to use £22.4 million from their budgets from 2011–12 and 2013–14 to cover the costs of schools becoming academies (Local Government Association, 2014). Benn describes how 'the aim was to create a majority of privately managed institutions … leaving a rump of struggling schools within the ambit of the local authorities, themselves undermined by savage budget cuts' (2011: 29). This extension of academies has altered the rationale behind New Labour's original policy, shifting funding away from poorer areas and creating an opening for wholesale privatisation.

The Education Act of 2011 further centralised power by giving the Secretary of State the right to direct the closure of schools causing concern. While the National Governor's Association added a clause to the bill requiring governing bodies to consult the local community before converting, these consultations have been criticised as toothless exercises. Former Secretary of State Michael Gove wielded this power with great controversy, publicly overriding parental opposition to conversions. Despite 94 per cent of parents voting 'no' to the conversion of a London primary school, it was taken over by the Harris Federation which runs a chain of 38 academies across the capital and is sponsored by Carpetright millionaire and Conservative Party peer and donor Lord Philip Harris (Aston, 2012; Sahota, 2012). Gove dubiously justified this forced conversion by appealing to racial and social inequality. Twisting the lines of causality, he referred to dissenting parents as 'ideologues who are happy with failure' who are really saying: 'If you're poor, if you're Turkish, if you're Somali, then we don't expect you to succeed. You will always be second-class and it's no surprise your schools are second-class' (Harrison, 2012). Parents at a Croydon primary school who unsuccessfully tried to block another Harris conversion called the Department for Education's (DfE) 'consultation' processes 'farcical' (Baynes, 2013). Invoking 'inequality' to impose further inequality is an ingenious discursive conflation whereby resisting the privatisation of public services is equated with promoting prejudice.

While the Education Bill 2011 was presented as raising standards through a return to discipline and promoting localism by reducing bureaucracy, in practice it further centralised government control and deregulated labour (Harrison, 2011). Teachers were given new powers to search and discipline pupils, while parents lost the right to complain to a local commissioner. Parents' right to redress was also curtailed, as the independent appeal panel considering permanent exclusion cases was replaced by an independent review panel (IRP) without the power to direct the reinstatement of a student, even when the original decision was flawed (see Kulz, 2015). Control was further centralised by abolishing quangos like the General Teaching Council for England and the Young People's Learning Agency and transferring their powers directly to the Secretary of State. The School Support Staff Negotiating Body was also abolished without any replacement, with Gove commenting that this body did not fit with the DfE's deregulation priorities. These authoritarian tactics and the limiting of democratic process both mirrors and legitimates Culford's 'short, sharp' approach discussed in Chapter 4. While

Culford once worked outside the bounds of the law, his maverick approach has become government policy.

Changes to the Ofsted rating system in January 2012 both complemented and accelerated the changes instigated by these two bills. The category 'satisfactory' was changed to 'requires improvement' with the idea that this relabelling would prevent mediocre schools from coasting. Recalibrating the yardstick of measurement does important work by remaking what is and what is not within the framework of possibility. As teaching unions argued, reclassification functions as a mechanism for academisation as many more schools automatically become eligible for government intervention.

The move towards total academisation continued with the passage of the Education and Adoption Bill in March 2016 under a Conservative government with Nicky Morgan as education minister. The bill abolished any form of local consultation process prior to conversion, with schools deemed to be 'coasting' eligible for intervention and conversion. 'Coasting' was defined as less than 60 per cent of students achieving five or more good GCSEs. This twenty percentage-point increase on the previous floor target of 40 per cent automatically makes more local authority schools available for academisation. Coasting schools must create an improvement plan that will be assessed for credibility by one of eight regional school commissioners. If commissioners do not support the plan, the school will be converted. Yet regional commissioners are not elected, but appointed, and act on behalf of the Secretary of State. Many have previous experience as chief executives of academy chains and trusts or as management consultants, while a leaked internal DfE report described how they should act as 'advocates for the academies programme' (Mansell, 2014). Hardly impartial actors, commissioners are active promoters of academisation.

Scrapping local consultation has been presented as cutting through bureaucratic and legal loopholes exploited by parents and teachers to hold back school improvement (Adams and Perraudin, 2015). Instead of local debate and decision making being valued, it is portrayed as selfish and damaging to children. Parents and teachers are depicted as blindly ideological while the government claims to be altruistically motivated. Yet one Liberal Democrat MP highlighted the ideological drive towards full academisation by asking Morgan if coasting academies would also be turned back into schools (Crace, 2015). Neither the House of Commons Education Select Committee nor a report by the Sutton Trust has found any evidence that academies raise educational standards more than maintained schools (Hutchings, Francis and Kirby, 2015). Yet these pieces of legislation and Ofsted reclassifications show how a pincer movement is being used to accelerate conversion. A fast-tracked voluntary process for outstanding and good schools is met by the mandatory conversion of inadequate and now 'coasting' schools to cover each end of the spectrum.

Meanwhile the shrinking and professionalisation of governing bodies also downsizes local participation in education. Lord Nash, Parliamentary Under-Secretary of State for Schools, has described how local parents are not needed on governing bodies because there are better places for them to offer their opinions;

however it is not clear where these places are located. The May 2016 White Paper 'Educational excellence everywhere' furthered Nash's comments by announcing that parents would no longer have two seats on an academy's governing body. It also announced that heads could award teaching qualifications and, most controversially, that all state schools would become academies by 2022. Compulsory academisation and doing away with parent governors met substantial opposition from Tory-led local councils and backbenchers, prompting the government to back down on these issues. Yet Morgan commented that the 'goal' of academisation remains the same, but will be pursued by a 'different path' (Adams, 2016). Justine Greening has since taken up the role of education minister in Theresa May's cabinet since the resignation of David Cameron in the wake of Britain voting to leave the European Union. Although Greening is the first education minister to have attended a comprehensive school, she is reportedly open to the return of grammar schools – a policy championed by May. While both Greening and May have described their passion for social mobility, with May keen to fight the 'burning injustice' of inequality, it is difficult to see how raising tuition fees, restricting young people's access to training and cutting benefits will achieve this goal (Mortimer, 2016).

Education as mobility miracle

Academies like Dreamfields are consistently portrayed as engines of social mobility, with Gove proclaiming that one chain was 'the biggest force for social progress and social mobility in the whole of the south of London' (Davies, 2012). Education has long been promoted as a miracle salve curing urban deprivation and balancing capitalism's inequalities, yet Basil Bernstein famously commented that 'education cannot compensate for society' (1970: 26). Still, the faulty notion persists that if teachers are skilled enough, the social context of education will become irrelevant (Reay, 2006: 291). Although the UK has one of the poorest records on social mobility in the developed world, mobility is presented as synonymous with social justice (Causa and Johansson, 2010). Reay describes how social mobility occupies a 'totemic role in UK society', featuring in elite policy yet 'also capturing the popular imaginary' (2013: 664). The academy programme deftly combines elite and popular dreamscapes, championing the aspirational self and creating potent confections as social mobility's 'mythical qualities' make it 'an extremely generative and productive myth that does an enormous amount of work for neoliberal capitalism' (Reay, 2013: 664). Rather than critiquing a lack of practical equality within and beyond the school gates, the emphasis rests on providing individualised equal opportunities through school effectiveness. This was reflected in Culford's speech detailed earlier in this chapter.

Former Prime Minister David Cameron announced that many academies were 'working miracles' in deprived areas and signalled a 'great revolution in education' (Cameron 2012). Cameron concluded that success stemmed from autonomy, transparency and parental choice, adding: 'these things happen if you trust in schools, believe in choice and give parents more information'. All of this culminates in 'real discipline' and 'rigorous standards'. Not only are these narratives of freedom and trust at odds with centralised regimes of inspection and testing that all schools must follow, they are also contradicted by a recent report charting the performance outcomes of disadvantaged pupils in sponsored academy chains. The report found that the majority of chains still underperformed the mainstream average for disadvantaged pupils (Hutchings, Francis and De Vries, 2014). The political rhetoric surrounding academies frequently does not match the realities within schools.

National imaginaries, militarism and discipline in schooling

Marketised educational confections are frequently coated in a romanticised neo-conservative glaze. Reverting to what Culford terms 'a traditional approach' plays a role in restoring Great Britain's faded grandeur post-empire. This safe return to a bygone era becomes a remedy to the destabilisation caused by the unravelling of the post-war settlement: discipline will prompt the return of 'true' British culture. Or, as Ball (2011) comments, there are two political fictions: 'One is a fantasy market of perfect choice and perfect competition. The other is a fantasy curriculum based on Boy's Own comics and a vision of England rooted in the one-nation Toryism of Disraeli, Baldwin and Butler.' Authoritarian approaches are presented as the obvious response to England slipping down the international league tables and wider anxieties over national decline. The Coalition's 2010 White Paper on education claimed strong discipline, 'traditional' uniforms and a Troops to Teachers programme to attract 'natural leaders' from the Armed Forces would make Britain 'an aspiration nation once more' (DfE, 2010). Introduced in 2013, Troops to Teachers seeks to discipline racialised, poor young people living in urban areas, and as Chadderton (2014) describes, is both informed by and feeds on discourses of white supremacy while devaluing teacher education. Hard structure is presented as what problematic raced and classed populations need to succeed; rather than being eschewed, aggression is promoted (Leonardo, 2009; Zirkel et al., 2011). Gove also enlisted right-wing empire-apologist Niall Ferguson to assist with rewriting the history curriculum which will discontinue the 'trashing' of Britain's illustrious imperial past and Britain's inspiring 'island story' (Gove, 2010). A story of western domination led by a triumphant Britain will be restored to history's centre, yet this story suffers from a continuing, damaging amnesia as historical narratives are reshaped to present Britain as a tolerant place advocating fair play (Alexander, Chatterji and Weekes-Bernard, 2012).

Rather than attending to structural issues of poverty and discrimination, poorer students are portrayed as lacking the character traits for success. Nicky Morgan announced how a Character Intervention Fund of £9.8 million supporting projects teaching character in schools is part of the Conservative Government's 'core mission to deliver real social justice' (DfE, 2015b). Former Labour Shadow Education Secretary Tristram Hunt embraced this initiative, describing how 'resilience and the ability to bounce back' was part of the 'great British spirit' and essential for young people competing for jobs and university places (Hunt, 2014). Students can beat the competition by being taught a nationalistic spirit that is contradictorily regarded as innately British. Several projects receiving funding described how they increased the motivation, confidence, leadership skills, curiosity, behaviour and aspiration of disadvantaged students. Poorer students are seen to be at a disadvantage because they lack the character traits of their more privileged counterparts; however it has been shown that poor students possess similar aspirations, but these aspirations can seldom be realised due to structural obstacles (see Baker et al., 2014; MacLeod, 2009). Similarly, Dreamfields' 'structure liberates' ethos assumes that disadvantage stems from the defects of individuals and their families and that grafting appropriate capitals onto the bodies of its students will solve this problem.

Reverting to authoritarian educational methods in the face of global competition, coupled with the denouncement of multiculturalism and a desired return to some happier, traditional culture via education carries all the symptoms of Paul Gilroy's 'complex ailment' of post-colonial melancholia. Gilroy argues that the continuing power of Second-World-War images of Britain signals a neurotic search for the juncture when Britain's national culture felt more liveable. He urges us to understand how 'wholesome militarism has combined pleasurably with the unchallenging moral architecture of a Manichean world' to produce a 'warm glow' that is relied upon to do cultural work in the present (2004: 95–6). It overlooks growing inequalities at home, while recalling a time when Britain faced indisputably diabolical enemies. This melancholia attempts to locate 'the place or moment before the country lost its moral and cultural bearings'. This desire for 'reorientation' cannot be severed from homogeneity's lure or an aversion to newcomers, for wanting to turn back is a rejection of 'the perceived dangers of pluralism and from the irreversible fact of multiculture' (2004: 97).

While tacitly acknowledging that these citizen-migrants and their children are here to stay, New Labour's academy policy responded to these disorientations by attempting to reorientate these 'others' by grafting on legitimate forms of cultural capital. This reorientation applies not only to ethnic minorities, but to the working classes. Conservative education policy has shown more aggressive, delusional attempts to impose celebratory imperial histories. Rather than simply trying to transform and incorporate disadvantaged urban populations, Conservative policies have also instigated the physical removal of poor populations from urban areas through draconian cuts to housing and social benefits (see Cooper, 2014). Meanwhile racism and class-based discrimination and the fundamental incompatibility of equality with capitalist modes of production remain unaddressed.

Structure of the book

This book draws on a long tradition of educational and cultural studies ethnographies that have unpicked and interrogated how race, class and gender are reproduced in and through institutional practices and negotiated by actors from situated locations. Paul Willis's landmark study *Learning to Labour* (Willis, 1977) departed from pathological representations of working-class boys' culture to show how boys enacted agency through counter-school culture. Yet the labour market has substantially altered since the mid-1970s; many of the jobs once available to Willis's lads no longer exist. Qualifications are now a necessary prerequisite for employment, while little space is permitted for a counter-school culture at Dreamfields. These changes affect how and to what ends agency can be employed by students. In *Young, Gifted and Black* (1988), Máirtín Mac An Ghaill rejected culturalist perspectives positioning black and Asian communities as hindering students from assimilation and achievement; however this culturalist perspective endures in new incarnations and runs throughout academy rhetoric, as racialised urban culture is blamed for holding students back.

The book also draws on Heidi Mirza's seminal work, *Young, Female and Black* (1992), which unsettles the mythology of ethnic minority underachievement. Mirza shows how young black girls exemplify the inegalitarian nature of our society: although they perform well in school compared with their peers, this educational success does not translate into labour market gains. Over twenty years later, these findings are echoed in subsequent research showing that while ethnic minorities perform well in school and achieve higher qualifications than their white peers, this does not protect them from unemployment (see Burgess, 2015; Li, 2015). A blanket assumption of ethnic-minority underachievement is reflected through Dreamfields' attitude towards 'urban children' and, as Chapter 7 suggests, is likely to have consequences on the type of qualifications available to ethnic-minority and working-class pupils. Finally, in *Formations of Class and Gender* (1997), Bev Skeggs shows how respectability was an issue for the working-class women in her study and encapsulates judgements of class, race, gender and sexuality as groups have different access to the means of generating respectability. Skeggs describes how their 'attempts to claim respectability locked them into systems of self-regulation and monitoring, producing themselves as governable subjects' (162). Similar issues of value and judgement play out at Dreamfields, where students must concede to disciplinary systems to access future gains. Prior to the advent of academies, David Gillborn and Deborah Youdell's *Rationing Education* (2000) used critical race theory to show how teachers and students felt caught within an education system dictated by larger, external forces which disadvantaged working-class and ethnic-minority students (2000: 43). These forces 'setting the pace that all must follow' are readily evident at Dreamfields as teachers and students try to live within and negotiate rigid boundaries.

There have been several qualitative and quantitative studies exploring academies by gauging attainment levels, concluding that the programme was low on effectiveness but high on expense and unaccountable to local communities (Beckett, 2007; Gorard, 2005, 2009). Ball (2007) has interrogated New Labour academies and the webs of actors comprising these public–private partnerships, while Melissa Benn (2011) has condemned the dismissal of the comprehensive model in favour of academies and free schools. While these studies rely primarily on documents to make their arguments, this book aims to extend current understandings of the social and cultural impact of the neoliberal academy model through an intensive empirical engagement with an institution at the vanguard of these changes.

This book does not seek to excoriate individual teachers, many of who are extremely dedicated, but examines how people are placed in relations of production, signification and complex power relations (Foucault, 2002: 327). Chapter 2 examines how Dreamfields acts as part of a long trajectory of interventions aimed at individualising and transforming a volatile 'urban residuum', while also engaging with the theoretical and methodological underpinnings of the study. Dreamfields' ordering of space, time and the body through a dense web of disciplinary practices is explored in Chapter 3, while Chapter 4 moves on to explore how Dreamfields' disciplinary structures are endured, negotiated and often welcomed by many staff and students. Chapter 5 examines how marketisation privileges the white middle-class student as an ideal 'buffer zone' against urban children, while Chapter 6 shows how students negotiate the demands of Dreamfields' conveyor belt against the backdrop of this 'buffer zone'. Chapter 7 moves beyond Dreamfields' gates to examine how parents negotiate the institution from a variety of social locations and how their relationship with Dreamfields is shaped by this location. Finally the book concludes by exploring the endurance of neoliberal subjects in pursuit of 'good-life' fantasies, as Dreamfields changes urban culture and rearranges hierarchies. Rather than alleviating inequality, hierarchies are remade through schools like Dreamfields despite their meritocratic, post-racial rhetoric.

Notes

1 The name of the school, borough and all participants are pseudonyms in order to protect their anonymity. In a few sensitive cases, I have also changed a participant's country of origin in order to protect their identity.
2 I have used italics to indicate when I am using ethnographic fieldnotes.
3 Several sponsors never paid the required amount, which had to be covered by the government.
4 Free schools operate on a very similar basis to academies, but are meant to be initiated by groups of parents, teachers, charities, trusts and religious or voluntary groups.
5 It is interesting to the note the fusion of celebrity with education at events like ARK's annual £5,000 per head fundraising gala attended by Sir Philip Green, Elton John, Liz Hurley, Boris Johnson, Mariella Frostrup and Busson's wife Uma Thurman, among others. This also raises question of how much additional capital is being ploughed into these academies to ensure they are 'winners'.

Research frameworks: historical representations and formations of race and class meet neoliberal governance

This chapter sketches out the key features of Dreamfields' ethos before reflecting on the historical trajectories that underpin how education, urban space and formations of race, class and gender are discussed in the present. Current discourses draw on historical representations rooted in the development of industrial capitalism, classificatory mechanisms and empire. The chapter also explores the post-structural, feminist and post-colonial thinkers that I will draw upon to approach Dreamfields' vision of the racialised, working-class urban child. Finally, the chapter reflects on the methodological process of producing qualitative data.

The architect's blueprint

Mr Culford was specially selected to act as Dreamfields' head, and his authoritarian management style means his vision is applied by teaching staff each day. He believes a clear philosophy and 'radical' leadership make a school successful, something he realised 'not by reading a book about it, but by trial and error and experience'. He implements the ethos with unswerving conviction and support from his Senior Management Team (SMT). Cultivating a position of supreme authority, Culford does not casually banter in corridors; appointments are made through his personal assistant. Culford sets Dreamfields' fundamental parameters, delegating daily tasks to his SMT and reserving his direct participation for assemblies, staff briefings and special occasions. Yet his leadership is clear as he routinely paces up and down the corridors, momentarily pausing in doorways to scrutinise lessons.

My interview with Culford took place in his corner office, a glass-walled room on the top floor overlooking the playground. He wore a pinstriped suit and looked relaxed as he rocked up and down in his black leather executive chair. Accustomed to the interview format, he answered my questions without any of the reluctant suspicion displayed by some of his more junior staff. Culford described the 'structure liberates' ethos as resting on a philosophy that altruistically seeks to provide poor children with the same opportunities wealthier children enjoy, in order 'to show that poor kids, working-class kids, can do as well as middle-class kids do'.

The second one [part of his vision] is the belief that children who come from
unstructured backgrounds, as many of our children do, and often very unhappy
ones, should be given more structure in their lives … if they come from unstructured backgrounds where anything goes and rules and boundaries are not clear
in their home, we need to ensure that they're clear here.

While Culford wants to provide working-class kids with opportunities, he simultaneously assumes these children come from unstructured, unhappy families. The
implementation of 'tight systems' results in what Culford calls a 'traditional or
formal approach' designed around various rituals and routines that provide the
structure allegedly absent from the home.

Yet not every Dreamfields student requires this intervention. Culford goes on
to differentiate between those who need structure and those who come to school
with structure built in:

So it's a realisation that you need more structure rather than less through experience in dealing with urban children, and that you can be a lot more relaxed and
free and easy in a nice, leafy middle-class area where the ground rules are clear
before they come in, where children go home to lots of books and stuff like that.
You need lots of rituals and routines in urban education than you do in more
prosperous areas.

The term 'urban children' or 'Urbanderry children' is used by several teachers to
describe a predominantly ethnic minority and working-class student body. This
urban child is contrasted with a middle-class and predominantly white child
from leafy suburbia. Culford feels routines are not necessary when dealing with
middle-class children because they come from disciplined homes with 'lots of
books'. He ties unstructured backgrounds to unhappiness and then aligns this with
the working-class, ethnic-minority 'urban child'. Dreamfields' disciplinarian structures are seen to aid this child by instigating academic success that creates happiness.

Poverty is briefly mentioned. However Culford's concern centres on creating
opportunity and supplementing poor parenting practices. He names class, not
ethnicity, as the biggest hurdle to achieving academic success:

I think class would be the biggest issue. A child going home to a home which
doesn't value education, doesn't support their child, where there are no books,
where there is no experience of higher education … that's the bigger problem.

Working-class parents are regarded as the 'problem' because of their detrimental
parenting practices. However, Culford feels this problem can be overcome, which
ties to his own experience as the mixed-race son of a lorry driver. Culford jests
about being mixed race: 'People think this is just a suntan.'[1] Being working-class,
not mixed-race, was the problem he overcame:

Economically I am working-class, but in terms of attitude, middle-class because
my parents were always aspirational, even though they didn't have any money.

> I think class is about attitude to life, as well as a financial position and what sort of job you hold.

Aspirational attitudes are seen to transcend material realities, and teachers expedite this transcendence by acting as 'surrogate parents' in possession of the 'right' attitudes. Culford emphasises how Dreamfields creates a culture and belief structure that 'works' in urban areas. He feels Dreamfields' mission is to drive up standards across the area through leadership and showing what students can achieve, proclaiming: 'We'll spread the message of Dreamfields to other schools. Dreamfields will become an empire.' Culford's desire to apply the Dreamfields credo to other institutions is being steadily realised through his influential advisory roles. Although Culford appears to acts as a sovereign authoritative figure, his approach is not the vision of one man, but draws on historical representations and subverts educational research to arrive at his common-sense approach.

Urban natives and their white middle-class others

Dreamfields' neocolonial stance of virtuous missionary saving urban children follows a long trajectory of interventions aimed at Britain's urban poor. As Jane M. Jacobs argues, the cultural dimensions of colonialism forged through the designation of categories and marking out of difference are imagined and remade in our postcolonial present through signs, narratives and metaphors circulating officially and otherwise (1996: 2). By the mid-1800s the industrial revolution and its demand for wage labour was creating dense urban populations within British cities like Goldport. These slums acted as fascinating, yet repellent sites of exploration for late middle-class Victorians. Referencing London, Anne McClintock discusses how poor urban port areas evocatively represented 'the conduit to empire – a threshold space, lying exotic, yet within easy reach, on the cusp of industry and empire' (1995: 120). She shows how race, class and gender have been mutually constituted as categories in conjunction with one another through encounters at home and abroad where 'race, class and gender are not distinct realms of experience, existing in splendid isolation from each other … rather they come into existence in and through relation to each other – if in contradictory and conflictual ways' (1995: 5). This ties to Dreamfields' intertwining of race and class through the notion of urban children, which is further explored in Chapter 4.

Poor urban areas generated middle-class anxiety and led to the classification of the poor and the assertion of middle-class respectability. Gareth Stedman-Jones (1971) examines how the Victorian middle classes worried that a 'residuum' of casual labourers deemed lazy, rough and irredeemable might radicalise the labouring working classes. The question of what to do about poverty and the volatile 'residuum' permeated political thought. In a curious twist of causality, pauperism – not poverty – was seen as the problem. The 1834 Poor Law designated poverty as a condition requiring effort and correction, not relief. Individual cases were compiled, investigated and categorised to differentiate between the deserving and undeserving poor. This logic continues in current policy, where individuals are presented as rational actors 'choosing' their fate.

British urban sociology's beginnings are linked to this rise of the middle-class subject as surveyor and judge. Social reformers' solutions to the moral failings of the urban 'residuum' are the harbinger to Dreamfields' teachers acting as surrogate parents. The accounts of nineteenth-century social reformers and researchers spurned sociology's birth as a discipline while producing knowledge and objects of study. Friedrich Engels's ethnographic exploration of abject slum poverty in the newly industrialised city of Manchester in *The Condition of the Working Class in England in 1844* (1892) was an early example of urban sociology. Working from a very different philosophical premise, Charles Booth's study *Life and Labour of the People of London* (1889) took a liberal, reformist approach, generating colour-coded poverty maps that classified London's streets and inhabitants by income and occupation. Booth enacted moral judgements and argued that adopting appropriate culture could alleviate poverty. Similarly, London settlement houses placed university-educated men alongside the working classes with the aim of bringing civilisation to slums (Gidley, 2000). It was frequently asserted that the absence of a 'better class' of resident made slums repellent and the poor would benefit from the establishment of a 'resident gentry' (Stedman-Jones, 1971: 258–9). Dreamfields' need to attract Urbanderry's middle classes shows how the bourgeoisie continue to act as resident gentry (see Chapters 5 and 8). The belief that poverty could be eradicated by adopting 'appropriate' cultural forms continues to be seen in the academy programme's stated goal of transforming urban culture.

Class and race were created together, with those outside the bourgeoisie regarded as other. In *London Labour and the London Poor* (1861) Henry Mayhew used ethnographic sensibilities to create rich narrative portraits of costermongers, scavengers and vagrants. He compared his intervention to that of colonial explorers searching for distant tribes, where the working classes were 'other forms of life' regarded 'with the same eyes as a comparative anatomist loves to lay bare the organism … or an ape in the hope of linking together the lower and higher forms of animal existence' (1864: 118). Inspired by the evolutionary assumptions of science and anthropology, Mayhew racialises the working classes. As Jacobs describes, categories like race and class are fluid:

> Indeed, the vitality of such binary constructs is most likely a result of their being anxiously reinscribed in the face of their contested or uncontainable certainty. It is, in part, this anxious vitality that gives racialised categorisations elaborated under colonialism such a long life and allows them to remain cogent features even of those contemporary societies that are formally 'beyond' colonialism. (1996: 3)

Race and class have rarely occupied stable, discrete categories; instead their meaning has continually altered throughout the centuries. Ann Laura Stoler (1995, 2002) highlights the porous instability of the boundaries between middle-class bodies and their others as racialised discourses travelled between British cities and colonies to craft bourgeois hegemony. This othering was necessary to stabilise an imagined cultural superiority rooted in material advantages. Stoler describes how discourses of race preceded nineteenth-century social classifications, making race not a function of social hierarchies, but constitutive of those hierarchies (1995: 95). Discourses blending desire, fear and repulsion highlight the 'anxious vitality' of boundary drawing and social reproduction that continues within Dreamfields, as a disciplinary gaze is directed at bodies that might threaten these fragile boundaries.

Civilising urban natives

Dreamfields' mission reflects the school's historical role as a potentially trans-formative institution where children and their families can be monitored and regulated (Foucault, 1991a: 212). Compulsory education was often regarded as a means of cultivating good character and appropriate culture in workers (Carey, 1992). Contrary to the idea of education as a liberating gift, an emergent English bourgeoisie instead 'recognised the value of education in its battle for ideological hegemony over other groups' (Green, 1990: 210). There were varying amounts of working-class resistance to state involvement in education. While some Chartists rejected a state-financed, compulsory system, others advocated a state-financed system of non-sectarian schools if they were under local democratic control (CCCS, 1981). This proviso has been removed through academisation.

Schools were also a space where natives could be turned into civilised Europeans; the French and Dutch authorities debated if mixed-race 'metis' and 'indos' in colonial Southeast Asia could be transformed through education (Stoler, 2002: 94–9). The colonial state's regulatory mechanisms were not only used on the colonised, but on problematic internal enemies. European colonial forays were used 'as models, inspirations, and testing grounds for modes of social discipline' which were augmented and imported back into Europe to create the bourgeois order (Pratt, 1992: 36; also see Cowen, 2004; Hall, 2002). Processes of standardi-sation, bureaucracy and normalisation went hand in hand with the systemisation of nature, the slave trade, plantation systems, colonial genocide and rebellion. The effects of these 'massive experiments in social engineering and discipline, serial production, the systemisation of human life, the standardising of persons' still haunt the present (Pratt, 1992: 36). Urban populations designated problematic continue to be regulated through spaces like Dreamfields.

My focus rests on the redeployment of these techniques in urban space via education, as empire's tools returned to England's shores and former colonial subjects arrived as citizens. While Urbanderry's 'problem' is described as one of culture rather than race, the terminological replacement of 'race' with 'culture' does not necessarily signal progress. Joel Kahn points out continual slippages between race–culture distinctions where nineteenth-century biological catego-ries were frequently cultured (2001: 53). Heidi Mirza argues that the cultural discourse on race needs to be rethought as a 'new post-biological discourse' on race because 'ideas about innate, genetic, scientifically provable difference are still at the heart of our thinking about race' (2009: 258). Just as nineteenth-century colonials might be remade through education, so too might the twenty-first-century urban residuum persisting in cosmopolitan hubs of capital like Goldport (see Rattansi, 1992). Now I will explore my theoretical approach to this vision of urban children in need of cultural transformation.

Subject making/making subjects

Foucault's work on the production of docile bodies through disciplinary mechanisms is pivotal to understanding Dreamfields' approach. The bourgeoisie's rise to become the dominant class in the eighteenth century was obscured by 'the establishment of an explicit, coded and formally egalitarian juridical framework' (Foucault 1991a: 222). The development of disciplinary mechanisms was the inverse 'dark side of these processes', as Foucault describes how systems of micropower comprise society's foundations through the employment of 'tiny, everyday, physical mechanisms' that counter egalitarian frameworks (1991a: 222–3). These mechanisms of power order the body through physical and cognitive disciplining, limiting unpredictability and reducing inefficiency. This is evidenced in Chapter 4 through Dreamfields' elimination of the staff room as a useless, divisive space. Student and teacher subjectification occurs not only through the mind as a conscious process, but also through regulating the body's practices and aesthetics (Youdell, 2006). As Chapter 4 shows, one student had to have the lines shaved into his eyebrows redrawn by his teacher to restore appropriate aesthetics, or face isolation. Processes of subjectification do not need to manipulate the ideas and beliefs constituting consciousness, but can operate through subtle mechanisms of power existing within institutions and regimes of truth. I draw on these theoretical perspectives to show how flexible, obedient bodies are cultivated.

Culford's discourses produce the effects of truth as power circulates through them. Instead of searching for 'truth', Foucault argues that truth effects are produced through discourses that are neither true nor false, but made true through the application of power and knowledge. Power is therefore not simply repressive, but productive. As Rabinow comments: 'What makes power hold good, what makes it accepted, is simply the fact that it doesn't only weigh on us as a force that says no, but that it traverses and produces things, it induces pleasures, forms knowledge, produces discourses' (1984: 61). The designation of Urbanderry as locked in a culture of failure allows Dreamfields to intervene and remedy this predicament. Many teachers and students submit to discipline because they can see the fruits of their labour in the production of results. Or, as Derek relates in Chapter 6, Dreamfields may have made him a 'little robot', but this is worthwhile; his submission is beneficial. Foucault describes how government has become about the disposition of things, where tactics are employed 'to arrange things in such a way that, through a certain number of means, such and such ends may be achieved' (1991b: 95). This text examines how Dreamfields governs things through their arrangement, rather than simply imposing rules.

While Foucault's work on discursive regimes and power is helpful for thinking about subjectification within the neoliberal market state, his refusal to base his theory in social forces like the state or society can make it difficult to empirically address how class and race are (re)produced daily by an institution (Beechy and Donald, 1985). Which students need to become 'little robots' to fit in? How does the missing staff room affect teachers? Feminist and postcolonial theory, sociologists of education focusing on issues of race, class and social justice, and Bourdieu's metaphors of capital, address and connect these patterns, providing an account of power relations that examines the (re)production of difference.

Legitimate cultures

Bourdieu's theoretical approach allows us to understand how non-egalitarian systems of micro-power play out in the social world. Although the Marxist conception that 'men make history, but not in conditions of their choosing' still underpins his approach, Bourdieu broadens class beyond the relations of production to give culture a larger role. He moves beyond rudimentary attempts at categorisation through occupation, for class is made through spatial and temporal relations, as 'the space of objective differences (with regard to economic and cultural capital) finds an expression in a symbolic space of visible distinctions' (1987: 11). Class is predicated on the movement of 'capital' through social space that is structured by the distribution of capital. This wider conception of class is crucial to understanding an institution that claims to transform urban culture.

The sociology of education interrogates the relationship between social and cultural reproduction; education functions as a site of class struggle where power relations are reproduced and dominant culture's values are transmitted (Bourdieu, 1977a: 487, 493). Bourdieu interrogates how the pedagogic power of educational institutions seems to 'demand the insignificant' while extracting 'the essential' by inciting 'respect for forms or forms of respect which are the most visible and most "natural" manifestations of respect for the established order' (1992: 96). Yet the established order is not simply formulated around class hierarchies, but also very much based around the idea of race. Recent research like *The Colour of Class* explores the intersection of race and class through the practices of black Caribbean middle-class parents against a landscape where the black middle classes do not automatically gain advantage through their class position (Rollock et al., 2015; see also Gillborn and Mirza, 2000; Strand, 2011; Vincent et al., 2012). Due to the mutual constitution of race and class through history, middle-classness continues to be attached to and infer whiteness. This ties to mixed-race sixth-former Olivia's description in Chapter 6 of how she has 'become more white' at Dreamfields, as learning how to fit into the established order requires specific adjustments. While aspirational mantras claim everyone can achieve if they try hard enough, Bourdieu disrupts this 'imaginary universe of perfect competition or perfect equality of opportunity' to acknowledge history's cumulative effects (1986: 241). This unsettles the common-sense view that academic success or failure correspond to 'natural aptitudes' (1986: 243).

The book also draws on Bourdieu's forms of capital that account for history's accumulated effects on the social world. He outlines three types of capital: economic, social and cultural. Economic capital is directly related to financial assets or income, while social capital relates to networks of human connections that can be converted into economic capital. Cultural capital can exist in three forms: as embodied, objectified or institutionalised. The embodied state is 'in the form of long-lasting dispositions of the body and mind', while the objectified state refers to cultural goods and the institutionalised state includes things like educational qualifications (1986: 243). Capitals must be recognised as legitimate before being converted into symbolic capital; only legitimated capital can accrue value and hold power. Forms of social and cultural capital held by students and parents are often devalued within Dreamfields' landscape, highlighting how capitals are context-specific. Only certain forms of culture – those bearing the hallmarks of whiteness and middle-classness – carry the sort of capitals recognised as legitimate by educational institutions (Yosso, 2005).

Bourdieu's concepts of symbolic power and symbolic violence are also integral to the analysis, as processes of legitimation exclude some, while including others. Bourdieu elaborates:

> Symbolic power, being the power to constitute the given by stating it, to create appearances and belief, to confirm and transform the vision of the world and thereby action in the world, and therefore the world itself, this quasi-magical power which makes it possible to obtain the equivalent of what is obtained by force (physical or economic) thanks to the specific mobilizing effect being only effective if it is recognized as legitimate (that is to say, if it is not recognized as arbitrary). (1977b: 117)

Symbolic power only produces these effects when both the speaker and their words are recognised as legitimate. Culford speaks from a legitimated position of authority and possesses symbolic power, while the legitimacy of parents, teachers and students varies considerably. Bourdieu describes the historic designation of the working classes as tasteless and suffering, and 'the peremptory verdicts which … condemn to ridicule, indignity, shame, silence … men and women who simply fall short, in the eyes of their judges, of the right way of being and doing' (2010: 512). These value judgements inflict symbolic violence. As Chapter 7 explores, middle-class parents often recognised their favoured status while other parents struggled to display the correct ways of being and doing to gain recognition.

Neoliberal governance and the pursuit of the 'good life'

The idea of the individual as a bounded, self-determined unit began to coalesce around the reformist interventions discussed above. Institutions like the workhouse rendered individuals legible by observing and recording difference, making it obvious who would or would not 'learn the lessons of the institution' (Rose, 1998: 106). Differentiating mechanisms were used across a variety of institutions, and as described earlier in this chapter, this was not simply a restrictive imposition, but also productive. The individuality these mechanisms created holds appeal, as individuals are 'seduced by their own perceived powers of freedom', yet this seduction also entails the loss of collective powers as heavy costs accompany the individualisation of responsibility (Davies and Bansel, 2007: 249). Dreamfields draws on this seductive, now common-sense discourse of individualised freedom to promise brighter futures.

The question of what Dreamfields' structures actually liberate individuals to is seldom considered, taking us back to Foucault's work on governmentality. He argues that a key feature of liberal governments is the 'extension of procedures of control, constraint, and coercion' alongside the advent of freedoms. Structure and control do not just counterbalance freedom, but 'become[s] its mainspring' (2008: 67). At the heart of liberalism is a productive/destructive relationship where freedom must be produced and organised, yet simultaneously limited and consumed (2008: 64). The 'structure liberates' ethos highlights the paradoxical contradictions of liberalism's reliance on freedom accessed through submission.

Neoliberal governance accelerates these interventions focused on the site of the individual. Nicholas Gane describes how neoliberalism emerged as a form of political economy in the 1920s in response to classical liberalism's decline. He outlines how neoliberalism is not anti-statist or about devolving the powers of the state to the individual, but instead its 'constant push to define and regulate social life' through market principles requires activity and intervention (2012: 613). This is not a laissez-faire approach, but a form of governance that requires continual effort and cultivation. Jodi Dean asserts that state privatisation does not dismantle state power, but radically redistributes wealth to the rich and restructures the state as an 'authoritarian tool for their protection' (2009: 9). Neoliberalism's presentation of its economic and political project as inevitable is 'one of the ways that the ideology instils in its subjects a belief in markets' (Dean, 2009: 49). The relentless activity of neoliberal governance is evidenced in Chapter 4 through Dreamfields' labour-intensive practices, where many participants felt this was the only approach that 'works'. Doreen Massey describes how a radical reimagination of ideology and the economic is necessary to alter neoliberal notions of a natural, external economy, as 'the very scaffolding of our political imaginations' has been financialised through neoliberal assumptions (2011: 31). Social democracy must recognise and challenge this fictitiously naturalised economy as an assortment of social relations in order to have real purchase.

Dreamfields' promotion of individualised, meritocratic dreams connects to Lauren Berlant's examination of our attachment to 'that moral-intimate-economic thing called "the good life"' (2011: 2). Berlant discusses how the optimistic ambition underpinning the pursuit of upward mobility can result in a relationship of 'cruel optimism' whereby what you desire actually obstructs your development. Optimistic relations are not intrinsically cruel, but become cruel 'when the object that draws your attachment actively impedes the aim that brought you to it initially' (2011: 1). She asks why people stay attached to 'conventional good-life fantasies' when there is so much evidence that they are unstable, fragile and come at a great cost. While fantasy may allow people to collect idealistic theories and imaginaries 'about how they and the world "add up to something"', Berlant asks what happens when these fantasies start to unravel (2011: 2). The academy programme responds to present-day unravellings by reinstating mobility dreams in more heroic, dynamic ways. Berlant provides a useful lens for examining these paradoxical, harmful attachments by offering an affective window onto the struggles of Foucauldian subjects who are both making and being made in complex ways.

Selfhood and value

While the reflexive modernisation thesis has suggested that class cultures are declining as individuals choose their own identity markers and form their own trajectories, Savage argues that these shifts are better conceptualised as a move 'from working-class to middle-class modes of individualisation' (Beck et al., 1994; Savage, 2000: xi). Possessive selfhood presents the individual as capable of standing outside themselves, legitimating their interests and establishing authority 'by defining themselves against the "mass"' (Skeggs, 2004: 7). This possessive self is classed, as Walkerdine outlines how 'the neo-liberal subject is the autonomous liberal subject made in the image of the middle class' (2003: 239). Forms of individuality aligned with middle-classness carry value, while other, more relational selves are not regarded as unique or interesting.

Feminist researchers have long emphasised the cultural significance of class and addressed the affective dimensions of class struggle – namely the pain, shame and injury of lived class inequalities. Lawler outlines how cultural and symbolic mechanisms make social class 'real', although class cannot be reduced to cultural mechanisms or located outside politics (1999: 5). Her research on women from working-class origins who now occupy middle-class positions shows how class is not achieved through economics alone, but through an array of cultural practices that mark the subject. Lawler's participants felt they actualised their 'real selves' through becoming middle-class and adopting certain tastes. Dreamfields seeks to 'liberate' students through its structures to more middle-class forms of selfhood, yet Lawler shows how this transformation is incomplete and often painful – even after a supposed lack of 'taste' is overcome. Hierarchies of 'taste' depicted as simple preferences connect to wider inequalities.

Dreamfields also draws on the familiar rhetoric that poor parenting by single mothers causes social dysfunction; however, this view is challenged by Gillies's (2007) research with working-class mothers. Poor parenting did not sustain poverty, while adopting middle-class parenting modes did not alleviate social disadvantage. Her research highlights the resourcefulness of working-class mothers in the face of marginalisation and instability, where a relational sense of self made personal interest secondary and family and friends created an interdependent web. This relational sense of self is not valued within the neoliberal educational arena. These feminist thinkers help us imagine alternatives to neoliberal subjecthood, where there are different ways of being and knowing besides that of the possessive individual. Blaming the pathological home for poverty's effects is not confined to the white working class; a long legacy of the stigmatised black family is also folded into this discourse (see Gilroy, 2002; Lawrence, 1982; Phoenix, 1991; Reynolds, 2005). Beneath Dreamfields' normative middle-class subject of value lurks an aura of whiteness.

Reforming racialised subjects

Dreamfields' 'traditional values with a modern edge' offer a route back to a lost golden age of law and order where a racially homogenous nuclear family was tied to happy nationhood. This text is not only concerned with classed inequalities, but the reproduction of the fictitious, yet durable category of race and the complex interplay between processes of racialization and classification within Dreamfields. It would be impossible to examine class without interrogating race due to their historic mutual constitution, with race resting at the very heart of modernity's formation (Goldberg, 2001). While Culford does not name 'race' as a 'problem' like he does class, race thinking is implicit to 'urban children' as the majority of Dreamfields students are from ethnic-minority backgrounds.

In the 1970s, Stuart Hall argued that social exclusions were inherent to the UK's state organisation:

> There is, it seems to me, an overwhelming tendency to abstract questions of 'race' from what one might call their *internal* social and political basis and contexts in British society ... to deal with 'race' as if it has nothing intrinsically to do with the present 'condition of England'. It's viewed rather as an 'external' problem which has been foisted to some extent on English society from the outside: it's been visited on us, as it were, from the skies. (1978: 23–4; emphasis added)

Hall asserts that post-war racism flourished in the 1950s due the 'historical amnesia' regarding Britain's imperial past on the left and right, as the longstanding relationship between Britain, the Caribbean and the Indian subcontinent was repressed. The 1960s saw the end of the economic boom and assimilationist dream, as anxieties mounted over a permissive youth culture and more aggressive forms of racism developed. Race, although not the fundamental focus, became a signifier and metaphor for a moral crisis supposedly caused by a 'general liberal conspiracy' (1978: 30–2). While these ideological processes unfolded during an economic crisis, Hall argues they could not be reduced to it. Produced over thirty years ago, *The Empire Strikes Back* (CCCS, 1982) examined how British constructions of the authoritarian state were inextricably tied to popular racism during the 1970s. While there have been significant changes to how the state operates, focusing on how race is (re)produced through authoritarian modes of governance remains a prescient concern in the face of undemocratic, centralised education policy.

Racialised hierarchies may have grown more subtle, but exclusion remains central to the state's organisation (Alexander, 2010). British culture is often presented as a fixed, homogenous entity immigrants must be absorbed into; their supposed unwillingness to be absorbed has often been blamed for cultural decline. Nostalgic narratives lamenting the demise of a golden age can be located in accounts of Dreamfields' predecessor Larchmont Grove. A website created by Larchmont alumni showcases the school's heyday in the first half of the twentieth century: boys in gleaming cricket whites play in a park; a bespectacled science teacher brandishes a beaker; the local Cadet Corps march against the backdrop of a newly built estate. These positive images of community solidarity also silently showcase the whiteness of Larchmont's student body in the 1940s and 1950s. One Larchmont Grove alumnus blames the school's decline on uncontrolled immigration, multiculturalism hampering integration, and comprehensive methods. The decline of areas like Urbanderry in the latter half of the twentieth century is attributed to an impossible onslaught of foreigners too different to be absorbed into Britain's social fabric and permitted to remain apart.

Paul Gilroy describes how 'lazy commentators' have conflated the arrival of migrants with the corrosion of homogeneity, arguing that instead of focusing on difference as the source of national decline, the real causality stems from an eroded welfare state and the turn towards market liberalism (2004: 135). This need to assimilate difference ties in to the historic infantilisation of the colonised where they are positioned as requiring guidance from Western superiors (Fanon, 2001; Nandy, 1988). Dreamfields' attempts to change urban culture present a way for alien others to be transformed and integrated into the global city. It is essential for us to focus on how race is presently being reproduced through authoritarian modes of governance, as ideologically driven austerity accompanies the increasing securitisation of schools.

Concerns over parallel lives and community segregation expressed in the 2001 Cantle Report and the move towards community cohesion policies have been overlaid by more rigorous forms of regulation in the wake of 9/11 in the United States, 7/7 in the UK and increasing levels of Islamophobia. Under the Counter-Terrorism and Security Act 2015, schools are now required to carry out the 'Prevent' duty by having 'due regard to the need to prevent people from being drawn into terrorism' (DfE, 2015a). Prevent requires teachers to police their students, and has frequently resulted in the criminalisation of Muslim students who have no links to extremist activity, while silencing critical debate. Former Runnymede Trust director Rob Berkeley writes: 'Seen through the prism of risk, incompatible difference and self-segregation, Muslims in Britain have become the talisman of the "post-colonial melancholia" that typifies the UK's race relations debate' (2013: 2; see Bhattacharya, 2008; Kundnani, 2014). The older black folk devil described in *Policing the Crisis* (Hall, 1978) persists alongside this newer Muslim confection, and, unsurprisingly, these lenses shape educational outcomes. David Gillborn (2008) illustrates how the achievement gap between black and white students has not closed, as racial inequalities are not accidental but sustained through education. Meanwhile, white dominance is reasserted as discussions and funding for issues relating to black and ethnic-minority students are cut. Gillborn (2015) describes how anti-racism has been 'monsterised' as damaging and racist to white people as we shift to a climate where referencing race or race equality is regarded as racist. Within education, the white working class have been presented as a disadvantaged racial group through statistical manipulation, resulting in narratives of white victimhood (Gillborn 2015: 8). Despite some claims that we have entered a post-racial era, the Runnymede School Report shows how inequality and racism persist in UK schools (see also Mirza, 2005). Vini Lander (2011) ties this resurgence of racism to teachers' lack of training and understanding of race and racism as these terms are erased through teacher training reforms. This situation will be exacerbated by the 2016 Education White Paper's plan to dispense with a qualified teacher status, with trainees instead being accredited by headteachers.

Divided struggles

Raced and classed struggles became disarticulated from one another for a myriad of reasons during the post-war era, a division arguably aided by anti-racism's central concern of removing barriers to individual minority achievement and social mobility. This was a debate within anti-racist politics, and Bonnett (1990) has argued that anti-racism fitted within the context of liberal educationalism's unresolved ideological conflict between egalitarian impulses and capitalist orientations. This theoretical and political severing of race and class becomes a constrictive rupture dismissing the relationship between racism and imperialism (Sivanandan, 1985: 11–12). Barry Troyna (2002) argues that policymakers' failure to cohere 'race', class and gender inequalities into a more broad, coherent programme – coupled with an inattention to more precisely identify education's role in generating and reproducing racism – was a major problem. The dissociation of racism from other forms of inequality and portioning into individualised forms becomes 'the coat of paint theory of racism' (Gilroy, 1992: 52). Meanwhile, an emphasis on cultural styles shifted the focus away from 'the struggle against racism to the struggle for culture' (Sivanandan, 1985: 6). Troyna famously describes how a '3S interpretation (Saris, Samosas and Steel Bands)' of multi-cultural education focused on the cultural styles of black students 'subordinated political realities to cultural artefacts' (2002: 74). The historical production of raced, classed and gendered selves in relation to imperialist misadventures and the development of capitalism make the tidy separation of these mutually constituted categories a difficult, detrimental and obfuscating present-day problem. Recently, Rollock has pointed out the impossibly of tidily separating race and class as Savage et al.'s (2013) British class survey attempts to do, with the accounts of the black middle classes acting as 'a stark and necessary reflection of the ways in which whiteness continues to be insidiously and silently enacted' (2014: 449). Audre Lorde (1983) wrote in the early 1980s that there is no hierarchy of oppressions, as one group cannot ultimately profit from the oppression of another without diminishing themselves. Lorde also remarks on the right-wing tendency to encourage the oppressed to act against one another that prevents joining together in meaningful political action. Race and class are reunited through Dreamfields' term 'urban children', yet this reunion does not involve a progressive critique, but a renewed pathologisation of categories impossible to dismantle within a capitalist framework underpinning their logic.

Methodological approach

My research plans, neatly mapped out from my desk at Goldsmiths, were frequently disrupted by the field and spontaneously adapted to fit within the confines of Dreamfields' environment. The process of knowledge making is also a process of recognising or arriving at limits felt through the boundaries of structures, the limits of one's ability to know and describe, and the limits of being a situated person who incompletely understands their actions and their potential effects (Das, 2010: 143). The research used a mixed-method approach meshing 200 pages of ethnographic data generated over 18 months with 46 semi-structured interviews with 20 parents,[2] 20 teachers and 6 interviews with sixth-form students. A group of 17 students aged 12–13 and 15–16 in Years 9 and 11 formed the research's core, as I worked with them throughout an academic year using ethnographic and participatory methods. I conducted teacher interviews while still working at Dreamfields, while the bulk of the fieldwork took place one year later after receiving funding from the Economic and Social Research Council (ESRC). The fieldwork lasted for one year and focused on students and, secondarily, their parents. During this period I spent two to three days per week at Dreamfields. The methods came to be temporally and spatially shaped by Dreamfields' rhythm and pace. While Dreamfields' active elimination of spontaneity left few actions to chance, there were crevices and cracks in this routine. Both the research and I shared common ground with the participants, as we were all regulated through this space.

An ethics of negotiation

My shift of status from employee to researcher incited a barrage of ethical dilemmas. Although I handed out consent forms and explained the research to teachers, students and parents in line with the British Sociological Association's requirements, forms and signatures cannot replace an ethics embedded in a continual awareness of your participants, your relationship to others throughout the process, and how you choose to commit accounts to paper. Given my long-term relationship with many students and teachers at Dreamfields, I felt a particular responsibility to exercise care. This responsibility to do justice to the accounts of my participants rested in tension with the need to maintain a sound critique of institutional practices and connect them to a wider social context.

Several teachers suggested the research would prove the effectiveness of academies, while one commented that it must support Culford's aims for him to consent, adding that he would be angry if the outcomes were not positive. These assumptions – coupled with Dreamfields' lack of engagement or interest in the research – have often given me a feeling of discomfort. My long-term relationship with the school impacted upon the research with regard to trust, access and my own perceptions. When I first introduced the research to Culford, he brusquely asserted that I did not need to spend time studying Dreamfields; he could tell me why it worked, and it had nothing to do with being an academy. Upon receiving a funded studentship, I offered to meet with Culford before starting the fieldwork to review the research questions and methods, but simply received an email from his personal assistant reading 'research proposal approved'. I wanted to give a brief presentation to staff outlining the research process, but the SMT decided this was unnecessary. While opening up a generally closed institution exhibited trust, I continually questioned how this trust was gained – by assuming research outcomes due to family ties, or my prior employment? By misunderstanding what sociological research is, or through a dismissive attitude towards research? Upon their completion I sent the thesis and executive summary to Dreamfields and asked to run a participatory workshop with the student council to debate the findings, or at least meet with the SMT; however, Dreamfields did not respond to my correspondence.

Reflexive knowledge-making

When interacting with teachers, students and parents, I inhabited a perspective shaped by my social and cultural position. As Donna Haraway (1991) writes, a disembodied and decontextualised gaze is impossible. All gazes are inherently embedded within a context, yet this partial perspective should not dissuade us from participating in the social world through empirical research. Partiality does not devalue empirical research or the political projects that can be supported and enabled by feminist knowledge production. Although all knowledge is contingent on positioning, context and power dynamics, these constructed realities still affect daily lives and determine life chances (Archer and Francis, 2007: 27). Sociology is a listener's art, harnessed to the art of descriptions that 'theorise as they describe and describe as they theorise' (Back, 2007: 21). This position informed my approach, which seeks to blend theory with rich pictures of the social world, allowing description and analysis to work together to examine how people attach value to themselves within their sociohistorical context where wider structural forces are working in tandem with popular discourses.

Reflexivity via the author's self-conscious awareness of their position has been advocated as a remedy to realism. While acknowledging these considerations, I do not want to place myself at the heart of the research by making it a narcissistic confessional device. However, I would like to mention a few biographical factors that drew me to the research. I grew up in a white, middle-class suburban area outside Boston in the United States, although I have lived in the UK for over seventeen years. As the only child of aspirational parents, I watched and participated in their precarious struggle to escape their working-class roots by acquiring the 'right' middle-class tastes (Lawler, 1999). Despite promising academic beginnings, I was discouraged by my high school's intense competition and ranking regimes. I was never an 'honors society' student and quietly concluded by the age of 17 that I was a mediocre failure at best. I was also troubled by my school's racial and social segregation. My intelligent Hispanic friends were consistently consigned to lower set-groupings than me despite similar grades, while I felt intimidated by the wealthier students with brand-name clothes. Being curious or capable did not seem to necessarily translate into educational success. These structural positions directed my interest in the research, albeit in uncertain ways where 'being' A does not necessarily equate with thinking or feeling B.

Making data through methods

Methodologies do not innocently discover pre-existent information, but create and provide different ways for participants to articulate themselves and for knowledge to be created. Ethnographic methods examined how action occurred within the spatial, physical parameters of Dreamfields. This allowed me to observe daily procedures and engage with students and teachers informally. Unlike the self-conscious pronouncements often made in an interview situation, ethnography places subjects within a collective context rather than isolating the individual as a unit of measurement. It allows an observation of how groups inhabit spaces and how the built environment shapes their actions. Connecting young people's comments about their social spaces with my playground observations drew attention to social divides. Ethnography makes incongruities between what individuals say they do and what they actually do in the context of daily life readily apparent. These gaps demonstrate the multiplicity of positions we shift between in the negotiation of numerous contexts with differing value systems and demands. Ethnography situates individuals within the social, cultural, historical and economic conditions in which they live. Skeggs writes: 'Ethnography is the only method that takes into account multifaceted ways in which subjects are produced through the historical categories and context in which they are placed and which they precariously inhabit' (2007: 433). This focus on daily processes and positions aims to examine and deconstruct essentialised categories by interrogating how they are produced instead of reproducing them.

Participatory activities were used with students to move away from relying solely on text and talk. Asking students to take me on a tour of Dreamfields allowed us to leave the confines of the interview table, and this mobility created space for spontaneous conversations and after-school loitering. Compiling photo diaries about their lives beyond school also gave students a visual means of producing knowledge while instigating reflection around topics beyond Dreamfields. Photo diaries generated discussion around how they chose to represent their lives to me, and although their photos are not included in this book, the exploration of space and visuals enhanced other elements of the research (Pink, 2001: 5). I did not record conversations with students – aside from two at the end of the project – as I felt it amplified the heavily surveyed atmosphere. Instead I treated our interactions as semi-structured ethnographic encounters that attempted to foster relaxed exchanges. This is why the majority of young people's comments are paraphrased, except for particular sentences or phrases I could recall verbatim or scribbled down during our meeting. However I did record my interviews with sixth-formers, teachers and all but one of the parents, as these lengthily one-off encounters made note-taking unreliable.

Finally, the research used the semi-structured interview. A ubiquitous element of modern life, the interview is present in a vast range of places, from radio to television to the job centre. Like Rapley (2007), I do not entertain any positivist notions of objectifying and standardising the interview to avoid bias; instead I regard it as a social encounter with a specific person in a particular context where an active collaboration produces accounts of the social world. Approaching the interview as a social relationship steers us away from adhering to standardising methodologies that 'imitate the external signs of the rigor of the most established scientific disciplines' and instead urges us to focus on developing an 'active and methodical listening' (Bourdieu, 1999: 607–9). Yet active listening cannot alleviate or compensate for the historical baggage our bodies carry. The interview's classed history must be considered, as Steedman (2000) describes how the English administrative state historically demanded the working-class poor to repetitively tell the self. Skeggs, Thumin and Wood (2008) highlight how class is made through methodologies, as middle-class participants generally seemed more comfortable with this format, positioned as fellow professionals and social equals to their interviewers, while working-class participants often seemed more uneasy. These orientations were apparent in my interviews with parents. While one middle-class family interviewed me about my research before starting their interview, this easy confidence was largely absent in interviews with working-class parents.

Raced, classed productions and power

The participants are described within the text using the ethnic, and sometimes national descriptors they related to me. I did not want to deterministically position how people ethnically described themselves as forming the basis of their ontology. Anoop Nayak describes how social constructionism still perceives race as an ontological category:

> In contrast, post-race writing subverts this position by adopting an anti-foundational perspective which claims that race is a fiction only ever given substance to through the illusion of performance, action and utterance, where repetition makes it appear as-if-real. (2006a: 416)

Drawing on Derrida, Nayak describes how the power of repetition can make objects like race appear and become true; the power inherent in repetition and ambiguity runs throughout this book. Yasmin Gunaratnam asserts that 'despite theoretical understandings of "race" and ethnicity as relational and socially constructed, there is still a voracious appetite for approaches that freeze, objectify and tame "race"/ethnicity into unitary categories that can be easily understood and managed' (2003: 33). This book hopes to chart race's fluid flexibility; however I do not want to ignore the difference differences make or lose account of how power relations interact with these continuing differences (Ahmed, 1998).

Compared to ethnic or cultural orientations, discussing class was less straight-forward. Middle-class participants readily named themselves as such, claiming this valued position. Other participants reiterated that they were just 'normal' or 'ordinary' people, actively disidentifying from a working-class label (Savage, Bagnall and Longhurst, 2001; Skeggs, 1997). For the purposes of letting the research speak to inequitable relations of power, I have named participants who figure as more working-class within the remit of institutional power relations and who did not readily adopt the 'middle-class' label as working-class; however I realise this is problematic as several parents occupy grey areas. Sarah, the daughter of a coal miner who went on to get a degree and work as a teacher, did not comfortably claim middle-classness. Esther, a university-educated woman from a wealthy middle-class Nigerian family, lived on a demonised estate and had lost her status through migration. This flux highlights how class-making is not static, but a dynamic and continuous process (Savage, 2000). Now I will explore how Dreamfields' parameters were collectively constituted through numerous individuating disciplinary practices.

Notes

1 How Culford interprets and negotiates this 'suntan' comment within institutional life is very different from the accounts offered by Sara Ahmed (see 1997).
2 Mothers were disproportionately represented in this 'parent' category, with sixteen mothers and four fathers participating.

3

Disciplining Dreamfields Academy: a 'well-oiled machine' to combat urban chaos

The end product is such that the school is so well disciplined in so many different areas of its operation, including things like the behaviour of the children, that it means that the machine – if that's what the academy is – works. It's a well-oiled machine, it's well serviced, it's kept up to good operational standards and it's regularly fixed if it goes wrong. So it's able to deliver, if you like, its passengers. It can deliver what it's aim, I mean the train has got an aim to deliver something from A to B, that's what the school's doing. The school's taking the children from one position and getting them to the other. And if a wheel falls off, that can hinder, so what we need to be sure of is that in every single aspect of this school, the academy works. Every aspect of the school works. (Mr Davis, SMT)

This chapter describes how Dreamfields responds to narratives of failure, the demands of the education market, and anxieties over national decline explored in Chapters 1 and 2. Dreamfields is disciplined through a variety of practices to ensure its 'well-oiled machine' routinely fashions its raw materials in accordance with global capital's needs. This chapter examines what 'operational standards' run throughout the institution to ensure every aspect 'works', exploring how this machine or 'train' literally 'moves' its cargo through the daily imposition of structure and how bodies are disciplined through this journey. Dreamfields showcases New Labour's communitarian agenda where visions of a British urban renaissance met and combined with a criminal justice agenda (Atkinson and Helms, 2007: 2). Teachers' language reflects how this agenda has permeated education, with phrases like 'zero tolerance' and 'a culture of no excuses' used by several teachers. Academisation becomes a way of escaping Urbanderry's pathologised 'place-image' by transforming narratives of failure (Shields, 1991: 6–7). Ironically, these stigmas are overwritten through the reiteration of pathology as the 'urban chaos' discourse is drawn upon to justify using 'boot-camp' tactics.

This chapter maps the contours of the physical environment through which students and teachers are funnelled. It describes how space, time and the body are (re)ordered through repetitive routines and surveillance which mesh various modes of discipline, ranging from panoptic surveillance to verbal chastisement to audit systems' measurement to create the neoliberal subject. Drawing on de Certeau's concept of strategies, it describes how Dreamfields as a subject with

'will and power' isolates itself, establishing a 'break between a place appropri-
ated as one's own and its other' (1988: 36). This is a useful way to think through
Dreamfields' demarcation of itself as a space apart from Urbanderry from where
it can manage exterior threats (1988: 36). While in the following chapters I will
examine how different bodies receive different interventions and negotiate the
landscape in disparate ways, this chapter focuses on how the institutional landscape is ideally and reflexively envisioned and the types of subjectivities it seeks
to cultivate.

Regimentation, transparency and predictability: 'keep things tight and remain vigilant'

Panoptic surveillance is a key disciplinary technique employed at Dreamfields. In
1787 Jeremy Bentham proposed his Panopticon as a 'new principle of construction' that could be used in institutions including prisons, factories and schools.
This 'inspection house' comprised a circular building with occupants based
around its circumference in separate partitioned cells surveyed by an unseen
inspector located in the centre. This configuration promoted a 'new mode of
obtaining power of mind over mind' through inspection's perpetual gaze (1995:
31). While Bentham acknowledges that this perpetual gaze is 'impossible', the
next best solution is to have occupants 'conceive' themselves to be under surveillance (1995: 33–4). Although the Panopticon was never realised, Foucault
warns against seeing it simply as a 'dream building'; instead it is 'the diagram of
a mechanism of power reduced to its ideal form ... it is in fact a figure of political
technology that may and must be detached from any specific use' (1991a: 205).
The Panopticon differentiates a crowd of integrated individuals and produces
'a collection of separated individualities' by mapping, assessing, distinguishing,
comparing and classifying (1991a: 201–3). Bentham's Panopticon also represents
a wider historical shift away from negative, arresting forms of discipline to lighter
'discipline-mechanisms' where power is made more productive and subtly coercive (1991a: 209). Foucault's reading of the Panopticon as symbolic of the art
of liberal government broadens *Discipline and Punish*'s arguments beyond the
mechanics of particular institutions (Gane, 2012: 618). Nicholas Gane questions
how the political economy of surveillance has changed through subsequent shifts
towards a neoliberal state: 'if the Panopticon is a model of governmentality within
which the state is said to watch over and thereby discipline the market, what of a
post-panoptic or neoliberal arrangement whereby the market increasingly structures the form and activities of the state?' (2012: 612). Instead of acting alone, the
Panopticon comprises one aspect of Dreamfields' disciplinary repertoire, suggesting neoliberal governmentality assumes a multifaceted approach. Now I will
describe the panoptic qualities built into Dreamfields' daily routines and physical
structure.

Discipline begins early at Dreamfields. Many senior teachers arrive at 7.00am
for meetings or to catch up on work. At 8.00am the gate is unlocked and teachers
monitor the stream of arriving students. By 8.20am the gate is pulled shut and two

teachers are left at the entrance to stamp lunchtime detentions into latecomers' planners, while any late sixth-formers are required to arrive twice as early the next day. Teachers on playground duty end the basketball games and conversations, herding students towards the centre of the playground before line-up is signalled by the 8.25am whistle. As the whistle sounds, a startling wave of movement occurs with students hurriedly weaving in and out of one another in order to arrive at their designated space. A member of the SMT frequently times this procedure; it usually takes less than one minute for hundreds of children to assemble themselves in straight, silent alphabetised lines according to their year and form group. Each head of year (HOY) stands on a bench in front of their respective year group; students stand to attention, with their bags off their shoulders. Students must also remove their hats, scarves and coats, regardless of temperature, as no outerwear can be worn in the building. This scene of uniform squares of students assembled before each HOY could easily be mistaken for four military regiments awaiting inspection by their commanding officer. All teachers must assist with line-up and are repeatedly reminded during briefings not to stand towards the back talking, but to actively participate. An all-staff email stipulates that teachers should report to the playground not *during* or *after* the whistle, but *promptly before* it sounds at 8.25am, 11.07am, 12.05pm and 1.06pm. Any students slow to get in line, not facing the front, or daring to talk are reprimanded by teachers walking up and down the lines inspecting uniforms and behaviour. Poorly behaved students are called to the front by their HOY who will verbally chastise them or occasionally make them face the wall. After relevant announcements, the HOY calls each member of staff teaching the next period. The respective teachers raise their hands and wait as students form another straight line. The HOY shouts not to cut across lines, but to walk straight to the back and around.

After ensuring the lines are silent and orderly, each class moves towards their respective learning area where another teacher stands on duty at each doorway to ensure students enter silently in single file. Additional teachers are stationed along the hallway and on each stairwell landing; between each lesson these duties are repeated so no spaces are unattended. SMT member Mr Vine, nicknamed 'Robocop' by students due to his rigid comportment and dress sense, patrols the playground, referencing his iPad outlining the duty rota to check teachers are in position. If any teachers are not in their allocated spaces, an all-staff email is sent asking them to report for duty immediately. Students perform this line-up three times a day: before school, after break time and lunchtime. It is one of the key procedures used to collectively discipline the student body. Teacher Mr Turner describes its precision as 'phenomenal', attributing its success to 'abnormal' strictness' on everything … from the uniform to the way that they stand to the not making any noise whatsoever if they are in a line'. He videoed it to show his old colleagues at a private school who were astonished this order was possible in Urbanderry.

Dreamfields was designed by a prominent architectural partnership. It sits back from the road and along the front runs a 12-foot-high corrugated metal fence. Its 'U' shape creates two wings, with all classrooms facing out to the playground, while the back is solid concrete. The front of the 'U' is largely glass, placing all classrooms and teacher office areas on display. All activity is conducted within the bounds of this U, making movements visible through the glass frontage. The only facilities behind the school are parking spaces, rubbish bins, PE changing rooms, a smoker's hut, and a complex of Portakabins that house the Learning Support Unit (LSU) where excluded students work in silent isolation. There is no staff room at Dreamfields; instead teachers share departmental offices dispersed along the ground floor. Teacher Mr Arkanel describes how 'every department has got their own little box', while Mr Mitchell suggests the glass-fronted offices 'encourage staff to be high-profile and vigilant at all times. The whole building is designed to be very open and so it's visibility, very good visibility at all times in the school. You can see what the students are doing.' More senior members of staff have glass-fronted offices on the first or second floors. Dreamfields' built-in visibility and business-style office arrangements were an intentional design decision. The architects have described how Dreamfields' design reflects Culford's educational approach and aspired to create a sense of inclusion, openness and accessibility while also offering a feeling of place and security. While openness or accessibility were rarely mentioned, openness, surveillance, safety and security feature throughout teacher, student and parent narratives. Mr Davis describes how Dreamfields' design fosters accountability:

> Well, it's purely by eyes and ears. It's about observation of all the senior management. It's about expectations of the head and the headteacher being around the school, measuring and quality, assuring what he knows should be happening. So by having visible presence in every part of this school the quality assurance procedures are that much more efficient and far-reaching. Because there is nowhere in this school where anyone can hide. It's an open school. The school is open because there is literally, literally transparency in the building. You know, the rooms are transparent … You can see what is happening in people's offices and children know that they are being observed, which is the same for staff, they know they are being observed, even if it's just a passing glance. Even if it's just an informal visit, as well as all the formal things. There is nothing that the management team, nothing that the head doesn't get to see or know about. So it's constant inspection.

Transparency induces a state of 'constant inspection'. One lunchtime Mr Turner announced Dreamfields' prison-style architecture was bothering him, joking that he wanted a place to pick his nose in peace. Ms Taylor, who had recently started at Dreamfields, said when she pulled up on her first day the taxi driver asked her if it was a prison or a school – and she wasn't sure! She described it to her former colleagues as 'like being in a science experiment' because of all the glass. Ms Burke laughed in agreement, adding it was like a factory. This laboratory-machine functions as an ideal setting for experiments correcting individuals (Foucault, 1991a: 203). Visual transparency enables the SMT to enact perpetual surveillance through frequent observations and 'passing glances'. Ms Hatcher said that she often felt like one of the students, and her department joked about surveillance:

And yeah, definitely, we used to call it SMTV *(laughs)* – have you been on SMTV in the last couple of weeks? They are just constantly observing everything that you do. But I suppose, in some ways, it could be construed as a supportive thing to make sure that you are okay, but it certainly didn't feel like that.

Visibility makes teachers' arrivals and departures evident; several discussed the dangers of being seen leaving too early after school finished. Glass offices make bodies out of place immediately obvious.

The playground area functions as a stage where teachers must perform their dedication to Dreamfields' ethos and students must visibly submit to discipline. Ms Hatcher describes these demonstrations: 'You have to be seen to be singing from the same hymn sheet ... you do have to make it very clear that you are very much behind the whole thing and yeah, that you are willing to shout and you're not willing to stand for walking past a kid with a top button undone or whatever.' Several newer teachers were advised on how to perform by more experienced colleagues. Ms Hatcher was told to 'make sure in the first couple of months you are seen shouting at a kid in the playground, 'cause that will look really good with SMT'. Ms Austin was warned that 'people are watching you', so she was to make sure students walked in quietly from the playground.

Pupil movements and whole-school events are carefully choreographed. Culford congratulated physical education (PE) staff on a meticulously organised sports day that showed Dreamfields was 'a professional organisation with attention to the details'. Staff briefings routinely contain reminders to 'keep things tight and remain vigilant' on behaviour. The emphasis is placed on execution, not content, yet detailed planning prevents undesirable content from surfacing. At a Parent Teacher Association (PTA) meeting, parents eagerly discussed having a karaoke stall at the winter fair. A couple of mothers had already selected videos and others enthusiastically offered suggestions; however karaoke was promptly vetoed. Teacher Ms Stuart explained that karaoke would have to be 'vetted': these were student performances and must be previewed because of the behaviour issues that could arise if they were inappropriate. The PTA chair looked deflated and the women reluctantly stuffed their videos back into their bags. There is no room for unpredictability at Dreamfields; self-expression must be pre-approved to prevent subversive behaviour. This elimination of spontaneity and continual visibility relates to de Certeau's description of one of strategies' key effects: the establishment of an autonomous space. Strategies are defined as actions 'capable of articulating an ensemble of physical places in which forces are distributed' (1988: 38). This division of space enables panoptic practices, providing 'a mastery of places through sight' where 'the eye can transform foreign forces into objects that can be observed and measured, and thus control and "include" them within its scope of vision' (1988: 36). The ability to see across a vast distance makes prediction possible through being able 'to run ahead of time by reading a space' (1988: 36). This pre-emptive, managerial stance is also applied to teachers through the eradication of the communal staff room.

Dividing spaces and bodies

A staple in most schools, the omission of a staff room was another design decision described by SMT members as a positive move to prevent factionalism and increase productivity. Mr Vine feels staff rooms are places 'where staff go and hide out and try to avoid students' and are 'a breeding ground for negativity … where people get together and talk about others or moan'. Mr Davis thinks the lack of a staff room fits 'the businesslike nature of the school'. Administrator Mr Fields feels private-sector businesses and Dreamfields share a similar work ethic:

> There is no doubt that people at the school work very hard … it's not a question of, well, you come here and you can relax for the first hour and have a cup of tea and have a long lunch break, which I think is probably still the case in some local authorities, but here people do work really hard.

Eradicating the staff room symbolically severs Dreamfields from the perception that local authorities are unproductive spaces in comparison to private businesses, responding to narratives of public-sector failure. Staff taking a break or talking to one another are framed as troublesome activities eliminated by preventing congregation.

The majority of teaching staff connected the missing staff room to poor communication and cohesion. Many teachers did not know all their colleagues' names and attributed this to the absence of communal space and Dreamfields' non-stop pace. Several teachers felt manipulated by the lack of a staff room, regarding it as a clever management decision. Mr Arkanel describes it as intentionally divisive:

> Well, looking at the design of the school I think it's been planned very well to split, control … because if you look at the school, every department has got their own little box where teachers are stuck in those offices and they can't come out and talk to another person. For example, I've been there this year and I have not had a word with one of the English teachers because they are on the other side of the building and I am on the other side, and we don't see each other. And I can't ask them, you know, basic things, like, 'how is this student doing in your class?' I can email them, but I can't talk to them.

He suggests these divisions stop teachers from communicating about their labour conditions: 'if everyone knew that people weren't happy with staying in school until six, maybe people could have said something or they could have pressured the senior management'. Ms Watson thinks it is 'very clever that we don't have a staff room 'cause it means that people work harder then, and they can moan, but they moan less because there are not so many people gathered together, moaning together'. While reflexively acknowledged as a decision to increase productivity, management also claims that it benefits students because they can continually access teachers.

This dividing and distribution are more rigidly replicated with students. As Culford announced during a briefing: 'We have a rule about groups of children that we should go over for any new members of staff … We do not have groups of more than six or seven congregating together. If you see large groups of children, you need to break them up so they do not cause silliness and mayhem.' In a briefing several months later, SMT member Ms Butler emphasised the need for teachers to weave in and out of large groups of boys during playground duties. Teachers should use their 'gut instincts' and intervene if people looked suspicious; hugging or any sort of physical contact were off limits. These dividing practices stop the formation of troublesome collective dispositions and the 'dangerous coagulation' of bodies (Foucault, 1991a: 143). Focusing on the prevention of transgressive acts through policing the 'suspicious'-looking bodies of young people mirrors New Labour's regime of Anti-Social Behaviour Orders (ASBOs) and Disorder Acts. Curfews and dispersal orders specifically designed for youth aimed to shape the use of public space, with groups of two or more dispersed and minors removed to their homes between certain hours (see Squires and Stephen, 2005). Students are also divided through rigorous subject setting, a hierarchical sorting mechanism with real spatial consequences through its distancing or collecting of bodies. The playground is also spatially divided by year groupings, preventing different ages from intermingling. In addition to spatial techniques, Dreamfields also utilises more time-honoured coercive methods.

The verbal cane

One afternoon a male teacher was loudly shouting at a 12-year-old boy in his office, attracting the attention of passing students going to lessons.

'You do not argue with me. Ever.'

The teacher repeated this a few times.

'You don't answer me back and give attitude.'

The volume increased as the teacher bent his face closer to the boy's, whose back was against the wall.

'Come on – you want to get angry? You want to get aggressive with me? Come on. I dare you. I dare you.'

One passing student abruptly stopped, recognising the boy was his little brother. I asked him to carry on. He went a few paces, but as the bellowing increased he stopped, looking torn over what action he could take until another teacher hurried him along. The shouting sent goose bumps down my spine as I walked down the stairs. The sound filtered through the atrium to the ground floor where students whispered, looked scared or giggled. One teaching assistant with a perplexed grimace whispered to me that all students were affected by this noise.

Shouting features frequently around the corridors, instilling what Mr Turner calls 'the fear factor'. Several teachers are known for their lung capacity, their booming shouts periodically cascading through the building. Culford announced in one briefing that the Shadow Secretary for Education would be visiting the school, so no screaming and shouting should occur between 8.30am and 10am; if teachers wanted to shout at a pupil after 10am, that was up to them. Emails reminding teachers to keep down shouting in learning areas were periodically sent before VIP visitors arrived. This concealment puzzled two long-term staff members: if what Dreamfields did was shout at children to get results, they suggested this should not be stopped when Ofsted or other guests arrived. They concluded Dreamfields should either have confidence in what they do and how they do it, or do something else. Prohibiting shouting when Dreamfields assumes its role as a display case highlights a sense of guilt, or at least recognition, that verbal aggression is widely frowned upon.

Several teachers also took issue with this practice. Ms Adewumi described how she wanted students to respect her and learn not because they were forced to, but because of her guidance. She felt there were other ways to discipline children; students should not have to be 'humiliated or treated like animals' to learn. This was a central factor in her decision to leave Dreamfields. Ms Hatcher also felt the application of discipline could be inappropriate: 'I remember seeing ... very tall members of male staff screaming in the faces of Year 7 girls or boys and I found that very hard to digest. And even today – it is still around the building today – and I still think it is unnecessary.' Mr Bello felt discipline was necessary, but doubted Dreamfields' methods:

> *Mr Bello*: So the ethos seems to be working at the moment, but I'm not sure – is it right? Is it wrong? Are the kids being mistreated?
>
> *CK*: Do you think it's right?
>
> *Mr Bello*: I think the shouting, the bellowing ... I don't think that's right. I don't think you need to scream as if you want to almost harm a child to some extent. I don't think that's necessary. I think the structure that they have that the teachers can fall back on is enough. I think if we depended more on that structure instead of impinging on the health of the teachers – because it's not healthy, is it? I think the kids would learn better ways because maybe they are getting that at home, you see, so ...
>
> *CK*: Ah, yes.
>
> *Mr Bello*: Well, you know, it's a form of verbal aggression, isn't it? Do you know what I mean? Is it going to work to their advantage or are they going to learn and think that this is what you have to do to get people to do things? When they have children they might try the same thing but then they might escalate a little bit. There are a lot of issues, social issues, so ...

Mr Bello feels surveillance and routine provide enough structure without the addition of verbal aggression and its potentially negative effects on teachers and students. Verbal chastisement acts as a stand-in for physical punishment, violating without unlawfully touching the body. Panoptic surveillance is reinforced by more old-fashioned punitive techniques, creating docile, pliable bodies open to the inscription of capital. Students must both learn to self-regulate through perpetual surveillance while being punitively coerced.

Enclosure/dislocation: 'You could be anywhere, really'

Changing urban culture means physically demarcating Dreamfields as a space and culture apart from Urbanderry, severing students from 'urban chaos'. Dreamfields' gates remain shut, except when students go for PE classes at the park, until the first group of students depart at 3.10pm. Sixth-formers can leave for lunch, but must remain on site throughout the day, whether or not they have lessons. Teachers stand inside and outside the gates after school, ensuring students do not loiter but go directly home, while students from surrounding schools lingering near Dreamfields' entrance in an attempt to meet their friends are moved on. Staff 'sign in' via biometric fingerprint recognition at security-guard huts stationed next to two entrances. Mr Vine describes how the gates act as a sieve excluding malignant cultures: 'It's not allowing the bad elements of the community to come into the school gates. So once they [students] come into the school gates, anything that's not wanted is left outside. It's another set of rules once they enter ... and all of that must be left behind.' The site remains closed to surroundings that are seen as potentially threatening to Dreamfields' structures. Ms Carrier explains: 'When you've got structures as rigorous as this, you don't want anything to dilute them.'

Teachers also noted this separation, often in less positive terms than SMT members. Ms Hatcher compared it to her old school in Cumbria where she knew teachers at surrounding schools and met with them to share practices. Regrettably, this interaction did not happen at Dreamfields, which was 'kind of like a little bubble' where community involvement was not valued. Ms Austin also described Dreamfields as 'a little bit closed off from things ... it's all a bit kind of prison – keep it in ...'. Although they had helped the elderly with food hampers, she did not think Dreamfields did much within Urbanderry:

> You could be anywhere, really. You know we are in Urbanderry because of the kids and they come in and they talk about it, but I never see them in their environment unless I see them in the street, but I never, as a teacher, kind of see them work with the community and, you know, they don't go and do many things.

She relates this enclosure to security:

> I think it's this big fear of this area, it's like a denial of – get in here and kind of sort yourself out and be really good and get home as quickly as you can. Although they [the SMT] are kind of like, 'we can do this anywhere, this is amazing, it's in Urbanderry', there's none of that kind of 'yeah, well we're outside as well and we will branch out'.

Parent Alexander feels that although Dreamfields attracts very good staff, he doubts how much they know about the community, saying that the school's only less than excellent grading in its Ofsted report was in regard to community relations.[1] However, he adds: 'I do not think it bothers them too much because they know what the real goals are and that's what they are going to go for.' Alexander had discussed earlier in his interview that Dreamfields' 'real goals' were exam results.

Teachers were consistently frustrated that permission was seldom granted to take students on school trips. Mr Dean felt excursions were limited by a prevalent 'sense of anxiety – it's all results, results, results':

> It's contact time in the classroom. If you're not in the classroom and you're away, particularly during term time, it would be unheard of to go off gallivanting into Europe. For the last few years [in his previous school] I've done a trip to Madrid as a part of my course. If you ask any of the pupils was it beneficial to them in terms of the course, yes, absolutely. And did it detract from them passing their exams? Well, I'd say no … Whereas at the moment, I do not think we are at the point where we can do things like that because we are so results-driven. Which is understandable; again, it's not a criticism. I think anyone else would be in the same position. There is a lot of pressure on this academy to perform.

As Culford announced in a governor's meeting: 'We will live or die by those [GCSE] results – it's the first thing that people look at, even before Key Stage 3 or even A-levels.' Parent Veronica also describes Dreamfields' contradictory position:

> Um, plus the fact the school are in between a rock and a hard place – part of their remit is to reach out to the community and involve them, however then there are these rules in place – dare I say almost to keep them out or filter whoever comes in. It's the gatekeeping thing; I can understand why that happens.

Alexander highlights how this closed-gate stance contradicts a market model: 'It could be brimstone and lightning – parents will be made to wait and stand outside in snow, rain, or lightning. No one will say come inside, come in out of the cold, you are parents and our product are your kids, so effectively you guys are the customers – but we are not seen as that.' Alexander assumes the position of consumer, but this relationship does not practically exist. Both parents understand the need for security, but point out its downsides. Veronica says:

> It's security – security before all. Security and safety. It's a bit of, well, fear, there's a bit of fear, kind of, you know, that culture of fear. Which is part of my mixed feelings towards it, even though it works for my daughter. It's fantastic, whatever, but there is this doubt, there's this thing – this negative feeling which perhaps has more significance with other groups.

Veronica, a white middle-class mother, reflexively acknowledges this 'culture of fear' may affect ethnic-minority or working-class parents more. Alexander, black British and middle-class, suggests 'heavy' security was intended to prevent challenging parents from entering the site, but feels this is 'a bit rough because people are improving a lot in Urbanderry'. These visions of Urbanderry as home to a deficit culture brimming with danger draw on the historic framings explored in Chapter 2.

Despite Dreamfields' enclosure, the architects intended to build an inclusive environment. The initial designs depict the playground area as open to the community and merging seamlessly onto adjacent public space. Yet the play-ground has become an enclosed space, bounded by a gate and security points. The conversion of this idealistic vision into a securitised fortress both symbolises and embodies the tensions of New Labour's approach to urban regeneration, where the promotion of social justice and inclusion sits uncomfortably beside the pathologisation and exclusion of communities (Atkinson and Helms, 2007; see also Keith and Rogers, 1991; Young, 1999). Ruth Levitas explores the inherent contradictions of New Labour's third-way politics that deny 'structural conflicts of interest', exemplified by Blair's 1996 conference speech where he announced: 'Forget the past. No more bosses versus workers. You are on the same side' (1998: 114). This inversion exemplifies the flexibility of these conflicting ideali-sations; what takes precedence in practice is security. Schools are not measured and ranked through community accessibility, thus the 'real' aims of producing results dictate the agenda and structure the physical landscape. Surveillance is also extended to external spaces, where Dreamfields becomes not part of the commu-nity, but places its tentacles into it.

Unstable thresholds and the policing of liminal space

Dreamfields' use of rituals and routines seeks to transform students, instigate a particular culture, and return them changed to Urbanderry. Culford continually reiterates the importance of these techniques:

> You need lots of rituals and routines in urban education, more than you do in more prosperous areas ... You reflect on what works, so again my philosophy is more structure and not less. That's why children stand up when teachers walk into a room, that's why they say a mantra, that's why there is a uniform, that's why they are expected to say 'sir' and 'miss'.

Rituals are central to transformation, as old ways are discarded and new ways are embedded. Anthropologist Victor Turner's research regarding how rites of passage, symbolism and liminality work within the Ndembu tribe in Zambia is relevant to Dreamfields' transformative experiences. Turner describes how rituals separate people from everyday life, placing them in a limbo from which they return altered in some way (1988: 25). These rituals correspond to de Certeau's strategies that create bounded places where external threats can be managed; however, rituals provide a more performative lens that highlights the delicate process of transformation and movement between spaces. Turner's reflections on the anthropology of performance draw on folklorist Arnold van Gennep's work outlining three phases of a rite of passage: separation, transition and incor-poration. Separation 'clearly demarcates sacred space and time from profane or secular space and time' (Turner, 1982: 24). Separation not only spatially secludes, but involves additional rites altering the quality of time and inducing symbolic behaviour, which 'represents the detachment of the rituals' subjects ... from their previous social statuses' (1982: 24). This separation and detachment 'implies collectively moving from all that is socially and culturally involved ... from a previous socio-cultural state or condition, to a new state or condition' (1982: 24). Only through removal from the profane space of Urbanderry and its associated symbols can students access the sacred world of economic productivity via employment; passengers are delivered from 'point A to point B' through this process.

Liminality is the second, ambiguous transition phase. Turner describes this as a betwixt-and-between threshold space where things are not as they have been or will be, and is particularly relevant to Dreamfields' policing of public space. Unlike Turner's cultural performances, Dreamfields cannot enact a state of permanent separation from Urbanderry: teachers, and students go home at the end of each day and during the holidays.[2] Ms Fletcher laments this limited influence:

> I think, well, you know, we teach, we constantly go on to these kids about what is right and what is wrong, and I know that they have lots of different agencies provided for them to sort of try, and things like that [a former student's arrest] make me realise that there is only so much we can do. What was it that Ms Carrier said? We only see them for 195 days a year and then the rest of the time they are out there in the world with their friends or their parents.

Patrolling liminal spaces after school is an integral part of controlling how students behave in a less contained environment.

Senior staff members are despatched in pairs to walk the streets after school, ensuring students wear the uniform correctly and do not enter shops or loiter on their journey home. Teachers can visibly monitor whether or not the institutional structures have permeated the body or if they have been discarded once past the gate. Mr Richards describes how 'having the senior management team out on the streets of an evening, making sure the pupils are well-behaved and there is good discipline – having that structure out and about also helps as a public relations exercise'. Not only are students monitored, but structure is displayed to the public. By getting 'out and about', it becomes a structure with legs. Ms Butler describes how all 'our systems' work together to create an order which extends beyond the gates. Ms Carrier feels after-school staff surveillance creates a good image of Dreamfields:

> I think when our children go out into the local community they are seen very positively because they are not allowed to collect in large groups. Because they look smart ... they have that level of politeness, like, I quite often watch our kids get on the bus and they will let members of the public on first, for example.

The continual circulation of after-school patrols ensures that bodies correctly bear the symbols and behaviour demanded of the uniform, while continually separating Dreamfields students from less desirable youngsters. In addition to duties on foot, a more speedy patrol is also conducted. Mr Clark and Mr Dupont, two heavy-set men who work as security guards and administrative staff, jokingly call this the 'chicken-shop patrol'. This duty involves driving around to ensure students are not visiting chicken shops further afield. The following passage of fieldnotes describes my afternoon 'on patrol'.

Chicken-shop patrol

It was a cold Friday afternoon in February. We grabbed our coats and walked to the back of the building with Mr Clark instructing children to tuck in their shirts on the way. He said he was taking off his caring face and putting on his mean face for the job. We met Mr Dupont in the car park; he chuckled to see I was actually coming and had made sure to drive his black Mercedes so I could fit in the back. They joked about making me get students out of the chicken shops as we piled in and passed through the security gate; I said I would just make disapproving faces from the back. As the saloon coasted towards the junction with Acacia Road, I got a fleeting glimpse of how it must feel to be a cop looking out of the windows of your patrol car. Students on the pavement glared back with trepidation or relief that they had not been caught, clearly recognising the black Mercedes. Mr Dupont took a right and headed up Ruxley Road as Mr Clark scanned the pavement for mis-worn uniforms, potential fights or eating. They discussed the array of repeat chicken-shop offenders who could not help but indulge on their way home. Mr Clark laughed, recounting how one kid had spotted him just as he was tucking into his chicken and threw it to the ground in panic. Mr Clark told him that he'd wasted perfectly good chicken. The boy protested it was not his, but a large piece of chicken was stuck to the side of his mouth. When Mr Clark asked how he had got chicken glued to his cheek, the boy screwed up his face in exasperation: he'd been caught red-handed and no amount of fast-talking could hide his chicken-smeared face. Although we laughed at this unfortunate student, Mr Clark said he never took students' food or phones away from them, although Mr Richards sometimes did. Occasionally he even ate their chicken, because he was 'a rule unto himself'.

We went past Ashmead Estate and a dingy string of corner shops on Kemble Road. 'Nope, no one in there, no one in there, not any of ours', Mr Clark commented as Mr Dupont slowed at the entrance to each shop so he could peer inside. The pavements were lined with students from the nearby Grove Academy. Many of their ties were undone; some carried the coveted orange boxes of chicken. I asked what Grove Academy was like. Mr Clark said it was bad – they had no discipline and ran wild. The car continued up Kemble Road, leaving these students behind. Mr Dupont suggested we hit Bob's Chicken, an offending hot spot. As we approached Bob's on Monroe Avenue, sure enough, a congregation of Dreamfields students stood outside, possibly contemplating their next purchase. Mr Dupont pulled into a side street. The turning heads and sudden movements indicated the saloon had been spotted. Two girls gingerly trotted down the pavement as Mr Clark jumped out and crossed the busy road. Mr Dupont said it was always this lot. They would not take their planners today because it was Friday and Mr Richards was overloaded, but Mr Clark would chase them off. Mr Dupont explained how they used to make them return to Dreamfields immediately, but now took their planners and gave them to their HOY. That way students received their detention when retrieving their planner the next morning. It was usually a two-hour 6.00pm detention for being in a shop; for other things it might be the LSU or worse. I asked if any parents had complained. He said not so far, because it's good to get them off the street after school. Mr Clark came back to the car as several boys reluctantly skulked away from Bob's.

We continued down Monroe Avenue. Mr Clark said most of the middle-class kids cut through the alleyway and went into the corner shop near Sussex Square; apparently they were not chicken-shop goers. Mr Dupont said one of the independent shopkeepers had asked why they didn't patrol Tesco because he'd seen loads of students go in and no one stopped them, whereas they were banned from his shop. This reminded me of Ms Carrier saying Dreamfields had put two nearby chicken shops out of business. Without inspecting the middle-class corner shop, we turned onto Holly Close to find fifteen or twenty Dreamfields students standing on the pavement. Mr Dupont pulled over; Mr Clark jumped out again. Mr Dupont said they needed dispersing because if they were gathered like this they were probably up to no good. Mr Dupont related how one afternoon he had gone back to Dreamfields and told Mr Richards they had caught twenty kids wearing hoodies (which students are prohibited from wearing unless it is raining.) Mr Richards got upset, for twenty hoodies meant arranging twenty detentions. It took him ten minutes to realise it was raining. Mr Dupont laughed, revelling in Mr Richard's despair at illicit hoods. Mr Clark returned, reporting that two boys were just saying things to each other as everyone watched, but he'd sent them home.

As we went up Priory Lane to check the new Tesco Metro, Mr Dupont and Mr Clark went down memory lane. Mr Dupont, who is black British and was in the army before working as a security guard, recounted growing up around here and the expensive Italian shoe shop that was out of sync with the area's general poverty. Mr Clark, who is white British and lives in a nearby suburb, commented on how he used to drive down Priory Lane in three seconds flat when he worked nearby. Initially I attributed this to his love for speed, but he explained how this street was ground zero back then – full of drug dealers with Mercedes parked out front, plus he was the wrong colour to be driving through. They chuckled as we rounded the corner past Tesco. Their disparate stories, mixing a bit of nostalgia for the old days with fear and racial polarisation, now collided on a now achingly trendy, yet continually impoverished street. Although their routes had been littered with different experiences and positions, the present had rather absurdly landed these men together on this changed street, cruising in Mr Dupont's Mercedes – not drug dealers, but co-pilots on a private policing mission hunting down chicken-eating children.[3]

This patrol of liminal space around the Academy highlights how some children, particularly those fond of fried chicken, are not free to go where they like after school. While wearing their Dreamfields uniform, students continue to represent what Dreamfields stands for – and this does not include a child who eats chicken or wears a hoodie. Why is the chicken shop presented as a particularly perilous destination? Why is wearing a hoodie perceived as illicit unless it is justified by rainfall? These consumptive and stylistic choices readily tie to pathological representations of Urbanderry as a poor, racialised area, where black and white working-class criminality underlies the specific prohibition of the chicken shop. To go there is a 'poor choice' Dreamfields must prohibit in order to change urban culture. Public disorder and criminality are linked to these spaces; meanwhile, middle-class students visiting a corner shop seem to draw much less interest. With its fresh fruit and vegetables stacked outside, the corner shop does not represent a place of danger. It is also worth noting who gets sent on this patrol: two solidly built men – one white, one black – who both grew up nearby. These men do not work as teachers, but in more peripheral positions, and represent brawny symbols of masculine force. They become the muscle behind the Dreamfields ethos, the arm of the law extending into the community demanding compliance. This vignette also signals the changing dynamics of Urbanderry as an urban space, as chain shops and trendy bars move in, and there are new uses for the Mercedes.

Measuring and making

Discipline is not only enacted through brawn, but through numbers and the worlds they create. Sitting in his office, SMT member Mr Vine waves a thick bound booklet in his hand; it is the pack produced for governors detailing Dreamfields' GCSE performance. He flips through its numerous pages detailing student grades and departmental targets to ensure Dreamfields falls into the top one per cent. It tells governors what teachers predicted students would get overall and what they actually got. The pack outlines how accurate teacher predictions were individually and at departmental level, offering a class-by-class breakdown. It shows how students performed in individual subjects relative to other subjects, broken down by department and class by class, followed by the progression rates for English, maths and other subjects from when students arrive until they leave. Any other factors used by the government to rank schools are also included, and Mr Vine neatly concludes before plopping it down on his desk: 'that is the GCSE pack'.

The continual measurement, ranking and quantification of staff and students through testing and performance management regimes are a key component of Dreamfields' landscape, adding another disciplinary layer to guarantee the well-oiled machine delivers. Mr Davis puts Dreamfields' success down to 'more accountability, more monitoring, more quality assurance, higher expectations and higher levels of organisation'. He defensively describes how, as a 'self-evaluating school', Dreamfields must analyse data in detailed ways to allow for a 'quality check' of what is being delivered. Calculating residuals are a key part of this check, a process Mr Vine explains. First grades are converted into numbers, where A-star is eight, A is seven, B is six, and so forth. Each student is given an average grade across all subjects and then for each subject they work out how far above or below it is from the average grade. This calculation gives each student a number for each subject: if their average grade is a B and they got an A in a subject that would be plus one, whereas a C would be minus one. All of these are averaged up to give the residual for that subject.

After I digest how this assessment system functions, Mr Vine continues:

What it does is it tells you, if for example somebody says, 'Well, my A-stars to Cs are low because I've got a weak group, I've got a set four.' What I can then say, 'Well, actually, you're right actually, because in your class they did really well compared to how they did in all of their other classes.' Or, 'Actually, in your class they did worse than they did everywhere else across the curriculum.' And for one student that might be the case, i.e. someone who is better in maths than they are in English, but when you start looking across groups of twenty or thirty students, it bears out. And it comes very, very clearly out.

I then asked Mr Vine how these residuals are used:

So if I am not happy with something I will meet with the teacher and I will pick out individual students and I will say: 'Why has this student done worse in your class? Please explain. Why have you not picked this up? Why did you say they were going to get one grade and they got something completely different? Please explain this to me.'

Mr Vine thinks this direct approach is an effective way to manage teachers, after engaging them with the process:

Once they realise that that's how they are being measured, people tend to engage with it on a higher level and then the accuracy and the information going into the system is more accurate. And therefore the information coming out and the decisions being made based on the information becomes more accurate. It's only as good as what you put into the system.

'Teacher tracking' is presented as a reliable tool for monitoring teacher performance; however, Mr Davis admits this is often contentious:

The tendency for teachers is to worry about that and say, 'Well, that system is being used to pick us out and punish us or discipline us for underperformance', but in fact it's fairer to say that that department, if it is a department that is underachieving in some way, could be supported easier or more professionally if that is known about.

Mr Vine also talks about assisting underperforming teachers:

So we may start off with something as simple as a basic intervention, so somebody observing them or helping them and supporting them in their practice. That may be stepped up to more regular things like that going on very regularly, that in turn might be stepped up to them being watched by a senior team. It may be stepped up by the person in charge of teaching, and learning may get involved. So making somebody outside the department, making it the responsibility of the SLT (senior leadership team) to deal with, and they then develop a programme of watching lessons, being observed, being supported, book marking, checking.

Regular observation is seen as the best way to support teachers, yet Mr Vine's repeated use of 'stepped up' alludes to increasing levels of pressure and surveillance. The 'support' of performance management merges into a stressful, change-able experience, generating insecurity.

'Teacher tracking' was introduced in a staff briefing during 2008–9, and several teachers like Ms Hatcher repudiated its purported helpfulness:

> They [the SMT] sold it as a way of saying 'well, you know, if one person in a department is performing better, then they can help you to perform better'. And you know, that's bullshit. You know, it's basically, like this is going to be, you know, a list of who is performing the best and who's not having enough progress with their kids, and I just thought, that is outrageous! That's the sort of thing you do in sales, like 'who has had the most sales in one week?' And one thing you have got to remember is we are working with children [*emphasis*], we're not working with, um – there are just so many variables, it's not somebody's money – it's not sales, it's human beings.

This ordering and ranking of teachers mitigates trust and damages solidarities between teachers, signalling the further 'displacement of systems based on auton-omy and trust to one based on visibility and coercive accountability' (Shore and Wright, 2000: 77).

When I asked Mr Vine how he responded to teacher resistance, he adamantly asserted that teachers cannot be allowed to 'sit in the middle' and produce so-so outcomes which failed children: 'Because teaching only takes place if they learn something on the other side. So if they did not learn it and if they cannot repro-duce it in an exam, then you didn't teach. So you didn't do your job.' Teaching is equated with enabling information reproduction for exams, while Mr Vine inverts Ms Hatcher's rejection of the school-as-business: 'Yeah, you know we're not in a sort of a business where if you kind of just make a little bit of profit that's okay because you aren't costing the company any money, but you are costing chil-dren their lives. Especially somewhere like this, like Urbanderry.' An ambitious teacher who earnestly describes how he wants to help Urbanderry's children, Mr Vine describes himself as born 'lower working-class'. The school becomes a sacred business responsible for producing life-or-death outcomes which either allow students to escape urban chaos, or condemn them to be forever mired in what Mr Vine calls 'the council estate cycle'. Teacher auditing is given a redemptive purpose by drawing on the urban chaos discourse, ignoring how measurement functions as a political technology of the self. Although it may be described as supportive and thus democratically orchestrated and participatory, this obscures how audit practices like performance management are premised on hierarchical relationships and coercion where 'challenging the terms of reference is not an option' (Shore and Wright, 2000: 62). To resist is not only to sacrifice children's lives, but one's job.

In addition to the production of results, Mr Vine details the other key work numbers do:

> These are a bunch of numbers, but the reality is each one of those numbers is a child who is in this school, that's here to learn. And we sell ourselves, and we

do, sell ourselves as a school that lets no child slip through the cracks or fall behind or fail. So we've got to be, to have a way of ensuring that that is actually true. Parents send their children to this school and children come to this school believing that. So if I don't question when that doesn't happen, it would just happen more and more. So yes, we're a tough school, but we give something else and the answer is that they don't have to worry about behaviour, they don't have to worry about discipline, all these other factors – like a nice environment, a lovely building, is all taken care of. So they are answerable for kind of one thing … And if the student results aren't what they should be, then what have they been doing in the last year?

Numbers make Dreamfields' promises come true. This exemplifies the demands of forcing schools to 'sell' themselves through the education market, narrowing learning's remit to successful examination. After promoting Dreamfields' aspirational dream with its good grade guarantee, management must employ whatever techniques will make these promises come true. It must produce the advertised product. Teachers are responsible for generating these numbers, as well as collectively producing the disciplined bodies that Mr Vine asserts are simply provided.

Mr Arkanel queries the actual value of these numbers, asserting that Dreamfields is successful because it teaches to the examination and its 'excellent' assessment system 'allows' students to progress:

> For example, the assessment system says that each student must progress two sub-levels every year, and if that's the case then all the students will succeed; even if they come in with a very low grade they will come out with a C. Even if they come in with a level one, when they finish in five years, they will be out with a C. And when the teachers are not putting those grades into the system and it pops out red then someone will go to them and say, 'Why is that student not achieving?' And the teachers have to do something to make sure that the students are achieving and it's a green light on the assessment system, so that shows the government and the school that they are progressing, but from, you know, experience as well, sometimes you put a grade in that satisfies the system instead of it satisfying the student's knowledge and needs.

This assessment conveyor belt pushes the student along, but Mr Arkanel questions what this pushing accomplishes, lamenting how his 'real job' as a teacher is not to teach students to understand how his subject area really works, but to get students to produce a set product quickly and accurately so he can enter this into the system. Teachers and students produce what needs to be measured, as results-driven quantification directs learning.

The workings of power are obfuscated as these practices are presented as obvious, neutral and efficient management strategies, yet they are based on highly normative positions (Shore and Wright, 2000: 61). While Mr Vine says the data only reveal things he already knew from frequent observations – quantification practices remake the landscape by imposing new meanings and discarding old ones, rather than innocently describing the already present (Porter, 1995). These performance management practices shape and dictate institutions; what 'counts' determines what is cared about. This is a political technology for exercising power and imposing a 'culture of compliance' where conformity is mandatory (Dreyfus and Rabinow, 1982). This intensification of measurement, ranking and classification and the accompanying vocabulary of audit facilitate the emergence of a new ethics and politics of governance, signalling the narrowing of neoliberal governmentalities (Foucault, 1991b). Teachers must submit themselves to these laborious regimes to gain a sense of empowerment, yet 'far from controlling the contours and boundaries of this regime, the regime is set by the terms of the neoliberal policy discourse, articulated by government and policed by the market mechanisms that the discourse emphasises and empowers' (Wright 2012: 291).

Similarly, academic labour is not immune from audit, as academic institutions have been remade as financial bodies. Burrows (2012) queries how responses to metrics are distributed along raced, classed and gendered lines. Expanding on audit culture's move from trust to accountability, Burrows explores how forms of 'quantified control' evidenced through myriad metrics autonomously create markets. These technologies have unanticipated applications; citation indexes were initially developed to trace the history of ideas, but now rank academic journals. Burrows points out how 'it is not the conceptualisation, reliability, validity or any other set of methodological concerns that really matter' as metric indices assume a life of their own, becoming rhetorical devices enacting value in the neoliberal academy, and, as academics, 'we are fully implicated in their enactment' (2012: 361, 368). At Dreamfields these metric indices work to rearrange social hierarchies in new ways that present themselves as detached from the social and cultural dynamics sustaining them.

Conclusion: what is the machine making?

I was waiting for a student to finish an exam when Mr Davis came out of his office. We had always got along well and started chatting. He asked what the research was about; it had been two years since our tense interview that was uncharacteristic of our usual easy banter. I described the project and he said it was interesting but sighed, adding: 'Oh dear, is this going to be all over the Times Educational Supplement?' *Mr Davis mentioned the Education Bill and the latest educational news – a drive to fire all headteachers with an under fifty per cent GCSE pass rate. He asked if this fifty per cent constituted a 'failing' school if it was based in a deprived urban area. Would fifty per cent actually be an achievement in some areas where thirty-five per cent was more standard? He said this sort of pressure demanded an entirely new sort of automaton – they could not just keep examining and examining them. Common sense counted for nothing, he facetiously exclaimed; what counted was being able to write stuff onto paper – that was real learning! And if they examined badly, they could be examined again. Meanwhile, other forms of knowledge were not taken into account – what about being able to form human relationships, or draw, or play sports? Every child had at least one talent and not all of them could be academic. What constituted a failure?*

Questioning what counts as knowledge reminded me of Mr Davis's interview where he had described his own educational experience:

> Whatever they [students] come to the school with, whether it be class, resources, money, wealth, position, working, unemployed or not, there is obviously going to be a fit between what the child has and what the school expects in terms of its own values. So there are always going to be mismatches, and that's where the friction comes. I mean, for myself at school I was, you know, my parents were typically working-class. We didn't have books at home. Going to school for me was a nightmare because I was being asked to sit behind a desk all day and write things which was, you know, it was not a culture I could access or understand. It was alien to me. Whereas if they said to me, and they often did, 'Right, Bob, you can go and do music or you can go and do art or you can go and do textiles', I was very happy in those areas.

Aware of the continuing 'disparity of esteem' between forms of knowledge, as well as the relationship institutional values have to students' class location, Mr Davis was clearly agitated by recent developments. He illustrates the precarious and uncomfortable position of making an institution and being made by it, which is symptomatic of Dreamfields' individuating, yet totalising space.

Dreamfields' supposed return to more 'traditional' disciplinarian methods includes the deployment of surveillance, coercion, division and audit to guarantee the consistent production of quantifiable outcomes. This complex of systems does not revert back to the imagined good old days when students respected authority and were proficient in the three R's. As Foucault reminds us: 'one should totally and absolutely suspect anything that claims to be a return. One reason is a logical one: there is, in fact, no such thing as a return. History, and the meticulous interest applied to history, is certainly one of the best defences against this theme of the return' (2002: 359). At Dreamfields, multiple logics of power are at work on the body, creating a narrow, dense web of disciplines where both sovereign and disciplinary power dispose subjects.

Dreamfields' panoptic architecture does not work on its own, but requires a matrix of interventions to work. The Panopticon's classical liberalism has been augmented and built upon by disciplinary forms. These structures work to both hold the body in place while also moving and structuring the body via classed, raced and gendered neoliberal norms; this enabling tourniquet simultaneously produces and reduces. This empirically supports Gane's theoretical suggestion that neoliberal governmentalities could be explored using 'a fourfold typology of surveillance' where surveillance is conceived as discipline, control, interactivity, and a way of promoting competition (2012: 614). While the academy programme claims to promote creativity and innovation through enhanced freedoms, these qualities are limited through the result imperative. Success is read through the register of exams; there is no 'freedom' from this continually tightening constriction which demands an 'entirely new automaton'.

Pitting the transgressive space of Urbanderry against the reformative space of Dreamfields shows how culture and value are marked out through physical space where Urbanderry's external culture is positioned as valueless. Rendering Urbanderry's culture and knowledge as incompatible and contrary to education has classed and raced implications hinted at by Mr Davis and which I will explore in Chapters 5, 6 and 7. Dreamfields' easy conversion to a heavily securitised fortress from its initial design as an accessible landscape illustrates the inevitable exclusions that inclusion implies. This enclosure also relates to the overwhelming pressure to produce results. Results are the yardstick measuring and valuing the space; community accessibility ultimately does not 'count'. A concern with 'community' issues only detracts labour and attention away from pressing priorities. Despite the many demands of Dreamfields' well-oiled machine, it remains a sought-after school. The next chapter explores how Dreamfields cultivates an evangelical belief in both the institution and the self, which makes its requirements bearable and often desirable.

Notes

1 Notably, promoting social cohesion and community engagement was removed from the Ofsted inspection criteria in 2010.
2 Although the school does run a Saturday school throughout the year and holds mandatory GCSE revision sessions for designated borderline-C students held during school holidays.
3 This patrol can also occur in reverse, as students were also collected and brought to school if they were absent from mandatory GCSE revision sessions. All this shifting and moving of bodies is performed in the service of results.

4

Cohering contradictions and manufacturing belief in Dreamfields' 'good empire'

Throughout this lesson I aspire to maintain an inquisitive mind, a calm demeanour and an attuned ear so that in this class, and all classes, I can reach my true potential. (Dreamfields' Academy reflection)

The golden opportunity you are seeking is in yourself. It is not in your environment, it is not in luck or chance, or the help of others; it is in yourself alone. (poster on a Dreamfields' classroom wall)

At the start of each class students must put their planners on their desks alongside all the necessary materials for that lesson, place their bags on the floor and stand straight behind their desks before reciting the reflection. This dutiful standing and recitation in unison reminded me of pledging allegiance to the flag as a student growing up in the United States; each morning we stood with our right hands on our hearts and declared our loyalty to the Republic. As we progressed from children to teenagers, our initial enthusiasm waned, the 'one Nation under God, indivisible, with liberty and justice for all' dissipating into a mumbled murmur, our hands reluctantly resting on stomachs or dangling by our sides. Dreamfields students' recitation of the reflection also loses its vigour as students pass from being generally eager 11-year-olds to wearily lethargic 15-year-olds. Yet unlike my US high school, Dreamfields students must recite the reflection six times per day and are often punished if it is not pronounced with 'the appropriate respect'. Most notably, Dreamfields' reflection is not a vow of loyalty to a nation-state or a collectivity of any description; instead it is a pledge of allegiance to the self and its aspirational fulfilment. This appeal to the self with unlimited potential is a powerful trope continually employed at Dreamfields to cultivate belief and compliance.

This chapter explores how the techniques of discipline described in Chapter 3 are made palatable and even welcomed through promoting a belief in the institution, its methods and its benefits to individual futures. Belief is cultivated through the use of repetition and morality tales that smooth over the various contradictions and ambiguities inherent in Dreamfields' approach. Culford's position as principal and archetypal masculine figurehead is paramount due to his dictatorial management style and his embodiment of the ethos. He assumes the combined role of saviour, hero, military commander and business executive in this rigidly hierarchical operation. He leads a redemptive troupe of teachers-as-surrogate parents who labour to redeem a twenty-first-century 'urban residuum'. Culford symbolises Dreamfields' mission, embodying its mantra as a self-made, mixed-race man of modest working-class origins who has made it to the top. Crafting 'appropriate' aesthetic appearances and reiterating Dreamfields' superior position in the education market are also facets of this indoctrination process, offering powerful proof of institutional validity and providing a sweetener, allowing the often unpleasant medicine of discipline to go down smoothly.

Dreamfields staff recite the universally high expectations of students. Mr Davis describes how a teacher at a nearby school nearly fell off his chair when he told him Dreamfields' predicted GCSE 80 per cent pass rate, adding that many urban schools would never dream this was possible, blaming factors like the children being from Urbanderry. Yet this chapter examines how Dreamfields' 'high expectations' are steeped in raced and classed norms that extirpate heterogeneity. Culford's polysemous positioning acts as a powerful stance, obscuring the particularity of Dreamfields' universals, as education functions as a coercive tool inducing parents, students and teachers into the dominant symbolic in return for a chance to live out good-life fantasies.

A sermon in the church of the self: 'may good triumph over evil'

The entire school was assembled in the sports hall for the end-of-term Christmas assembly. The SMT took their seats on stage, the band came to the last bar of a carol and Culford assumed his customary place behind the podium. He touched on three themes currently in the news: the terrible economic recession that would probably carry on into the New Year; the horrible abuse of children by their families; and most importantly, the election of Barack Obama as the first black president of the United States. Culford showed a clip of Obama's acceptance speech in Chicago; students looked on, the vast majority captivated and inspired. He asked who would have thought that after so many years of prejudice and civil rights struggles the US would elect a black president? This triumph confounded conventions and expectations. He offered three reasons for Obama's victory: first, he had wanted to succeed and was determined. He worked hard to beat the odds and had the will to overcome prejudice. Secondly, Obama was educated. Culford again rhetorically asked if Obama would be where he was now if he were not an educated man. No way, he answered, adding that anybody who thought education and qualifications did not matter was bonkers – they were the key to success. Thirdly, Obama had excellent communication skills, capable of conjuring up a feeling in just a few words, referencing his 'yes we can' speeches. Directing this to the Year 11 students sitting in front of him, brimming with enthusiasm, Culford added: 'We can give you a great building, good equipment, fantastic teachers, but you have to meet us half-way. The other half is you – you have to want it.'

An image of the baby Jesus now filled the screen. Culford described how

Christians reflected on Jesus' birth and the love his earthly family gave him at this time of year. Referring to the now infamous murder of Baby Peter[1] in London, he said some families were not giving love. Family was key; when you become the head of a family you have to give your family care. This was more important than how much money you had or going on nice holidays. Family values were important for the Obamas; they had good morals and a clear idea of right and wrong. Finally Culford tied these themes to Andrew Moore, Dreamfields' late sponsor, who came from a poor background but became a very wealthy, successful businessman. Even when Moore had faced economic problems and struggles, he still got out of bed happy because he liked facing a new challenge and seeing what new solutions he could find. At this point, Culford asked everyone to bow his or her heads, leaving a pregnant pause.

The cavernous hall was completely silent, save the occasional cough or sneeze.

After a few moments Culford asked students to remember Mr Spencer, a teacher who had recently died, commending his determination to come to work each day despite his terminal illness.

Another pause.

Culford finally broke the silence, sombrely pronouncing: 'May good triumph over evil.' Slowly everyone opened their eyes and raised their heads as the band struck up a rousing rendition of Curtis Mayfield's 'Move On Up' – the perfect Motown soundtrack to accompany a rags-to-riches escape from the urban ghetto via a magical combination of willpower and education.

This neoliberal church of the self and its morality tales promote several key ideas. We are given a cast of masculine heroes who have triumphed over evil: Barack Obama, Andrew Moore, Mr Spencer, Jesus, and Culford himself as the mixed-raced son of a lorry driver. These masculine heroes conquer all manner of hardship – from racial prejudice to poverty to physical infirmity – to reign victorious over their lives and forge their own destinies. Dreamfields' mission is aligned with Obama, a much-respected figure among students, suggesting the school provides the necessary tools to fashion themselves into future Obamas. It portrays itself as a revolutionary project breaking with convention, rather than a conservative force trying to reinstate a nostalgic version of traditional British values infused with a hefty dose of the American dream. Culford uses the Baby Peter case to exemplify what a lack of family values can produce. By employing this extreme, heart-breaking example as a worst-case scenario of moral lapse and contrasting it to the Obamas' wholesome portrayal of family values, a sensational tale with clear binaries of good versus evil is created. This drama removes its characters from a social context, placing them in a heroes and villains scenario to make persuasive rhetorical points. Tales and legends 'are deployed, like games, in a space outside of and isolated from daily competition, that of the past, the marvellous, the original' (de Certeau, 1988: 23). The morality of Jesus is tied to the nation-state led by the nuclear, heterosexual family, which is wedded to the success and wealth of Dreamfields' sponsor. Meanwhile poor parenting techniques, largely propagated by single mothers, are instigators of moral dissolution.

> The formality of everyday practices is indicated in these tales, which frequently reverse the relationships of power and, like the stories of miracles, ensure the victory of the unfortunate in a fabulous, utopian space. This space protects the weapons of the weak against the reality of the established order. It also hides them from the social categories which 'make history' because they dominate it.
> (de Certeau, 1988: 23)

Dreamfields aligns its mission with the pursuit of equality, while simultaneously refuting the structuring importance of race and class on positioning. Individuals can overcome prejudice through individualised determination. These magniloquent speeches serve as cogent, emotive vehicles admonishing students and staff to feel part of a progressive project.

The empire-builder and bringer of happiness

This mission not only promises access to the good life, it also fuses happiness with cultural transformation. As described in Chapter 2, Culford claims 'urban children' from 'unstructured backgrounds … and often very unhappy ones' need more structure. The term 'urban children' or 'Urbanderry children' is used by several teachers to describe a largely ethnic minority and working-class student body; unstructured unhappiness is tied to the working-class, ethnic-minority 'urban child'. Sara Ahmed's re-description of empire's civilising mission as a happiness mission, where 'human happiness is increased through the courts (law/justice), knowledge (reason), and manners (culture, habits)', where 'Empire becomes a gift that cannot be refused, a forced gift', illuminates Culford's linking of urban children to unhappiness (2010: 124–5). Ahmed outlines how the unhappy Other provides the premise of action, where 'colonial knowledges constitute the other as … being unhappy, as lacking the qualities or attributes required for a happier state of existence' (2010: 125). Moving towards this more middle-class position requires 'acquiring good habits' and an 'affective disposition' where 'you learn to be affected in the right way by the right things' (2010: 129). Urbanderry natives old and new can be structured into dominant value systems while broader structural issues are ignored, yet simultaneously drawn upon to make value judgements. Dreamfields' mission functions as a gift to urban children, forcing them to become less ethnic and more middle-class so they can move towards happy futures.

Culford thinks people with a clear vision run good schools, ideas he claims he developed not by reading a book, but through 'trial and error' in urban schools. Dreamfields' approach is something he vows to disseminate: 'We'll spread the message of Dreamfields to other schools. Dreamfields will become an empire … Not an evil empire. A good empire.' He asserted that the ethos should not be tied to one person, but be part of a wider culture that teachers 'lower down the pyramid buy into' and then carry out by becoming leaders themselves: 'We want to train, develop, nurture, encourage deputy heads, assistant heads, heads of department, people lower, to say, "Hey, I believe in this." You know? "This is a credo I can repeat in other institutions.'" The ethos takes on religious dimensions as a doctrine teachers can invest in and export to other deprived areas as truth, combining the language of church and market. At the close of the interview, when I asked if he had any other comments, Culford laughed, saying: 'No, that's the gospel according to St Culford!' Dreamfields' gospel has been subsequently spread through Culford's increasing influence on education policy.

Culford's 'good empire' rhetoric has taken on increasingly strident, masculinised tones since our interview. He courted controversy by publicly suggesting heads should be powerful empire-builders crafted in the guise of gun-slinging action heroes. He did not believe in distributed leadership, but instead felt that heads should enjoy exercising dictatorial power. Critics questioned if Culford's approach was a little too reminiscent of the well-meaning white missionaries of yesteryear dispatched to the colonies to show them the Christian way. Yet, as previously mentioned, Culford is not white, but mixed race. Nor is he leading a Christian organisation; however he effectively synthesises the masculine action hero with religious and militaristic overtones to create a powerful message. His position highlights the elasticity of race and class, advantageously employed to claim authenticity within certain contexts without implying a progressive political position, despite numerous references to equality. By embodying the heroic individualism he promotes, Culford proves his statements are true.

Culford's depiction as the tough-love saviour of poor and ethnic-minority children has been bolstered by press coverage, turning the Panopticon explored in the previous chapter outwards and converting it momentarily into a display case where the public can behold bodies redeemed through Dreamfields' training. This posturing is more than a media guise, but a management style that filters throughout the practices and norms of the institution, working its way into the language employed. During a briefing before half-term break, one SMT member announced that although teachers were tired, we needed to 'stick to our guns and remain vigilant'. Police-style language is frequently used, with announcements and emails describing how a student is being held in someone's office 'pending an investigation', while staff are continually reminded to log student incidents onto the School Information Management System (SIMS) – particularly those involving 'repeat offenders'.[2]

Father Teresa's universal attraction

Despite Culford's rhetoric, Dreamfields does not just serve Urbanderry's 'urban children', but middle-class children dislocated from the leafy suburbs. Ms Carrier relates how students from a variety of backgrounds attend Dreamfields, adding: 'I think it's a school that is attractive to absolutely everyone in the borough. It's got universal attraction.' Ms Carrier describes parents' differing reactions to discipline:

> The biggest contentious issue, I think, is the behavioural policy. And there's a mixture, I think there's some parents who, um, really like it, who can see that

it's done a lot of good for their child … and there are some parents, tend to be the middle-class parents actually, who tolerate the behaviour system and the discipline because they know that on a whole school level it's good. They may not necessarily think that their child needs it, but they can see that it allows their child to go to a comprehensive urban school.

Dreamfields' stringent policing of potentially unruly urban others 'allows' middle-class children to safely attend a 'comprehensive urban school'; this creation of a middle-class space is examined in Chapter 7. Yet Florence, an 18-year-old black British sixth-former, points out how Culford's comments about unhappy, urban children benefit his image at the expense of students like herself:

It's kind of his way – I know this sounds really bad – but his way of making this place [Dreamfields] seem better than it actually is because a lot of us are from okay backgrounds. We are not living in the slums or anything. I think it is his way of trying to become like Mother Teresa, but I just think he is not necessarily doing it in the right way, if that makes sense. And I don't know, it's a bit mean saying that because Urbanderry itself has a stigma already, so just to say poor deprived background, blah, blah, blah.

Invoking historical stigmas becomes an easy, convincing route to sainthood. Reiterating images of pathological urban chaos creates a more impressive media story where Dreamfields boldly stands out as 'an oasis in the desert'. This hyperbole is also propelled by the marketisation of education where schools frequently employ public relations agencies to cultivate a successful image to avoid being 'ordinary' (Maguire et al., 2011).

For most parents, Dreamfields was anything but ordinary. Many proudly cited its notoriety and positive impact on Urbanderry's reputation, describing how Dreamfields had filled an educational vacuum after years of poor provision. Both Julia and Eve felt Urbanderry 'deserved Dreamfields'. Eve simply wanted a non-faith mixed-gender local school to send her children to, while Julia thought Urbanderry 'had waited for a long time for a glimmer of hope educationally'. Phil admits: 'I don't know what we would have done if they had not built Dreamfields, so we were pretty grateful', while Miriam thinks Dreamfields has 'done an incredible job, considering being in the heart of Urbanderry'. Celeste says: 'Everyone is just buzzing about Dreamfields.' Superlatives pepper the start of parental interviews. Veronica calls it 'a miracle', Nazia feels 'it's perfect' and Esther asserts: 'Dreamfields has been a dream come true for most parents.' While I will examine parents' differing and complex relationships to Dreamfields in Chapter 7, I have included these decontextualised sentiments to emphasise the widespread embrace of the institution and to reiterate how Dreamfields works to undo the pathology narratives explored in Chapter 1. Despite Culford's public ruminations on urban chaos, even parents with critical viewpoints attached the word 'good' to Dreamfields in some regard. Dreamfields' 'universal attraction' offers parents a school they can feel good about, and, like teachers, gives them something to invest in after a prolonged period of neglect.[3]

Tough love: boys will be boys

Crucially, Dreamfields' zero-tolerance tactics target a student population where boys comprise a small majority of the student body. Teachers consistently portray boys as more disruptive than girls, who are perceived as less overtly riotous, if more manipulative. Culford felt disciplinary tactics had to differ according to gender as the majority of underachievers were boys 'because boys will be boys will be boys, I suppose. Boys tend to be a bit slobbish between the ages of ten and sixteen and maybe a bit beyond that as well. Girls tend to be much more aspirational and self-motivated.' Culford thinks innate differences cannot be addressed by perceiving boys and girls as the same; there needs to a 'philosophy and a strategy' to deal with underachieving boys. Most teachers reiterated this 'natural' difference. Mr Davis feels the 'naughty-boy syndrome' means lessons need to be 'boy-friendly' and 'practical' by giving them 'a bit of a challenge, a competition' that girls might also enjoy. Mr Dean admits gender changes his disciplinary style: 'I would probably yell at boys ... more so than I would yell at girls, in terms of screaming and shouting. Rightly or wrongly ... I don't tend to be as, um, aggressive with girls.' Boys are positioned as slovenly, naughty, and in need of competitive challenges.

Despite his reservations described in Chapter 3, Mr Bello still suggests an aggressive approach is necessary in urban areas: 'But I presume because the kids have come from a hard background, they feel they need the discipline in school, which I am inclined to agree.' Hard backgrounds require hard treatment. The need to regulate and reform potentially dangerous masculinities ties to the presence of gangs. Mr Vine comments: 'If you live on an estate – and especially if you are a black man – the chances of not being involved in a gang is pretty much non-existent. You are involved in a gang just because of where you live.' The bodies specified as most susceptible to deviance are black boys on estates, as black, male working-class criminality is presented as almost inevitable (see Arday, 2015: 49).

Ms Wainwright describes how Dreamfields' structures save these boys from criminality through discipline, where even the 'most recalcitrant and the most bolshie' Year 11 students wanted to attend sixth form, admitting they had been 'a pain in the neck' and now understood why they had been punished. She adds:

> It's really interesting how the really difficult ones who have had the most time spent on them actually really want to stay and are desperate to stay, because they know if it wasn't for the structures of Dreamfields they would probably be, like, in prison or something by now.

Eventually difficult students realise Dreamfields has salvaged them. The masculine hero, played by men and women alike, takes over from single mothers and the lumbering bureaucracy of local councils to produce civilised, happy children. Pathology is located in the (working-class) black body as an unassimilable, underachieving cultural issue to be policed and contained, which 'constitutes black children as an alien group that present "problems" external to "normal" schooling' (Carby, 1982: 205). Over thirty years later, this culturalist perspective is echoed in many Dreamfields teacher narratives. While education is portrayed as a 'liberating force' enabling social mobility, Bourdieu describes how it is one of the most effective ways of reproducing the status quo, 'as it both provides an apparent justification for social inequalities and gives recognition to the cultural heritage, that is, to a *social* gift treated as a *natural* one' (1974: 32; emphasis added).

Risk-taking approaches are seen to be imperative when facing urban deprivation. Culford thinks heads in poor areas must be 'quite radical ... they need to think outside the box and take risks'. Misdemeanours face immediate consequences: 'There's none of this twenty-four-hour notice, but I'm sure if I looked up – now, I've never done this – the detail of statute, I'm probably forbidden by law to do that. But I don't. So it's a risky threat to make, that they stay there.' Pioneering strategies are rationalised and legitimated through Urbanderry's negative 'place-image'. Despite the potential illegality of his actions, transcending the law is seen as necessary, while Dreamfields' 'short, sharp, immediate, effective' punishments are part of a behavioural policy which parents and students must sign. Ironically, acting lawlessly is positioned as a means of preserving the law, acting as an antidote to the civil disorder caused by unruly youth. Usurping the law is only acceptable in the pursuit of goals legitimated by power.

In the wake of the English riots of August 2011, Culford claimed no Dreamfields students were involved because of the school's strict ethos and described how young people in Britain needed to respect authority again. Dreamfields crafts students into law-abiding, future-orientated selves, neutralising the threat of the gendered, classed and raced body of the potential gangster, while other educational approaches are aligned with public disorder. Culford's rhetoric draws on a diverse range of discourses, blending sociology with a common-sense amalgamation of Conservative and New Labour doctrine to craft persuasive arguments. While dismissing research as irrelevant to his pragmatic approach, Culford reflexively references and inverts research through his assertions. The nineteenth-century 'urban residuum' is recast as a multi-coloured cultural problem, and urban cowboy Culford stymies its contaminating effects by restoring respect for authority. Moral panics and anxiety coalescing around race, crime, youth and the disintegration of British society are reminiscent of the issues tackled in *Policing the Crisis* (Hall, 1978), prompting us to question how much debates and framings have shifted in three intervening decades.

Making the neutral professional

Potentially dangerous bodies are converted into respectable ones through the cultivation of 'appropriate' aesthetic representations. As the staff handbook comments, the uniform is 'one of the outward signs by which the local community recognises and makes judgements about the pupils', and should show students are proud to belong to a well-disciplined school, promote equality and simplify pupil management. The uniform acts as a shaper of judgement, overwriting and repackaging the student body. The school's blue blazer with grey piping, blue trousers or skirt, tie, blue jumper and plain white blouse or shirt reference a public school aesthetic. The uniform requirements are detailed and numerous: shoes must be plain black leather, not suede or patent leather, and without coloured stitching; hairbands must be black or blue; girls' hair can be worn in one neat ponytail; boys' hair cannot be shaved nor touch the collar; no logos, labels or markings are allowed on coats, which must be plain black, navy or grey; girls must wear white ankle socks or opaque black tights; dark, plain scarves and gloves and the Dreamfields woollen hat may be worn in colder months; no jewellery is allowed except gold or silver stud earrings and a watch; no makeup or hair dye is allowed. The PE kit has a similar litany of requirements, from blue polo and rugby shirts to white socks to grey shorts. Top buttons must be fastened and ties worn with seven stripes showing. Styles seen as affiliated with a gangster aesthetic – like wearing one glove, baggy trousers or wearing a hoodie when it is not raining, as Chapter 3 described, are vigilantly prohibited.

SMT member Ms Heart relates how Dreamfields' order needed to be made visible and readable by being worn on the body:

> This orderliness that I talked about, we felt that you need to have almost outward symbols of it. You need to be able to see it. And you can see it when you see the children come to school, the way they dress for school. That's almost the first vision you have of the children in school and so when we put out the uniform we had … and again, it wasn't just tensions with the community. There were discussions, some quite heated, with the sponsor and various people because they had a different notion. Again, everybody, when you start something new people want to be new. They want to be different. There is a temptation. And I've got to say, ah, I totally agreed with the head's idea that we didn't go down the route of trying to be too, too different, too trendy. And so there were some suggestions of the children wearing parkas and stuff like that to school and, ah, hooded tops, and after a discussion though, we did agree on a traditional uniform. We came out with the blue uniform with the blazer and edging around the blazer to finish it off and we didn't, I mean, we weren't totally inflexible … To be honest, as long as it was reasonably traditional and didn't make people stick out, because when you make people stick out, people want to look at them and want to point at them and say, 'Oh look at them, aren't they different?' We believed actually that, that working mode and being dressed for work and being like the rest of the population going off to work was quite important.

Dreamfields chose a traditional uniform aligning the student body with 'smart' middle-class professional bodies, signifying normality and announcing that Dreamfields students were just like other Goldport professionals heading to work. Ironically, in the context of Urbanderry, these uniforms did make students 'stick out' and get noticed for being 'posh'.

Ms Heart emphasises how difficult it was to achieve universal compliance initially. She jokes that it could have been a clown suit for all she cared, but once decisions were in place, they had to be enforced. On opening day five children – 'good children from good families' – were wearing suede shoes. Ms Heart describes how this minor infraction had to be stopped to prevent future problems:

> Now, again, that's a small thing but if you don't stop suede shoes on the first day, when are you going to stop them? When half the year group are wearing suede shoes? Because it ended up being a problem. So you do have to stop those things as they happen and so we started with a great deal of rigour and hopefully we have continued with that and it develops.

Although it might be difficult to imagine how problematic suede shoes could become, rigidly enforced rules are not just about aesthetic representations, but about demanding detailed compliance. A 'broken-window theory' of the uniform develops: first the finish of a shoe is disregarded, and this flouting of the rules escalates until disorder reigns. Ms Austin describes the uniform's containing effect: 'I think things like uniform and stuff like that just puts them in this box that they can't move out of, and that makes them feel like if they do something silly with their shoes or they do something silly with their hair then they are being really rebellious.' Regulating minuscule details narrows the range of possible actions, so that undoing a top button becomes subversive.

Ms Heart describes how boys' hair can neither be shaved past a number two nor hang below collar length, 'because that's an extreme style'. Hair with 'too many things sticking out of it' is banned because it is extreme: 'Anything that draws attention. Anything where other children will go, "Oh! Look at his hair!" We don't want that. We want professional dress. Would it be a hairstyle that any professional would have?' Professionals are neutral, proper, moderate; they represent the desired status quo. Mr Vine similarly outlines how uniform rules are designed to be 'non-fashionable' so they do not distract from learning. Crafting 'very plain, very neutral' bodies is supposed to make bodies fit in rather than stick out:

> Nothing that could be the centre of attention or allow a child to stand out in that way. Like, 'I am such and such' … but it also means that hopefully we get as close as possible to uniformity between the social economic classes, so everybody can – everybody has the same uniform, everybody has pretty much the same shoes, everybody pretty much has the same hairdo… so it's that sort of almost anonymity and conformity which allows them all to fit in, regardless of where they come from.

The uniform seeks to socially equalise the student population by providing anonymity through conformity. Yet conformity is distinctly classed, with its neutral position being that of the commuting professional. The removal of individuality does not create a neutral body, but attempts to graft cultural capital onto the body through imposing a regime of ideological symbols. Bourdieu describes how the imposition of these symbolic systems acts as an instrument of domination. He describes how, unlike myths that are collectively produced and consumed, 'ideologies serve sectional interests which they tend to present as universal interests common to the group as a whole' (1977b: 114). The sectional interests of the middle classes are positioned as universal modes of appearance, where certain individualities are more out of place than others. The fixity of these symbols ensures order; symbols out of place must be either corrected or removed from view. One student had shaved patterns into his eyebrows over a half-term break. They had not grown back by the start of term and he could either spend each day in the LSU until they grew back or report to his head of year's office each morning to have them drawn on with an eyebrow pencil. He chose the latter option; evidently having makeup applied by his teacher was preferable to isolation. With the appearance of appropriate eyebrows literally drawn on, he was allowed to circulate among his peers.

Exhibits of difference and the social injustice of sameness

On a summer day at the outset of the fieldwork I ran into Ms Frost in the playground. I had interviewed her the previous week, but the recorder seemed to have made her nervous; she asked me to pause it three times during the interview as she broke into peals of laughter. Although Ms Frost had mentioned how hair rules were not fairly applied to students and left some working-class pupils feeling that middle-class children were allowed more liberties, she did not elaborate. Now at break time Ms Frost took me firmly by the arm and said she would show me what she was talking about. First she steered me towards a white boy with messy, curly hair that fell past his collar and onto his face. Ms Frost said he was a good example of someone who would never be reprimanded about his hair. In practice, the staff handbook's 'appropriate style' means one neat bunch for girls, or as Ms Heart announced in briefing, 'no adventure playgrounds' – an implicit reference to black girls' hairstyles. For boys, hair must be off the collar and no shorter than a number two.

Ms Frost discreetly gestured to a black girl with a fringe who had been reprimanded and made to put it back; she then turned and pointed to a bunch of white girls with fringes hanging across their faces, sitting around a circular bench. Evidently these girls would never be told off either. Near the basketball courts, Ms Frost pointed to another boy who had been told his mid-length Afro was too messy. I commented that it was just his hair; vexed, she replied: 'Yes, I know.' As she signalled to another boy who had to tie his Afro back, a group of three white boys with long, loose hair sauntered past. Ms Frost gauged my reaction; the contrast was obvious. She turned to me, describing how she felt uncomfortable enforcing rules that she could not explain, telling students she did not make them. She understood why they felt it was unfair. I said that it seemed like the line was drawn by race. Although she silently nodded in agreement and signalled race through which children she pointed to, Ms Frost never used the word 'race', but repeatedly referenced class. Even black or minority-ethnic teachers are reluctant to name race and have difficulty addressing racism due to the pressures of fitting into a post-racial climate (Pearce, 2014). A short, white boy with long, unkempt hair walked past. I said his hair was messy; Ms Frost sarcastically replied: 'Of course it was, but this was messy middle-class hair!' She described how one boy was put in the LSU for patterned cornrows deemed 'too creative'. We shook our heads, sighed and laughed as the bell rang and children hurried to line up.

Ms Frost was not alone in her consternation. Despite assertions of neutral universality, Dreamfields' practices are based on specific, particular forms. As de Certeau (1984: 48) describes, 'panoptical procedures' have historically been used as 'a weapon ... in combatting and controlling heterogeneous practices', while Mohanty (2003: 18) asserts: 'colonisation almost invariably implies a relation of structural domination and a suppression – often violent – of the heterogeneity of the subject(s) in question'. In order to create readable, docile bodies, differences in appearance and practice must be flattened. Yet Dreamfields' wholesale imposition of 'appropriate' forms evidences how it works off a white middle-class model, as raced and classed connotations belie the rules' supposed neutrality.

Ms Watson felt hair rules ignored how black hair could be styled, sympathising with student complaints: 'I will see middle-class white students with their hair all over the place, which is against the rules that we have here. It is picked up on occasions, but not as much as it should be. And I think in that way there are discrepancies – big, big discrepancies!' Mr Dean also describes the difficulties:

> Hair is a difficult issue because to me a good, solid – okay here, I'm going to talk race – for a black boy having an all-over cut, without designs, just having it short, say to a number one can be very neat, very tidy, very presentable. Whereas on a white person that can be deemed to culturally be having a skinhead, which has different connotations. So there is that reason for getting away from it. Therefore do you have a uniform rule that nobody has a number one? I understand that kind of thinking. I don't like the rule in regards to longer hair because I do feel that all pupils that have Caucasian hair – whether it be Indian, Chinese, white – Caucasian hair can become very messy, which in this school that is deemed allowed and appropriate, whereas someone who has had their hair slightly too short, a black person with their hair slightly too short is not allowed. But when this has come up in meetings, which it has, who's got a solution? And the difficulty is, that there is no absolute solution, which is why lots of teachers try – which again creates problems – to use discretion.

Unlike Ms Frost, both Ms Watson and Mr Dean explicitly mention race; notably, the teachers highlighting these inconsistencies are themselves from ethnic-minority backgrounds. Significantly Mr Dean pauses before announcing he is going to 'talk race', almost asking me to brace myself before launching into potentially contentious terrain. Mr Dean points out the different aesthetic connotations of a white skinhead; while Dreamfields associates short hair on a white boy with far-right leanings, this not only ignores how short black hair is deemed smart, but the other connotations behind a white skinhead.[4] As Ms Frost showed me, black students were continually surveyed and reprimanded more than white students. Rather than addressing the problematic imposition of uniformity divorced from social context, Dreamfields adopts (mostly) white and middle-class styles as normative.

Essed and Goldberg's work on cultural cloning illuminates how Dreamfields' attempts to create sameness are inherently problematic, as 'the systematic reproduction of sameness' is a deeply ingrained feature in the very organisation of contemporary culture and structures of race, gender and class (2002: 1067). While biological cloning remains mostly a fiction, 'cultural cloning of preferred types … is everyday practice', as the desire for social sameness underpins biological cloning's material realisation of this desire. Attending to the 'socio-cultural fabric enabling cloning cultures' helps shift our focus from identity and difference to how social injustice and inequality are silently contained within the reproduction of sameness (2002: 1068–9).

> To speak of 'cloning culture' presupposes a society where productivity and efficiency occupy a prized position on the list of values (little time and energy wasted on the tensions and trials of difference and distinction), where one can expect a consumptive demand for certain types of children … as well as for other products, according to what, aesthetically, is considered the fashion of the day. (2002: 1072)

This vision of cultural cloning fits against Dreamfields' approach, where the difficulty of dealing with difference is alleviated by a meritocratic gloss focusing teachers and students on the most pivotal task at hand – the production of results and docile students who can easily be consumed by the labour market. Although the banning of white racism via the skinhead is a well-meaning gesture, a permissive attitude to white, middle-class hair continues, evidencing the difficulty of discussing problematic blanket approaches in a supposedly post-racial era. Dreamfields' universal body fashioned in the guise of a whitish middle-class one makes the creation of a uniform student body have uneven practical applications and realisations which are explored in the following chapters.

Business bodies

Bodies must be contained and repackaged not only to limit subversive elements, but to promote students' employability. As Mr Davis describes, the uniform is part of a 'first-class' experience:

> You've really got to ask yourself if what we are doing here is providing for children a first-class teaching and learning environment, a first-class education, then they are going to get qualified for that eventual place in work or in college, and one of the things that is very apparent with sixteen-, seventeen- and eighteen-year-olds is that they don't know how to present themselves to the world when it comes to work. And the discipline of the uniform, as much of a pain as it is to maintain and keep right, the discipline of a uniform code will give them an advantage, not a disadvantage. I don't think anyone gained an advantage by going to a job interview scruffy. And I don't think anyone gained advantage by, say, going to meet a colleague or going to meet someone who could make a difference in their life having messy hair and dirty shoes, so we have to look outside and ask ourselves how can we prepare Dreamfields children for that

world of work? And in the world of work, presentation is so important when you are talking to clients. You know, your manners, the respect you have, your telephone manner, the way you are punctual, you attend school, you don't try to dodge out of responsibilities, you present yourself well, you can mix with other people. All of that we can do here because we immerse them in this high-class culture. It rubs off on them.

'High-class culture' via clothing is extended into the sixth form where students must abide by a 'business dress code' that hopefully 'rubs off on them'. It is inferred that working-class students are primarily disadvantaged by their poor self-presentation, which can be remedied by applying 'high-class culture'. Boys must wear a 'smart' dark-coloured business suit and a business shirt with a button-down or stiff collar, tie and smart shoes. One earring is permissible, but other piercings and facial hair are banned. For girls, a dark tailored jacket, skirt, dress or trousers are required, with skirts and dresses falling on or below the knee. Only fitted blouses can be worn untucked, jumpers must be formal and tights must be either fine or opaque in navy, black or flesh colour – no fishnets or patterns are allowed. Jewellery must be 'minimal and discreet' with one piercing in each ear. Hair can be dyed in natural colours only. An array of pictures depicting appropriate and inappropriate clothing choices hung outside a sixth-form office to guide students; notably, there was considerably more advice for women (see Figure 4.1). Beside these photos hung a poster advertising a best-dressed competition sponsored by a financial services provider. It depicted a gaggle of smiling, suited young people in an office setting. This packaging attempts to fix and contain the body, as aesthetic appearances and moral values become intertwined. There is an assumed correspondence between the body's container or wrapper and its interior intentions and values; the repackaged body will do what its package indicates. The uniform becomes part of Mr Davis's machine referenced in Chapter 3, aiding the movement of the student from point A to point B.

A professional dress code also applies to staff, but is less specifically outlined; unlike sixth-formers, teachers are expected to understand the professional world's demands. And if they do not, they are reminded of them. Mr Turner recalls being reprimanded for wearing grey trousers that did not match his black suit jacket. Mr Wilson thought Dreamfields would accept his laid-back chinos and open-necked shirts; however, he was promptly taken aside and instructed to purchase a suit. Now Mr Wilson wondered how much longer he could get away with having shoulder-length hair. He was happy to use a hairband around school, but added that the SMT probably thought this made him look like a girl, highlighting the gender-essential underpinnings of this dress code where men and women are meant to not only act, but look different. Dreamfields becomes an officious parody of the corporate world, with dress requirements more dogmatic than most professional workplaces and bounded by extremely fixed, gendered ideals of how professionals look. Dreamfields' private-school aesthetic references an imagined, conservative past. Over forty years ago, Major Barnes (1950) offered a celebratory account of the history of British army uniforms, tying national pride and the glory

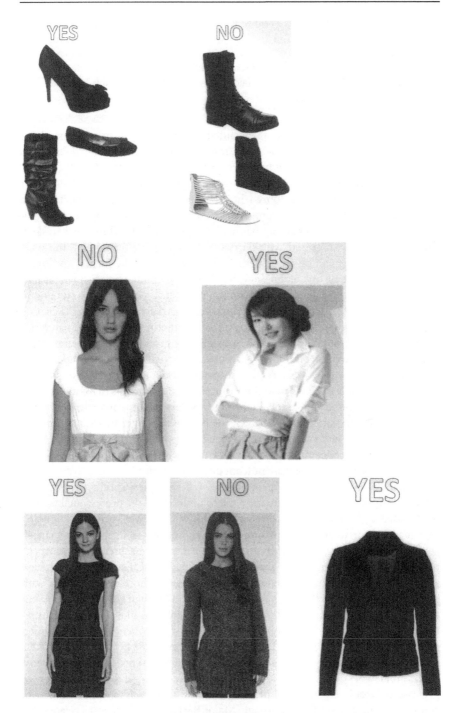

4.1 Sixth-form uniform requirements

of empire to the uniform's disciplined efficiency. This tradition continues into the twenty-first century, as Brian McVeigh's (2000) examination of school uniforms in Japan details how ideology comes to be worn on the body, attesting to the work uniforms continue to do.

A sixth-former 'board meeting' where students discussed strategies for selling advertising space to sponsor their young enterprise project highlights their awareness of the relationship between appearances and respect. One young man refused to wear his suit when selling advertising, but the group insisted, explaining no one would take him seriously. When he continued to resist, they jested his jeans were from Primark. He claimed they were from Hugo Boss. The argument led to a discussion of Culford's finances. Allegedly he was 'stacking it', with a house worth at least £600,000, and only wore clothes from Ralph Lauren and 'big stores' like Selfridges. Culford embodies Dreamfields' ethos through his consumption habits, serving as a mascot for progression from enterprising sixth-former to wealthy professional.

Labouring on the range

As Culford described in the Introduction, he wants staff that 'go the extra mile' and commit to taking on the role of surrogate parent. In order for the ethos to work, 'We can't have a staff here who just see it as an ordinary job where they are worrying about their total number of hours and the minutiae of their contract.' Working at Dreamfields is no routine job, but a calling where teachers act as modern-day missionaries redeeming urban students. Mr Mitchell describes this endeavour:

> There is still a kind of sense of mission, um, that you have here. It is very intense. As I said earlier, you are effectively on duty from the moment the children arrive until the last one leaves the building. That can at times be stressful. It's necessary … and I feel most staff understand that it is necessary.

Several staff relate Catholicism to the Dreamfields ethos. Mr Dean calls it a 'very Catholic school sort of ethos which is underpinned by a sense of discipline and structure, as the school mantra kind of shows'. Urbanderry is portrayed as a fragmented borough in constant flux, where Dreamfields creates stability. Mr Richards explains: 'It's all about maintaining the status quo, maintaining things that aren't going to change and making sure that we don't change our views and rules.' This perceived instability surrounding Dreamfields justifies non-negotiable authoritarian management strategies.

The rigid inflexibility of the ethos's rules stands in direct contrast to the flexibility of labour where teachers must go the 'extra mile'; staff cannot worry about the 'minutiae' of their contract, but must worry about the minutiae of everything else. Administrator Mr Fields describes how the management loves phrases like 'energetic and willing to go the extra mile', but he disliked them due their completely unquantifiable, vague nature, which he denounced as 'just stupid, really':

'Must be a self-starter who goes the extra mile' – well, how do you test that? I think it's just actually very old-fashioned, um, but they love it … and what they mean is that you work from dawn to dusk without a break and I think [*laughing*] but I think from an administrative point of view that is very unprofessional, because going the extra mile will mean something very different to you than to me. And it is very difficult to quantify, and if you were disciplined because you did not go the extra mile, well, that would not hold up in a tribunal, would it? Because we never set down what it means … they always look for teachers who will – who they think will work hard, but of course you don't know that until they start.

Although no hours are specified on teachers' contracts, all employment contracts are governed by the European working-time agreement which limits employees to a 48- hour week, unless an opt-out agreement is signed stating they are willing to work for longer. Mr Fields describes how most teachers at Dreamfields exceed this limit; however, no one has signed the opt-out agreement. While Mr Fields professes teachers ought to sign this as it makes Dreamfields 'vulnerable', he knows management would say this is unnecessary. While results and bodies are rigidly monitored and quantified, teacher labour is unregulated.

Mr Fields was working to establish 'proper approaches' through standardising policies and procedures. Previously Dreamfields was often doing 'whatever it liked', with Culford acting as an educational entrepreneur; however he felt variations in staff treatment and the lack of concrete rules could land Dreamfields in an employment tribunal. Dreamfields is registered as a private company and generally keeps to the high end of national salary ranges; however Mr Fields adds that it can be more 'draconian' and gets 'good value' from staff. With an average age of 33, Dreamfields has a youthful staff. Recruitment is described as a 'pretty ad hoc' search for the 'best teacher' with no effort made to recruit from the local area or within particular social or ethnic groups. Teacher turnover is higher than normal, something Mr Fields puts down to Dreamfields' distinct culture and pressure regarding results, which means teachers usually either like or hate it. Dreamfields can dismiss teachers after six to nine months. If a teacher is heading towards dismissal, Mr Fields notes it is preferable for them to voluntarily leave before the 'drawbridge is pulled up' and their record tarnished. He relates how some teachers felt 'in other schools they would be a good teacher, but I am being hounded out because I don't fit the Dreamfields way of doing things'. Mr Fields describes how one teacher who left was instructed by his line manager to be creative with lessons, but as the lessons had to follow strict norms, there was no allowance for creativity. He adds: 'And I can see that in Dreamfields – you have to get the syllabus done, you can't be a bit sort of left-field on things.' Despite the creative innovation promised by academies' 'freedom' from local authorities, this freedom is one-sided, as leaders like Culford can demand flexible labour, but teachers cannot deviate from strict norms.

Dictating culture

Culford remains resolutely unapologetic if teachers feel continually monitored, because that is what it takes. Engaging with staff quibbles distracts from the fundamentals:

> We are inspected to death. There's a testing regime now in schools. Examination results are published; everyone knows how a school is performing. I am account-able for the success of this school. If things go wrong here and I get or this school gets a poor inspection or children don't do well, I am accountable for that and I am likely to get the sack. I believe in passing that accountability down the line. People need to be aware that they are accountable for their performance and I am quite open about that. And there is nothing secret, and I'm not going to say that they're not. They are! And the only way that they can be accountable is by opening up their classroom. Now, this is not a big-brother institution. This is not about us looking … trying to create a 1984 culture.

Yet numerous teachers were frustrated by Dreamfields' management style, com-menting on the lack of transparency and communication. Ms Adewunmi did not agree with the SMT's covert decision making. She felt Dreamfields did not trust teachers and found it difficult to stay energetic under circumstances where trust and transparency were lacking. Ms Hatcher described how teachers felt manage-ment distrusted them with

> Decisions being made without proper consultations, decisions that are affecting you and your subjects … I think quite often the manner in which teachers get spoken to is like children by some of the senior management team … it's very much a culture of pointing the finger and, um, it's very much a stick rather than a carrot culture, I think.

This lack of consultation relates to the lack of union presence; if representation reached 40 per cent Dreamfields would be required to consult unions on par-ticular matters. Mr Fields reflected on the benefits and drawbacks of consulta-tion. Decisions could be made and implemented faster because Dreamfields did not have to build a robust case for action justifiable to a union representative. Conversely, Dreamfields could not demonstrate a consultation process and deci-sions would not be challenged like they might be at other schools; this could feel like a 'dictatorship'. Several teachers commented on an underlying hostility to unions. Although Ms Frost likes working at Dreamfields, she thought many academies 'did not want to dirty their hands with unions so they did not have them and if you don't like it then tough – leave'. Mr Vine said Dreamfields self-regulates through administering staff surveys, adding: 'The unions are there nor-mally to pick up trouble and at the moment there is no need for it, so why create it? [laughs] That's what I say.' This attitude links back to Chapter 1's concerns over the undemocratic nature of these structures, where surveys replace meaningful participation.

Covert management breeds an uneasy atmosphere, despite the collective tasks at hand. Ms Singer thought a backstabbing, paranoid culture was one of Dreamfields' biggest weaknesses. A feeling of suspicion where staff were not working together was common, and she found this unfortunate, given their common goal. Mr Dean explained how Dreamfields' strict hierarchy meant he had little contact with Culford and everything went through his line manager. Mr Dean envisioned being more approachable and talking to his staff if he became a headteacher. Ms Hatcher also described how Dreamfields was not the sort of environment where she would casually greet Culford. The SMT filters orders down through a hierarchy of teachers, as Ms Austin relates:

> There is not much choice in anything that we do … so although there's people in power and they are telling you what to do, it's not necessarily them who have actually made any kind of decision or agree with it, they're just – they have to tell you to do it and people lower down might want to do something or might want to change something or might have other ideas about how to do things, but they can't do things because it's not – that's just kind of tough.

Ms Watson portrays this rigidity more positively, describing how everything is tightly run through 'directives … very clearly passed down to the rest of the staff' so 'everyone knows what they are supposed to do'. Although Mr Mitchell agrees with Dreamfields' approach, he still jokingly refers to it as 'compassionate fascism'.

While teachers are responsible for their performance as accountability is passed down the line, consensual decision-making is not similarly distributed. Culford paints teachers as a generally idealistic bunch of good people who tend to be unmotivated by financial gain; however they also tend to be complainers. These 'whiners' need to 'stop moaning, get on with it', adding that he was once a whiner himself. If teachers do not agree with his 'philosophy', there are plenty of other schools to go and teach in: 'If they don't want to sign up to it, that's fine by me. But don't work here.' Management through dictation, not consensus building, is portrayed as a more pragmatic, efficient and effective strategy than taking the opinion of teachers, parents or students into account.

Dreamfields clearly has the right formula in place to produce results; interventions could disrupt the progress of Chapter 3's 'well-oiled machine'. Although the built space is visually transparent, the decisions of the SMT remain covert. Aesthetic transparency does not give way to procedural transparency as mechanisms for negotiation like unions are phased out. Chartists' fears about a state-organised education system without democratic participation referenced in Chapter 2 have been realised, while the conditions of labour become non-negotiable.

Culford dismisses concerns over teacher labour as trivial complaints remedied by self-help measures like counselling, which position the individual as failing to meet institutional demands, rather than the institution making unreasonable demands. As Mr Vine mentioned, surveys replace unions as a mechanism for measuring satisfaction. Ms Hatcher describes:

> We get these emails the other day: 'What do you think that Dreamfields is doing for the well-being of the staff?' and you're like, well … uh … I know there is that woman [counsellor] who like, sits there and if you want to go talk to her about stuff you can do that, but I just think there could be a lot more thought about how, just, little things.

Although these structural issues cannot be resolved within the self, many teachers persevere and feel it is worthwhile to work at Dreamfields despite mixed feelings.

Making a contract

> *CK*: Compared to other schools, what do you feel the atmosphere is among your colleagues?
>
> *Mr Bello*: I think they're, um, highly under pressure but they are always seeking to please. You know, they always want to do things right.
>
> *CK*: Who are they pleasing?
>
> *Mr Bello*: I think they are pleasing themselves because they obviously want to do things right for the school, they want to do things right for the kids, so they put the time in. And then obviously Mr Culford, because Mr Culford is quite an influential man, you know what I mean? And having that kind of influence will influence other people's behaviour. So I think it's a combination of things between the children and Mr Culford.

One route of gaining consent from teachers, students and parents is via Dreamfields' superior market position, reiterated through public acclaim. These badges of popular and political approval make teachers and students proud to be part of something officially recognised as outstanding. One autumn morning I arrived at Dreamfields in the wake of a media frenzy: teachers were excitedly passing around press clippings, boasting that ITV and BBC camera crews had just left. Dreamfields-related media is conscientiously circulated to staff via email, keeping them abreast of the school's public profile; however staff are also explicitly instructed not to communicate with the press on any school-related matters. Celebratory pep talks during staff briefings emphasise Dreamfields' moral mission while encouraging teachers to keep up the hard work. Culford described how Dreamfields was 'breaking the mould' in Urbanderry – something achievable only if everyone did their part. In another briefing he mentioned meeting with Michael Gove and how Dreamfields was taking over other schools to become an educational revolution that they were all part of.[5] This revolutionary undertaking justifies going 'the extra mile', excuses the discomfort of disciplinarian methods, and makes teachers part of a radical, acclaimed project. Now I will explore how teachers negotiate their dedication to the ethos against the demands it places on their lives.

'It took me a long time to be indoctrinated'

Several teachers described adjusting to Dreamfields' environment. As I turned off the recorder at the end of our interview, one teacher said I should have asked about her initial thoughts of Dreamfields, recalling her first day:

> I went home in tears. I was crying and saying, 'Oh my God, they have got them all in lines and they shout at the children and it's horrible.' I could not believe what I'd gotten myself into, but then the next day I taught a lesson and I understood why it was like that.

The orderly classroom allowed her to deliver her lesson, assuaged her qualms about shouting, and prompted her conversion. At the end of her contract, this teacher 'begged to stay' because she loved working in 'such an inspirational environment'. Ms Hatcher relates a more ambiguous conversion story:

> I think you really have to buy into the ethos to be able to stay here and you see it when people start working here, it does take – I mean I know it took me a good three or four months of just thinking, 'Gosh, I'm not sure if I can do this.' I thought it was terrible, I thought it was really bad. It took me a long time to be indoctrinated into the ethos, but now obviously I am now just as much a part of it as everybody else.

Although Ms Hatcher has been 'indoctrinated', she still has doubts, but finds it hard to contest Dreamfields' methods because of its results:

> But nowadays, but the thing is it's very difficult when you can see the fruits of what Dreamfields has produced and how much it works. It makes you think, well, you know, it makes you think, well, is that [aggressive discipline] justified then? So but yeah, it was those things that I found really difficult to begin with and I still do, I suppose, sometimes [nervous laugh].

While Ms Hatcher conforms and realises she actively participates in the production of Dreamfields' parameters, a level of ambivalence is maintained. Ms Wainwright asserts that it might seem too 'blanket disciplinarian if you are just looking at it from the outside', but once you know about the students' chaotic home lives it becomes clear that 'for some of the students it's the only place where they feel like anybody does actually care and give them strict boundaries to adhere to'. Not only do teachers provide education, they see themselves as providing safety and care. This theme runs throughout teacher interviews. Many teachers, while expressing regret, resigned themselves to the fact that Dreamfields would not work if it were run differently. Ms Fletcher describes her ambivalent feelings:

> I find being so sort of aggressive and shouty and strict, I find that quite difficult because I am slowly turning into a really mean person who shouts at children for no reason. So I find it difficult, there's lots of things that I don't agree with, but I think it does work and I think the kids love coming here.

The fact that 'it works' and that she thinks the children love it makes it bearable. Most teachers negotiated their tentative feelings about Dreamfields against its production of results and the urban chaos discourse to assuage any lingering reservations.

Benefits

Ms Carrier felt teachers were proud to work in an outstanding school where they could witness progress, presenting the long hours as a 'choice': 'I think people choose to work harder here than they would in other schools because they see what can be achieved if they do work harder.' Mr Vine echoes this sentiment, bragging that he happily works 12-hour days because 'you can see that what you are doing has an impact'. Making a 'difference' motivates him to work 'longer hours and harder hours'; he does not want to be the one to 'let the side down' by not 'maintaining this culture'. Ms Watson calls Dreamfields 'constantly full on', describing working without a break and eating lunch standing up on duty, yet she feels her labour is meaningful:

> I think that you have to have a passion for what you do for it to sort of mean, to
> sort of, you know, be meaningful just because it's so full on. But I love being here,
> bizarrely enough. I quite like the hard work … and I think the reason I like it so
> much is that you see immediately the fruits of your labour.

Her labour is justified through a passion for the job and its obvious outcomes. Ms Hatcher, however, felt teachers deserved more recognition for their toil, describing how 'we are willing to do the work, obviously, because we know the rewards but it's – I don't think it's understood how hard everybody works in this place'. Producing good student outcomes is rewarding, but this does not compensate for recognition or the toll it takes on teachers' lives.

The persuasive power of quantifiable results cannot be underestimated. Nearly every teacher attested to how initially problematic parents were gradually won over through the generation of excellent results that showed Dreamfields 'worked'. Ms Heart describes how discipline becomes positive:

> Because the head's belief, alongside of this orderliness, is that if you've got good
> lessons and lots of enrichment of the children's experience, then they will – then
> the orderliness will come, um, will be received as something that is good because
> it comes as part of a package of good lessons and an enriched experience.

Wrapping Dreamfields' authoritarian regime within an appealing package of high-quality provision makes it more digestible; the productivity of results means discipline is received as a necessary medicine.

Meanwhile teachers benefit from the silent classrooms discipline creates. Ms Carrier feels staff are 'generally very happy', if not tired by the long days, yet unlike other schools, where teacher absenteeism rises as teachers have their lessons 'thrown back at them', this does not happen at Dreamfields. Absenteeism is also less likely due to the fact that teachers must cover absent colleagues' lessons. This saves Dreamfields money by cutting out supply-teaching agencies, but also adds to already high workloads while making it readily apparent who is absent and how often.

Ms Carrier describes how teachers do not have 'that relentless battle at the beginning of every lesson' to get children sitting down and listening; students are ready to receive information, making teachers' jobs easier. Ms Fletcher describes how the discipline 'enables the teachers to sort of teach anything, because the students are very clear with boundaries'. Ms Wainwright admits there are extra demands in terms of duties and longer hours, 'but the upshot of that is that you can teach. You're not actually being harassed, sworn at, potentially in physical danger all the time.' For teachers this trade-off is presented as the only way urban education works. Ms Austin explains how silent classrooms demand innovative lessons: 'If you've got them quiet you'd better be teaching them something good.' Mr Bello says he actually has the opportunity to teach at Dreamfields, whereas most of his time elsewhere was spent dealing with poor behaviour. Ms Heart thinks orderliness 'frees everybody up to learn and the teachers to teach'. Yet this freedom afforded by docile bodies is not 'free', but achieved through the relentless labour of teachers.

Maintaining Dreamfields is a collective enterprise; many teachers feel it only 'works' because everyone is actively involved. Mr Turner says this makes Dreamfields a hard place to work:

> Every moment of every day is taken up with some sort of duty. You are con-stantly reminded of this all the time – we are permanently on duty. If you're not in a lesson we are expected to patrol ... You couldn't let a kid go past with his tie down or his shirt untucked without saying something, because if you get seen doing that, then maybe you'd be in trouble for letting it go past. And that goes all the way up to everything; every moment of your day is a duty.

This routine collective action contrasts with Culford's solitary leader motif. Rather than reiterating his individualistic, superhero fiction, teacher narratives emphasise the necessity of continuous collective action – even if this action is dictated and obscured. Despite Culford's binary tales and individualistic proclamations, daily routines show how Dreamfields' operation is not this straightforward. Teachers are under pressure to individually reproduce the institutional structures to create this collectivity, yet the demands placed on teachers often make their positions unsustainable.

Burn-out

Many teachers were concerned with Dreamfields' detrimental effects on their personal lives. Ms Singer feels that although most teachers appreciated working at Dreamfields, staff got fed up with the daily pressure. While she thinks Dreamfields must be run this way, reminding me that 'these are Urbanderry kids and probably put them in another school and I think some of them would change completely', she also feels working there is not a permanent option:

I don't think it's sustainable long term. I don't think you could stay here for … well, ten, fifteen years, have all of this pressure and work piled on you. Um, I think there will come a time when people say, 'Right, well I've done my four or five years here, I am going to move on now.' Which some members of staff are doing, you know … I mean some staff don't like the fact that there is no staff room so they can't mix or socialise … it takes a lot of time in the evenings, your free time, personal time, personal life, marking, working. And they probably think, 'Well, this isn't for me and I am going to move on now because I have done this for enough years.'

Mr Dean also questions how healthy it is to work at Dreamfields with its 'ridiculously high' workload where management 'certainly want their pound of flesh'. Several teachers felt younger staff were intentionally recruited, as newly qualified teachers without any yardstick of comparison were more compliant and willing to work longer hours. Mr Dean describes how this long-hours culture is not family-friendly, as parents were less able to stay until 6.00pm compared with young, single staff:

I know a couple of examples where it's caused staff to leave this academy, which I think is not fair. But it's the nature of the school. I think, yeah, it's … something that you almost become tainted with, you know. I always said, 'I'm not going to finish at those kind of hours', and sort of everyone does it and you get caught up in it, but I actually do not think it is healthy. I don't. Because I then go home and work.

Mr Dean admits becoming caught up in the requirements of this culture, staying late in his glass office to avoid a 'conversation with the powers that be'. Instead of seeking reform, many teachers like Mr Dean sympathised with Dreamfields' pressurised position. Mr Dean tried to understand Dreamfields' reasons for being overly conservative and blinkered, balancing these sentiments with his belief that Dreamfields is a place where students can achieve. While he thinks Dreamfields aims towards a multicultural society and breaks down stereotypes, he also hopes it will strike a better balance in the future and develop a 'soul' beyond its results.

This chapter has shown how selected past stories outlined in Chapters 1 and 2 are built on to (re)produce Dreamfields' present framing of urban chaos. De Certeau describes how we live in a 'recited society' defined by stories and fables which are cited and then endlessly recited to establish the 'real' (1988: 186). Culford's fables become common knowledge, cited and recited in Urbanderry and beyond via media interventions and self-publicity.

Culford and Dreamfields assume a slippery position, posing as both anti-establishment yet establishment; giving love, yet laying down the law; old-fashioned, yet brand new all at the same time. Queer, feminist and postcolonial theorists alike have highlighted the power of ambiguity. Homi Bhabha describes ambiguity's power in making and remaking race:

If I may adapt Samuel Weber's formulation of the marginalizing vision of castration, then colonial mimicry is the desire for a reformed, recognisable Other, *as a subject of a difference that is almost the same, but not quite.* Which is to say, that the discourse of mimicry is constructed around an *ambivalence*; in order to be effective, mimicry must continually produce its slippage, its excess, its difference … mimicry emerges as the representation of a difference that is itself a process of disavowal. Mimicry is, thus, the sign of a double articulation; a complex strategy of reform, regulation and discipline, which 'appropriates' the Other as it visualises power. (1994: 86; emphasis added)

Bhabha references Macaulay's 'Minute' and its colonialist musings which imagines creating this 'mimic man' through English schooling, resulting in 'a class of persons Indian in blood and colour, but English in tastes, opinions, in morals and in intellect' (Macaulay, 1835, cited in Bhabha, 1994: 87). This grey area of almost-not-quite means contrasts cannot be pinned down; power is diffuse and 'it is precisely ambivalence, always amenable to change and adaptability, which guarantees the survival of anything of a dispersed, repetitive and ambivalent nature' (Skeggs, 2004: 25). Repetition and ambiguity hold power, giving Culford's position weight while concealing inherent paradoxes.

Dreamfields' 'universal attraction' contrasts with its quashing of heterogeneity, where only certain forms are accorded value despite appeals to neutrality. Dreamfields' culture blends disparate ingredients to concoct a potent confection. It combines middle-class norms, as outlined by New Labour's education policy aimed at 'cloning the Blairs' or re-socialising working-class parents (Gewirtz, 2001), while applying 'old-fashioned' notions of dress, manners, morality and rote learning which are not 'high-class' as Mr Davis attests, but more lower middle-class in their cultivation of respectability and curtailing of individuality. These structures work to sever 'urban children' from imagined pathological cultures and police boundaries, and contain inherently problematic bodies. As Ms Carrier's comments reflect, Dreamfields would probably be more permissive and child-centred if it was solely catering to middle-class parents; however the school does protect the middle-class child from their urban Other by providing a safe space. Even though Dreamfields symbolically positions urban families as having the wrong culture, the provision of a shiny new school gains many parents' approval, despite Culford's urban chaos rhetoric. Education becomes a key site and tool through which people sign up to and can be assimilated into the dominant symbolic as rewards are promised in return for compliance. Critically, Dreamfields fills a vacuum left by previous educational neglect in the borough.

Notes

1 Baby Peter died from abuse inflicted by his family; this case resulted in a highly publicised inquiry of Haringey Council's child protection policies.
2 This compiled dossier of information is used to justify exclusions.
3 Notably, Dreamfields, as well as other academies, has probably helped stymie white migration out of Urbanderry for secondary education, as the numbers of students attending secondary schools outside the borough has fallen.
4 Including, less commonly, anti-racist activism.

5 This pep talk occurred during a special early Friday morning briefing prior to the day of industrial strike action the following Monday, which one teacher suggested was a special briefing called to indirectly persuade teachers against striking. Although this is purely speculation, it evidences the atmosphere within the school.

5

'Urban children' meet the 'buffer zone': mapping the inequitable foundations of Dreamfields' conveyor belt

> The formal equality which governs pedagogical practice is in fact a cloak for and a justification of indifference to the real inequalities with regard to the body of knowledge taught or rather demanded. (Bourdieu 1974: 37–8)

Some students fit on Dreamfields' conveyor belt with greater ease from the outset. This chapter will explore who functions as the ideal student and comes to represent the 'status quo' Mr Richards mentions in Chapter 4 by examining who can move along the production line relatively unimpeded while others require modification to advance. While Chapter 4 showed how Culford's heroic tales establish Dreamfields as a universalising force for good, this chapter maps the particularities of this vision through daily practices, as Dreamfields instates forms of structural bias while simultaneously ignoring their structuring capacity. Bourdieu describes how treating pupils 'as equal in rights and duties' in a highly inequitable society sanctions and reproduces inequalities (1974: 37). These cultural inequalities encompass not only a classed, but racialised vision (see Cole, 2004; Crozier, 2005; Gillborn, 1997, 2005; Mirza, 2009, 1992; Rollock et al., 2011). Through the reflections of teachers and students, the chapter outlines how Dreamfields' disciplinary interventions examined in Chapter 4 are neither neutral nor universal.

The structuring of groups in the playground ties to these institutional structures as groups of students reproduce, but also subvert dominant social structures. How students embody mobility and the altercations or eliminations necessary to achieve it produce and bring raced and classed positions into focus by highlighting who needs to 'adjust' themselves to accrue value. While market mechanisms privilege and perpetuate the white middle-class pupil as ideal, openings are also provided for other students to be incorporated into this valued space if they can fit the template. Meanwhile, many participants found naming and discussing persistent inequalities difficult within a supposedly post-racial, meritocratic environment. These institutional practices connect to the world beyond Dreamfields' gates, generating new hierarchies that correspond to the long lineage of policing and reform of the volatile twenty-first-century 'urban residuum' explored in Chapter 2.

Establishing the 'buffer zone':
nice, leafy (mostly white) middle-class children

Imagined as resident in Britain's greener areas, middle-class children are presented in binary opposition to their urban counterparts. As Culford described in
Chapter 2, while urban children need structure: 'You can be a lot more relaxed
and free and easy in a nice, leafy middle-class area where the ground rules are
clear before they come in, where children go home to lots of books and stuff
like that.' Structure is less necessary when dealing with middle-class children
from disciplined homes with 'lots of books'. The middle-class child's normative
status is inscribed within Dreamfields' ethos, signalling how the middle class 'has
become the "particular-universal" class' whereby a whole range of practices associated with it are 'regarded as universally "normal", "good" and "appropriate"'
(Savage 2003: 536). White middle-class children living in Urbanderry are not
perceived as urban 'natives', but retain their association with these 'nice, leafy
areas' despite living in the borough. They transcend pathological 'place-images'.
This transcendence has real effects on institutional perceptions and treatment, as
Ms Wainwright details:

> *Ms Wainwright*: We are potentially more classist, if you like, than racist, to be
> honest.
> *CK*: Hmm. How so?
> *Ms Wainwright*: I think that sometimes when I look at the white middle-class
> children I wonder if they are getting away with things that other children
> wouldn't. And I don't think that's because of the staff, I think that's because
> their parents will get on the phone. And complain.
> *CK*: So it's more parental pressure, maybe?
> *Ms Wainwright*: Yes, because the middle-class parents know how to work the
> system … I've quite often found myself saying, 'But if this was another child,
> a different child, you wouldn't have made this allowance because their parent
> won't get on the phone', and I've quite often put my neck on the line for that
> because I think in a way it's more classist there, potentially. Because at the
> end of the day, the school needs the middle class. We need those people who
> read the *Guardian* and want to send their children to a comprehensive school,
> but equally well would fork out fifteen grand if they had to. We need them to
> keep sending their kids to this school. And I find that quite a difficult battle
> sometimes.
> *CK*: Why do you need them?
> *Ms Wainwright*: Because, um, otherwise it's not a comprehensive school, it's a
> sink school, I suppose. Fundamentally. We need them because they tend to be
> high achievers, their parents will push them to get good grades, their parents
> will – when they are supportive of the school – will be amazingly supportive of
> the school and within the local community the school needs that reputation.
> Otherwise it's too much. If every single child in a thousand cohort is some-
> body who is really hard to keep safe with, who is defiant, who is involved in
> gangs – then that's too much. You almost need to have a buffer zone of, I don't
> know, three hundred kids who actually are not going to be any problem for

the most part – apart for having a whiny parent, I suppose. And it terms of its standing in the local community, you know, whether or not I personally agree with it from a moral point, I know that as a teacher in Goldport schools, you've got to have those kids and those parents on board. You've got to.

Dreamfields' survival in the education market is tied to the steady generation of exam results, and, as Ms Wainwright describes, the middle-class child – consistently envisioned as white – features as a valuable commodity. This reflects Reay and her colleagues' assertion that in a target-driven culture (white) middle-class children are perceived as valuably helping schools meet their targets (2011: 148). Although their favoured status may not promote equality, they are necessary for institutional survival. Ms Wainwright attributes this to their tendency for high achievement, parental support, and the promotion of a favourable image to the local community – or other middle-class parents. Their perceived compliance also makes process-ing them unproblematic – apart from the odd 'whiny parent'. Without them, Dreamfields would 'sink' under the weight of urban children. Rather than blaming individuals, Ms Wainwright points out wider structural issues – namely how middle-class parents' ability to 'work the system' converges with Dreamfields' need for these children – a dilemma that gives them a clear advantage. Ms Wainwright tries to defend pupils without these privileges and admits moral uncertainty, adding that maintaining fairness is 'quite a difficult battle sometimes'.

Scrutinising who is included and excluded from the category of 'urban chil-dren' and who functions as the 'surrogate parent' demonstrates that 'interpreta-tions of what children are and need patently reflect a white, middle-class cultural hegemony' (Gillies, 2007: 145). Although class is named as the 'biggest problem', with two-thirds of students coming from ethnic-minority backgrounds, there is a clear overlap between working-class children whose families are deemed inad-equate and children from ethnic-minority backgrounds. Race becomes classed as an embedded, yet unspoken element underpinning 'urban children'. The unspo-ken fusion of race and class is apparent through the comments of teachers like Ms Wainwright where the idealised middle-class child implies whiteness. Ethnic-minority children fall into the problematic working-class category. They are folded into the term 'urban children' and tied to pathologised urban space. The inferred whiteness of the middle classes signals how black middle-class students are not automatically granted access to 'buffer-zone' status, nor presumed educational success (see Gillborn and Mirza, 2000; Vincent et al., 2012). Gilroy discusses the historical relationship between race and urban space. Drawing on Langer (1984), he asserts how post-war visions of the urban have shaped ideas of race, where black settlement was aligned with conceptions of an unruly, violent jungle, cre-ating a context 'in which "race" and racism come to connote the urban crisis as a whole', and this crisis comes 'to embody racial problems even where they are not overtly acknowledged or defined' (2002: 312). Although Urbanderry's rapid gentrification means demonised spaces are once again considered desirable, this does not mean racialised rhetoric and readings have ceased. Instead the racialised urban is often conceptualised and spoken of through the register of class.

Unstable boundaries

The porous instability of race and class is evidenced through the shifting mean-ings attributed to these words and how they are employed. This was particularly evident in the case of Lorna, a white English and Afro-Caribbean middle-class 13-year-old. Lorna described how her white friends told her she was 'really white' while her black friends felt she was 'really black'. I asked her if her father was keen to give her a sense of his Barbadian heritage. She replied no, adding her father was 'actually quite middle-class too'. Lorna distances her father from black-ness through middle-classness, as do her white friends. Meanwhile her mother Eve describes how Lorna has more white middle-class friends since attending Dreamfields, adding: 'even the black children that she hangs out with I would cat-egorise as white middle-class'. Race and class are used to both do and undo each other, showing a flexible interchangeability that references their historic mutual formation.

Class is more readily named and discussed as problematic, which is unsur-prising, given the widely acceptable excoriation of the working classes through the use of derogatory terms like 'chav'. This heightened maliciousness cuts across political divides. Lawler interrogates what is 'respectably sayable within a given cultural formation' to show how the working classes are represented and othered by the middle classes in the process of constructing middle-class normativity (2005: 431). Tyler describes how abject class disgust performed through media outlets creates a borderline whiteness 'contaminated' by poverty-ridden estates and racialised via sexual relations with ethnic minorities; the respectable middle classes claim moral superiority through the working class's 'filthy whiteness' (2008: 25–6). Deficit representations of the working class underpin Dreamfields' rhetoric and practice, as the loud, illiterate 'chav mum' with her gaggle of multi-coloured, illegitimate children is replaced by the respectable middle-class (mostly white) surrogate parent-teacher.

Meanwhile the white working class are represented as an obstacle to what Chris Haylett (2001) terms 'multicultural modernisation', with their valueless culture obstructing the realisation of neoliberal modernity. This relates to mul-ticulturalism's alignment with modernity, while the white working class are aligned with racist regression. Dominant discourses of multiculturalism are fused with those of modernisation, working to 'discriminate between non-problematic "selves" and problematic "others" who become ciphers (or a dumping ground) for the heavy contradictions of a multicultural welfare society articulated within a neoliberal and middle-class imaginary' (2001: 357). These contradictions descend from Labour's paradoxical attempt to merge socialism with liberalism in the post-war period, as the Left's focus came to rest on the fair distribution of opportunities rather than the equality of outcomes (see CCCS, 1981). Haylett quotes *Times* jour-nalist Janet Daley describing how the 'indigenous working classes' were more dif-ficult to assimilate into a 'morally constructive social life' than immigrant groups. Not only did they block the progress of ethnic minorities who possessed 'cultural integrity', but 'long after Britain has become a successful multi-racial society it will be plagued by this diminishing (but increasingly alienated) detritus of the Industrial Revolution' (2001: 359). These leftovers from the last century, or the 'urban residuum,' as Chapter 2 discussed, are portrayed as incapable of becoming enterprising, modern selves, and not only block global capitalism, but also the (highly conditional) progress of culturally appropriate ethnic minorities. Instead of the historical attempts to incorporate the white working class into a homogeneous whiteness that marked out its social superiority through opposition to blackness, this racial homogeneity has been fragmented to designate the white working class as a 'hazard to modernity' (Skeggs, 2004: 91). This shows how categorisations can temporally shift to do different work at various historical junctures.

These subtle shifts are present in Culford's rhetoric, where racialised judgements continue to underpin his class problem. Class becomes an acceptable, indirect way to 'talk' race while sidestepping the need to address racism. While direct racism is denied, racism is silently present through the raced implications of class. Dreamfields makes 'a commitment to "colour-blindness" rather than equality', as anti-racism is seen as outdated in a supposedly post-racial era (Lentin, 2008: 313). Gilroy's (2000: 40) call for 'liberation from white supremacy' and 'from all racialising and raciological thought, from racialised seeing, thinking and thinking about thinking' goes unrealised, as class does the work of race. The historical splintering of these differing forms of discrimination and exploitation from one another, despite their continual entanglement, precludes avenues for a cohesive political opposition. This chapter signals how this disarticulation provides openings for blackness of the 'right kind', as class functions as the primary problematic and organisational tool, yet is continually focused through a racialised lens.

Privileges for the privileged

Variations in colour, gender and class fuse with ability levels to create differences in the desirability of bodies, their institutional monitoring, and responses to their behaviour. I asked Ms Fletcher if she could keep an eye on the children in the playground enclosure until my lunch-duty replacement arrived. Ms Fletcher looked over at the group of mostly white, middle-class students, commenting: 'Oh yes, from the children in there I expect a lot of bad behaviour!' Several months later, during her interview, Ms Fletcher described how 'We've got a long-haired, lovely middle-class crew ... sort of well-educated parents, um, professionals, and you've got those sort of students.' These students occupied the circular playground bench area: 'the long-haired lovelies all sit around there *(pointing)* at break time and they are all kind of involved in music lessons, you know, they all do drama productions ... they've got floppy fringes and nice bags.' Ms Fletcher says you can pick these 'lovely' middle-class students out of each year group.

The privileged status of the 'buffer zone' means discipline sticks to some bodies more readily than others. When a group of white middle-class girls were discovered to have bullied several boys for money over the course of a year, several teachers questioned how this was handled. One teacher confided to another teacher and myself that he thought these students were not being punished severely enough, particularly compared to Ted, a black working-class student who was promptly placed in the LSU after once stealing money. The teacher suggested that because these girls were middle class the punishment was light: all their parents were professionals, some with influential media positions. Numerous jokes were made about how the girls had probably been stealing to save up for their next skiing holiday. Mr Dean also commented about middle-class students' special status:

> I think as a school some of the middle-class pupils can have preferential treat-ment, certainly if they've got more influential parents, which has been the case in this school. If Mummy and Daddy have a direct line to the top, that can play a role. Which will, um, some poorer, more working-class pupils who have no say and have no status – parents have no status – that would not necessarily happen.

Despite this tendency, Mr Dean thinks overall Dreamfields is 'pretty fair' due to 'blanket rules' which make exceptions 'isolated examples'. Yet only a few minutes earlier, Mr Dean had critiqued the 'discretionary' nature of hair rules, as Chapter 4 explored. Arguably these girls committed a much more serious, premeditated series of acts sustained over a period of months compared to Ted's one-off theft, yet their actions do not carry the same weight. Anticipated pathology means the transgressions of ethnic-minority, working-class students are often read as more serious signs of future degeneracy, whereas similar actions are perceived as child-ish pranks when performed by the more benign white, middle-class girl. Another teacher decried the incredible rudeness displayed by a white middle-class boy who had recently lost a parent, adding that ongoing leniency in response to his defiant attitude would never be tolerated from boys like Ted, Shaun or Tevin, naming three black boys in lower sets. When asked where he thought this permissiveness stemmed from, the teacher pointed out how the boy came from a stable nuclear family with a receptive parent – assuming that these black working-class students did not have similar families.

Ms Hatcher also related her frustration over the permissive treatment of one disruptive student, linking class and race to results:

> I had an incident with a very white, middle-class – several incidents with a very white middle-class pupil who is extremely clever and I remember saying to a friend at the time, 'I swear if that kid was black, he would have been out of here.' Not out of here, but you know, it would have been taken a lot more seriously. I think not necessarily race all the time, but sometimes like ability-wise and stuff, you know, if that said kid had come in with a knife, for example, I know for a fact he would not have been expelled because of his ability. Then again, that's all the results-driven thing that everyone believes in here. In terms of the pupils, I don't think it has any effect in the classroom.

Ms Hatcher describes the complex range of factors at play in the passing of judgements. Although she feels a black boy doing the same thing would be taken much more seriously, she adds that differential treatment is not always racially motivated. Ms Hatcher attaches this permissiveness to a results-driven culture that 'everyone believes in here'. Anoop Nayak and Jane Kehily describe how raced and gendered categories generated through the materiality of institutions and neighbourhoods become a way of embedding globally circulating racialised myths about masculinities within local sites of meaning-making and the bodies contained in those sites (2008: 107). A wealth of literature exploring the criminalisation of young Afro-Caribbean men where they are represented as lacking a stable culture, disadvantaged through a supposedly matriarchal family life, and subsequently positioned negatively by educational institutions underlies Dreamfields' approach (see Carby, 1982; Ferguson, 2001; Lawrence, 1982; Mac an Ghaill, 1988, 1996; Sewell, 1997; Wright et al., 1998). Several teachers grappled with these legacies underpinning the perception and treatment of students.

Being ideal

While Ms Hatcher concludes these variations in treatment do not impact upon students in the classroom, students were aware of Dreamfields' hierarchies of value. Privilege coalesces on the bodies of some ideal students, like 13-year-old Poppy, who attested to her ability to remain largely under the institutional radar. Poppy is a white British student who lives with her two professional parents in a large Victorian house and designates herself as middle class. Although Poppy was born and raised in Urbanderry, she describes her social group as 'not typical Urbanderry kids', differentiating her and her friends from Urbanderry 'natives', much as Culford does. Poppy said she had noticed how the school picked on certain students, admitting that she could do many of the things boys got punished for without being yelled at, exclaiming: 'Oh yes, they always say that this school is fair, but it's not true!' Yet Poppy did not explicitly link unfairness to race or class, attributing it instead to 'reputation' and describing how Dreamfields focused its attention on the behaviour of young boys in lower sets. Poppy described how once these boys had done something wrong once or twice, teachers would then pick on them 'incessantly' and they would always be in trouble. While she understood this was to 'beat' the teenage rebellion out of them, Poppy added: 'What teenager is not silly and rebellious? That is the entire point of being a teenager!' She felt that some students might not even mean to be naughty, but simply did not 'socially fit' into Dreamfields' environment. Sometimes Poppy thought the people who got into trouble were cool, or not exactly 'cool', but she respected them for 'kicking back' and daring to rebel.

Poppy offered two reasons why she escaped punishment: she was a girl and she was in set one. Throughout the year I repeatedly observed Poppy talking in lessons without censure, but I had not realised that she was aware of the special treatment she was afforded. Poppy's narrative highlights how some students automatically fit into the institutional landscape better than others. It also highlights the lack of efficacy the female body is seen to carry; while boys are marked out as potentially threatening and disruptive, middle-class girls like Poppy are positioned as aspirational, ideal students. Middle-class women not only reproduce class society as wives and mothers, but 'as standard-bearers for middle-class family values, for certain norms of citizenship and also for safeguarding the valuable cultural capital accruing to them and their families through access to education, refinement and other privileges' (McRobbie, 2009: 133). Poppy senses her social fit with the landscape as standard-bearer, whereas some of her fellow students cannot access this position.

Bangladeshi British 13-year-old student Afra also described the importance of first impressions. Afra was also in set one, wore a hijab and was reserved, yet occasionally cheeky. Like Poppy, I frequently observed her chatting in lessons without reproach. Her advice to new students was to follow the rules and do what teachers say for the first year at least, to establish you are a good student. She described messing about in a lesson with a few other girls; while the teacher took their planners, they did not take hers because they knew she was 'usually good'. Once you have cemented a good reputation, you can get away with more. Although Afra cannot draw on white middle-class privilege to establish her value, she arguably plays on discourses of compliant Muslim femininity to stay under the radar and function as a 'model minority' student. Hardly submissive, Afra frequently asserted herself to rearrange our sessions because she was too busy – something no other Year 9 students attempted.

Deceptive bodies: looking the part

Mary, a diminutive 16-year-old white British student who was in set three and four lessons, described how ideal students frequently engaged in practices she deemed wrong. Before Mary joined the interview, her mother Sarah described how Mary's social group had changed since primary school:

> She went with a group from primary school who were actually pretty nasty girls. And I know that the school [Dreamfields] don't actually think they are nasty girls, but they have been very nasty to Mary in the past and she got really left out at that point when they all moved. And they were all set one kids that had come with her from Easton Primary, so she felt intimidated by that.

When Mary joined us, she described this exclusive, set-one group: 'All the posh people, like, hang out together. I don't like them at all. They are all snobby.' Mary describes how she does not care any more about being excluded, describing how they 'try to be like the people in *Skins* … All they do is take drugs and have sex.' Yet this social grouping was highly regarded by the institution.

> CK: So this group of 'nasty girls' is seen by the school as good?
> Mary: Yeah, they are always seen as being the good ones.
> Sarah: Well, one is a prefect.
> Mary: Yeah, all of the prefects are actually the bad people. It's true!
> Sarah: That's not on, though, is it? They should have given that black blazer to you, except you never went enough.[1] *[laughs]* You should have been head girl, Mary, imagine! Yeah, 'cause basically, I mean, they're bright and they go to school and so yes, from the school's perspective they are good.

Mary: They don't know what they are really like.
Sarah: But they were very bitchy as well. And quite nasty and said nasty things, which I don't think there is really any need for ...

Both Sarah and Mary admit this group predominantly comprised white middle-class students, while neither Mary nor Sarah readily claim this label. Notably they both designate Mary's older sister Charlotte as being a 'snob' – perhaps through her positioning as a set-one student. Mary, however, proudly asserts that her social group is much more socially and ethnically mixed.

Phil, a white middle-class parent, also remarked: 'I certainly know that there is quite widespread use of spliff[2] at Dreamfields, not at the school, but out of school ... and from what I am told – and this is hearsay – it is the white middle-class kids who are selling it. So the more wealthy the kid, the more likely they are meant to be selling it.' While I am not concerned with the veracity of Phil's story or want to suggest that all white middle-class kids are drug-taking snobs compared to ethnic-minority or working-class students, it is worth regarding the potential crevasse between institutionally perceived modes of looking and being 'good' and students' actual practices. Because idealised white middle-class students comprise the 'buffer zone' their potential transgressions lack gravity; they become 'normal' teenage high jinks legitimated through their social position, while other students' misdemeanours are more stringently policed.

Troublesome (black) boys

After initially denying that race or ethnicity was an issue, several Dreamfields teachers went on to express concern that some groups of students were disciplined more frequently and severely than others. Mr Turner initially says he has never noticed any racism, describing Dreamfields' multicultural atmosphere as an ideal mixing pot. Yet moments later, Mr Turner adds that he has 'certainly seen teachers who will be quicker to temper with black boys than they will be with anyone else'. He describes these disciplinary variations:

> Well, start off with boys, they'll be disciplined so much more quickly. So straight away, say a boy and a girl have both done the same thing, the boy will definitely get that discipline, the girl might not ... I don't know, I haven't got any solid facts that I could give you about whether people really do, but when you look around in the evenings and there's people sitting outside classrooms or sitting outside head-of-year offices, it's always young black boys. Very rarely anybody else around. Um, very rarely any girls, but maybe that is because young black boys are more likely to misbehave? I don't know, I don't know. I try to be absolutely as fair as I can, in fact I probably go a little bit too far the other way in trying to get them on side a little bit because I find if I can get them on side, I don't have the issues to deal with. So sometimes I might overlook something deliberately, knowing that it's going to pay dividends later on. Whereas if I was caught doing that, you know, I would be in trouble for that. I would have to write up a report explaining it and I have been in trouble for that. I have had to go and see senior

management and take a grilling for choosing not to punish somebody because I've felt it would be in their best interests and my interests and everybody's best interests if I didn't at that stage. I was told that was not my decision to make. So I didn't like that.

Mr Turner describes punishment as a matter of gender and colour, questioning why the overwhelming majority of students sitting outside teachers' offices are black boys – a phenomenon readily visible in my routine passage along the corridors. He ponders if this is due to black boys' more routine misbehaviour; in the absence of an answer, Mr Turner tries to be 'absolutely fair' and even makes a concerted effort to 'get them on side', although he is frustrated by the limited jurisdiction he has over his classroom. Ms Austin grappled with a similar point:

> There seems to be, this is well known as well and they are obviously trying to combat this, is the behaviour of young black boys. And it always does seem to be a lot of them who are in trouble and is that because they are known troublemakers and they have got themselves in trouble, but then after that they kind, we've been on them and teachers are on them all the time and focusing on them? Or I mean, it's boys in general? I don't know … But you know, you could say that about the Turkish boys, you know, when you see them together and think, 'Oh God, they are a nightmare!' But you know, um – but I don't know … is it because they are more troublesome or is it that we notice them more because we are concerned about their achievement and we are worried that they are not, you know, that they are potential troublemakers and they are a bit silly, so we notice when they do something because we are looking for them to you know, bring a knife in, or we're looking for them to, you know? Are there other kids that are getting up to things just like that but we aren't focusing on them because they don't look like troublemakers and they don't necessarily show themselves in the same way and kind of get the attention from teachers? I'm not sure, really. I definitely think you can start to fall into a stereotype of … you can start to think of it like, in that way, but you've got to really try not to. I think, you know?

Ms Austin's speculations highlight how deviance is anticipated from ethnic-minority boys who are frequently viewed as potentially dangerous; however she is wary of taking this position. Gill Crozier (2015) points out how there was little evidence to legitimise teachers feeling threatened by groups of South Asian boys in her research. Instead she feels this threat is more imagined than real – something hinted at by Ms Austin. Meanwhile students who do not 'look' deviant could be involved in similar things but go unnoticed. This ties back to Poppy's recognition of her lightly surveyed position and Mary's assertions that prefects were 'the bad ones'. These differing perceptions are also discussed by Mr Mitchell: while misbehaviour from a group of Kurdish children makes them an intimidating 'gang', the same behaviour coming from white middle-class children evokes a less serious response because they are seen as 'less threatening, more familiar and the rules are not enforced in the same way'. Ms Wainwright also invoked the imagery of the gangster to justify the need for middle-class students. Similarly, Claire Alexander (2000) showed how young Bengali men in inner London were frequently racialised and seen as a 'gang' despite having practices in line with other young men, which affected how they were perceived and treated within educational establishments. Assumptions about gang membership have also been applied to black Caribbean and black African young people in other research contexts, while groups of Kurdish and Turkish youth are recipients of this gaze at Dreamfields (see also Crozier and Davies, 2008; Joseph and Gunter, 2011; Shain, 2011). These perspectives also ignore how group solidarity is not born out of a desire to self-segregate, but can also function as a form of protection against racism in schools (see Miah, 2012, 2015).

Both Ms Austin and Mr Turner struggled with how to approach inequality; frequently repeating: 'I don't know.' Ms Fletcher also describes how middle-class children have external 'advantages' and she tries to be fair by overcompensating: 'Generally because I can consider myself to be middle-class and white, I am mean to the kids that are middle-class and white and not necessarily as mean to the other kids that aren't middle-class and white.' Some teachers try to favour the underprivileged through their own reflexive practice, yet removing the 'cloak' of formal equality which Bourdieu describes and Dreamfields wears by acknowledging pre-existing inequalities has resulted in reprimands for teachers like Mr Turner. The failure of teacher training to effectively confront racism feeds into Dreamfields' teachers feeling confused or confounded by what they experience within the institution. The lack of teacher education and professional development concerning race and racism does not challenge racist positioning of students, but works to maintain the status quo and aids the resurrection of racism in schools (Lander, 2011; Maylor, 2015: 28; Smith, 2013). Teachers are being moved away from acting as 'critical educators' and pedagogues to function as efficient service providers delivering results. Vini Lander writes:

> The erasure of race from the initial teacher training standards and the diminution of university-based teacher education in tandem with a colourblind stance has served to compound teachers' ignorance about racism, how it operates and how policy and practice serve to embed the dominant discourse, leaving BME pupils the victims of racism in their everyday school lives. (2015: 34)

This leaves teachers like Mr Turner and Ms Fletcher to take individualised, discretionary approaches to the suspected inequities they observe.

Within Dreamfields some ethnic-minority bodies – primarily those of black male students, but not always – have a heightened visibility that relies on wider discourses of ethnic-minority criminality. Despite claiming to be 'an oasis in the desert', Dreamfields does not operate in a vacuum; its practices connect to the outside world and reflect the surveillance of bodies on Urbanderry's streets. Nirmal Puwar explores how a 'racialised optics' is applied which amplifies the ethnic-minority body – not because these bodies are curious or unknown, but because they are 'known' in ways that threaten and intimidate (2004: 51). Black bodies are marked by race and under surveillance, yet contradictorily; 'the saliency of race is denied and repressed by the pervasive liberal ideology of colour-blindness and the necessity of professional collegiality' (2004: 139). However, unlike in Puwar's research, where adult ethnic-minority, professional bodies had already been vetted and provisionally approved, the child's body is still awaiting approval and must be carefully monitored for signs of potential deviance. The student's body must take on or at least convincingly perform Dreamfields' values or risk facing continual monitoring and punishment. Maylor (2015) describes how a majority white teaching body is often not equipped to teach black children, for being prepared to teach black children requires regarding them in the same way as white children. Research by Maylor and her colleagues (Maylor, 2014; Maylor et al., 2006) has shown how black students were treated more aggressively and punitively by teachers than white students engaging in similar actions. Black British parent Alexander describes how many Dreamfields teachers are not from Urbanderry and may be teaching kids 'they are not familiar with' and who might 'look challenging'. Yet Alexander refuses to tie black bodies being seen as 'challenging' to racism, instead saying: 'No, I think it is your history, it's what you're used to, it's what you've seen on TV.' In this post-racial era, we enter a state of denial described by Bonilla-Silva (2014) as 'racism without the racists'.

Sticky reputations: 'I am bad in this school'

Now I will move from examining the raced, classed and gendered parameters of Dreamfields' institutional structures to focus on how students and their social groupings are structured by these parameters. Gazi, aged 13, occupies the position Poppy outlined. As a young man in lower set groupings, he frequently discussed trying to shift his 'bad reputation' whilst under continual surveillance. Gazi is an energetic, outgoing student who is Turkish and Welsh. He lives on a nearby estate with his mother, stepfather and siblings and spends most evenings at cadets, the youth club or boxing. At the beginning of the year he proudly showed me his planner: despite being crammed with detentions for talking in class or 'immaturity' during the previous four weeks, the last three days were clear and his form tutor's comments cited improvement.

Yet a couple of months later the scrawls of red, blue and green ink in his planner had returned. Gazi sighed wearily, professing he did not know what was happening – 'things are out of control!' When I asked Gazi what advice he would give to a new pupil coming to Dreamfields, he blurted out: 'Don't come – go to another school!' He felt there were too many rules and he was constantly in trouble – sometimes for things he had not actually done, but once you have a reputation, you get in trouble more. Yet Gazi added that at least he could say it was a good education because some teachers were very dedicated and expected a lot. Gazi described how he decided not to be a bad boy and focus on his education after deciding you could not do both, adding that 'real bad boys' were not in school, but in court or a jail cell somewhere (see Archer and Yamashita, 2003a, 2003b; Shain, 2011). Gazi described how he was trying to change his reputation by not answering teachers back, looking interested and using the right body language; however, these alterations took time. When I asked about discipline being meted out fairly, Gazi asserted that there were some racist teachers in the school, and he hated this. Shaking his head and sighing, he described how some teachers ignored the poor behaviour of white people and picked on black people, pointing out that he fit into the latter category due to his olive complexion. This made him want to leave because even when he tried to be better, teachers still singled him out. Gazi's classmate Charlie, a 13-year-old white British boy, had also described how their English teacher would frequently shout at the black boys in the class, even if they were not the ones talking. He said the whole class noticed this, admitting that he and the Asian girls in the class often talked, but seldom got into trouble.[3]

A few months later, Gazi reiterated that turning over a new leaf was difficult, adding: 'I am just bad in this school.' Even though he had stopped getting numerous detentions and was trying to be good, he could not shake his bad reputation. I asked him how long he thought it would take to wear off and he laughed, speculating approximately five years. Adopting a resolute tone, Gazi pledged that he was going to try hard to show teachers he was a good student.

Tameka also describes how once you get a bad reputation, teachers always look for you to misbehave; they always think of you like that and it becomes really hard to get them to think anything else. Tameka is an outspoken and friendly 16-year-old who describes herself as 'a normal Urbanderry girl' whose family is from the Congo. She lives on a nearby estate with her parents and two siblings and is in set four for most subjects. While there were some teachers she liked, Tameka described how some just thought that because of your background and what you are like that you would never get anywhere or become anything. In a tone of passionate defiance, Tameka asserted that when she got her five good GCSEs she would push them in these teachers' faces to show them they were wrong about her.

The 'three C's' and racialised divisions

One Dreamfields rule dictates that groups of more than six children in the playground must be separated. Tameka and several others discussed how ethnic-minority student groups were continuously broken up while groups of white students were often overlooked. As we strolled around the perimeter of the playground one afternoon, I asked Tameka if some people got into trouble more than others. Exasperated, she exclaimed: 'Yeah, my group does!' She said they were always breaking them up in the playground, but there was another group that teachers left alone. Tameka thought this was due to racism and this discrimination had been going on for ages, but there was no point in mentioning it because if you told them they never did anything about it. When I asked her how she dealt with it, she sighed, saying it never changed so they just tried to ignore it, keep their heads down and get on with it. They only had five months left and Tameka was in no mood to get excluded. Besides, there was nothing they could do; they just thought some kids were bad. Both Gazi and Tameka's resigned attitude echoes Lander's (2015) research where students felt unable to do anything about racism in school.

Joshua also discussed the different treatment of groups in the playground, describing how a predominantly white group of students congregating around the circular bench was left alone. Unlike Tameka, Joshua did not attribute this to racism, but instead suggested that the different comportment of bodies by colour could justify discipline:

> It could be more or less the people in that group – like Tameka and Sharon – they actually love hype. They enjoy the whole, making it bigger, creating drama. They form big circles and crowds and get really loud and there is no need for it. In that whole frenzy problems can occur. Whereas white people just sit there and talk casually, you can't really blame them. No, they are actually quite interesting. They are just compact, controlled and concise. The three C's.

Larger gestures and louder sounds issuing from some black students like Tameka are seen to attract discipline, whereas stationary, quiet white students engaged in casual conversation are audibly and visually non-threatening. Regardless of whether or not students are doing anything subversive, different aesthetic forms are assigned differential values. Yet performing 'the three C's' is not limited to the white body. Joshua describes himself as Nigerian. He lives with his parents and siblings on a demonised estate; however his parents are both middle-class professionals. Joshua said he avoided loud groups and his ethnically mixed group routinely displayed the three C's. Nayak asserts: 'It transpires that whiteness or blackness is not attached to respective white and black bodies but rather that race signs are encoded into everyday practice' (2006a: 418–19); however, achieving academic success is still associated with 'acting white', or, as Fordham (1996) describes, by maintaining the existing hegemonic systems of power and domination. Joshua displays these ideal, aspirational behaviours and is accepted into the Dreamfields community as a valued set-one student and prefect.

Joshua connected heavier in-school policing of ethnic-minority groups to heavier out-of-school policing, describing how a group of black people were always seen as more frightening than a group of white people, suggesting this was due to being loud and a minority in Britain. Joshua described how when police saw black people, they thought: 'Hey, let's investigate them to see what they are up to.' This happened on his estate; the police would stop groups of black people being loud, whereas a group of white people would be regarded as a friendly gathering. Joshua said that if you looked around the school, black students tended to be naughtier than other students and the percentage of them who got into trouble was greater, suggesting this could be why teachers broke them up. Instead of positioning heavier surveillance as unjust, Joshua thought it was ultimately positive. I asked if this surveillance was problematic for him, and he replied no: he stayed out of trouble and tended not to hang out with loud people any more because loud noises hurt his ears and annoyed him, joking that he was getting old. Through distancing and differentiating himself from the 'loud' – and often more working-class – black students like Tameka and her friends, Joshua mitigates the possibility of featuring as a suspect.

Despite his previous explanations, Joshua resurrected the issue of playground divisions months later in our final discussion: while 'mixed crowds' were continuously divided, around the circular bench 'they gather in twelve and are there for the entirety of lunchtime, untouched and unmoved. And I wonder why.' Although unsatisfied by his prior conclusions, Joshua still rejected racism, exclaiming: 'Personally I don't want to think that racism happens at this school because I like this school, and if they were racist I would have a whole campaign against the school with flyers and poles and stuff.' Although Joshua felt racism probably still existed, he thought it was very unlikely to occur in a multi-ethnic school like Dreamfields, for surely teachers would teach elsewhere if they were racist? Still, he was stumped: 'I mean, I'm just guessing they have a logical explanation for why they treat the two groups differently. There must be some logical explanation, apart from skin colour.' Puwar describes how the physical presence of ethnic-minority bodies is assumed to create racial equality, where 'race' resides in these bodies and multiculturalism infers that more bodies of colour must imply equality (2004: 32). Joshua assumes that a critical mass of black and brown bodies creates racial parity at Dreamfields.

Samuel thought teachers were not 'up-front racists, but they just … I just think they have certain perceptions of certain people and then they just think … "Oh, this person, they might do something, they are a troublemaker … and they just like, as a group, they just look mischievous."' Samuel is also a set-one student, black British and a prefect who lives on an estate with his mother, a legal professional, and his younger sister. Samuel recalls being deemed 'mischievous' by teachers in Year 9 when he and his friends starting rapping during break time. Their clever, funny wordplay drew a small crowd until a teacher told them to stop because they were attracting too much attention. Samuel felt this was unfair, as they were only passing time and not trying to attract an audience. Recalling the ban on spontaneous karaoke performances at the winter fair discussed in Chapter 3, stopping Samuel and his friends from rapping banned both the 'street' culture excised from Dreamfields' landscape as well as any impromptu performances contravening the three C's.

While Joshua's hypothesising belies some uncertain perplexity, Tameka clearly states that racism is the problem. Samuel is more cautious in his assessment, yet shares Tameka's indignation. The different interpretations regarding why groups may or may not be broken up not only hinges on raced and classed norms of composure, but these interpretations are shaped by the students' different class backgrounds and their status within the achievement hierarchy. Although Joshua and Samuel live on estates, their parents are both educated professionals; it transpires that Mr Vine's assumption that most black boys on estates end up in gangs is inaccurate. Meanwhile, Tameka's family has a more precarious financial situation and little experience of higher education, affording them less legitimate cultural capital to draw upon and employ within the educational landscape.

Mobility and social space

Institutional structures shape social groupings in accordance with dominant value systems. Although Ms Fletcher says students are not 'necessarily aware of the fact that it's class that they separate themselves out into', students are acutely alive to social divisions, even if they do not always name 'class' as such. Gazi and Poppy each stay with their respective social groups in the playground and rarely attempt to circulate, yet they become fixed in very different social positions. Poppy says her group are conscious of being 'very middle-class', noting that she does not mean this in a 'snobby way'. Yet Poppy also referred to the students outside the 'skinny-jean crowd' as 'street kids', describing how her friends were 'very fashion-conscious' and could be called 'hipsters'. Poppy felt class no longer referenced money, but was about interests, how one spoke, and if they shopped at Urban Outfitters – a clothing store designated as denoting middle-class taste. She describes spending time in a fashionable area of Goldport, often referring to herself and her friends as 'special' or 'weird', drawing boundaries between herself and the rest of the cohort. Research on white middle-class families who send their children to comprehensive schools highlights how commitments to multi-ethnic spaces exists in tension with the defence of middle-class privilege and a 'belief in the "specialness" of white middle-class children' (Reay et al., 2007: 1043). The 'specialness' conferred on middle-class students resides in their claims to possess a unique individuality displayed by the cultural symbols their material position affords.

Poppy says there are divisions in the playground and people she never speaks to; while some people can move between groups, she is not one of them. When she first came to Dreamfields, Poppy describes how she had enormous glasses and spoke very properly, but quickly toned down her accent, realising 'it was a bit much'. Like many students, she thinks group divisions correspond to speaking style. She recounts trying to speak slang once, amusingly contorting her mouth in an uncomfortable shape before announcing 'it didn't suit me' and 'just sounded wrong'. Poppy adds that her friend Lorna is 'pretty good at doing both accents', although she did not literally move between groups. When I ask her to describe the other social group, her initially diplomatic response of 'I don't like to put labels on things' moves to a guilty admission of calling them chavs. Although Poppy acknowledges it is 'bad to say chavs', she adds: 'It is just so true.' She reflected on a recent textiles project where they presented a designer's work. Some students presented Ed Hardy or Baby Phat, which Poppy derided as 'not real brands', but showed how potentially nice things could be 'over-branded until they were skanky'. Poppy's report was about Vivienne Westwood, 'not famous people who decided to pretend to be designers'. As Bourdieu outlines in *Distinction* (1984), 'skanky' fashion preferences are tied to a purported lack of taste and appropriate knowledge of what is good. Poppy expressed regret for her admissions, but described how some people criticised how she spoke and referred to her as a nerd. In a posh accent, Poppy joked: 'Sorry, darling, but I am speaking English.' While her group's middle-classness is clearly asserted, any reference to ethnicity playing a role in social formations is emphatically rejected. The majority of Poppy's group are white, but a few friends like Lorna and Daniel are not. It is not a tidy picture of social distance determined by either/or dichotomies.

Meanwhile, Gazi sits at the opposite end of the social spectrum. While walking around the playground, Gazi pointed to the circular bench, designating it the 'blond nerd area'. This is the same bench referenced by Joshua, Samuel and Tameka in Year 11, and it is also where Poppy and her friends in Year 9 congregate. Although many of them are not blond, this area has the largest concentration of blond-ish and white bodies in the playground. Gazi recalls being introduced to them when he was new; they did not understand what he was saying and stared at him blankly. He says they speak English, but I point out he speaks English too. He says no, it was different – they speak 'posh English', they are posh people whom he does not 'get' and who aren't 'normal people'. Gazi thinks these nerds are boring goody-goodies who never have fun and always follow the rules. After the disclaimer 'not to be rude or nothing', Gazi goes on to describe how they have 'no style' because they work constantly, listen to horrible rock music and cut themselves. He suggests nerds hang out in parks, eat roast dinners and play in rock bands, while he likes to go to the cinema, listen to rap and eat chicken and chips. He accurately speculates that the nerds probably call him a chav, but Gazi refutes this label. After his passionate diatribe, Gazi pauses and admits he is prejudiced against them but he does not actually know what they are really like.

Despite this segregation, there were limited attempts at mixing. Gazi had one friend from the nerd group called Fred with 'long floppy hair'. Even though Fred was a 'semi-emo', Gazi described him as 'cool' because he understood what Gazi liked and didn't play rock music around him. Several months later, Gazi told me that he had made three new 'nerd' friends during PE, actively adopting their style of slang and greeting them with 'hey dude'. During this mixed-ability lesson, space was created for mixing. Gazi connected his mixing to his efforts to lose his bad-boy reputation and take school more seriously. Poppy also expressed wanting to be closer friends with a black classmate who had a great sense of humour; however, she found it difficult to make this social leap.

Poppy and Gazi's largely stationary stances may appear evenly sided; however, their immobility has very different consequences. Their respective practices and 'styles' actively make class and carry unequal currency. Bourdieu distinguishes between those who only have to be what they are as opposed to those who are what they do, and who therefore have to constantly prove that they are capable of carrying the signs and capital of national belonging (quoted in Skeggs 2004: 19). Poppy does not need to learn how to speak slang to acquire value – she is already positioned as the ideal student. Conversely, Gazi is continually being pushed to reform his behaviour and self-presentation. His limited ability to modulate his speech and self-presentation means he lacks the right affective disposition; he is not carrying the necessary signs and capital. Gazi needs to speak properly, as his social forms are undervalued and deemed incompatible with success. Yet judgements about linguistic codes are a function of power rather than an accurate assessment of the inherent superiority of one code over another (see Harris, Schwab and Whitman, 1990). Roxy Harris asserts that many working-class and some lower middle-class students in UK cities share a generally understood speech code that Roger Hewitt called 'local multi-ethnic vernacular' (2009: 89). Yet this local multi-ethnic vernacular that Gazi describes using has no place at

Dreamfields as it seeks to rid the student body of these denigrated cultural forms. Gazi is the one who needs to 'move up', not Poppy, for she has already arrived. While social mixing may be optional for some students, I will now consider a few students who describe mixing as necessary for acquiring social mobility and value.

Mobility and the dynamic self

Institutional and social structures are also manipulated or contested by students in pursuit of their own needs, yet these structures are navigated in relation to their position within it. Several students described circulating between groupings as a positive practice. Joshua says he moves from the Afro-Caribbean to the Asian to the 'Caucasian' group, 'having a laugh with each'. He describes how mixing 'opens you up' and prevents narrowmindedness; you have to interact with and understand a range of people to discover the 'true beauty of life'. The capacity to move between ethnic groups was part of becoming a 'diverse' and 'dynamic person', because 'being British had changed'. Language features heavily once again, as Joshua describes Britain as a diverse country where you need to know how to converse with different people. He describes how some of his black friends don't feel comfortable with his white friends because there are expressions the white kids do not understand. Yet Joshua says he has 'achieved' an ethnically varied social group and can go anywhere with relative ease. Samuel also describes how he 'is not one of those people who just stuck to one group', explaining how he moves between groups to avoid pigeonholing himself.

Isaac, a black British, middle-class 16-year-old, relates social mobility to his interest in other people and how they 'get on'. Like Joshua, he feels one should embrace different groups rather than 'try to separate yourself off from others and be afraid of people who are different from you'. He thinks mixing around makes things better and it is what you need to do to get along in life. Mobility has personal benefits, for Isaac adds he is 'lucky' to circulate, 'zipping in and out' with ease. By the end of Year 11, Isaac had decided to attend Dreamfields' sixth form, proclaiming that his days of 'messing about' were over because he had realized this was a competition and he was going to turn it on 'full-blast next year … to be on top'. One strategy Isaac described for getting on top involved shifting his friendship group to hang out with high-achievers and thus gain entrance to sixth-form head Ms Harding's 'private sly little club' that 'herd around her' and visited Oxbridge. He speculated that you needed a minimum of five A-stars to go on these trips. Isaac felt being seen to be friends with the set-one group would get him in her 'good graces', as the Oxbridge candidates were 'more serious students' who Ms Harding was particularly friendly with. Isaac described how this partnership was advantageous because it was not simply you trying to get yourself to Oxbridge, but you *and* Ms Harding 'working with each other' to get you there. This shift involves Isaac deliberately moving from a more ethnically mixed social group to a whiter, middle-class group to accrue benefits. This shift is also similar to Gazi associating his mixing with middle-class students with his attempts to erase his 'bad-boy' reputation. Future social relations become welded to the acquisition of educational advantages, and this shift of self can be visually displayed through physical placement.

These boys' narratives highlight a combination of altruistic and self-serving motivations for social mixing. While pointing to the importance of understanding others, circulating also aids the development of a dynamic self, capable of moving across social space. Mixing is related to social mobility, both spatially and culturally. A key element of this mobility is the capacity to modulate speech styles. Mixing becomes a way of resourcing the self as mobility becomes an achievement, unfixing students from ethnicity or class so they can accrue value. Ethnicity becomes a positive asset, provided they can effectively perform white middle-class norms as promoted by Dreamfields' training. Reay and her colleagues (2007) highlight how white middle-class parents depicted their children's proximity to students like Joshua, Samuel and Isaac as desirable as they accrued 'multi-cultural capital'. Aspirational ethnic-minority children also functioned as symbolic barriers demarcating the white middle classes from their undesirable white working-class 'others'. These students arguably function as what Ahmed calls 'conversion points' (2010: 44). Their positive social integration promises happiness, as social mixing turns bad feelings into good. These young black men are actively converting themselves and acquiring capital that can be deployed in the future through taking up the idea of integration and happy multiculturalism. They have converted the threat of the pathological black body found in Dreamfields' urban chaos discourse into an exemplary black body.

Immanent subjects

Although Tameka says she can talk to anyone, her account of social mixing is more complicated and exemplifies what practices need to be discarded to embody mobility. Tameka explains that 'just because her friends "spud"[4] does not mean they are selling drugs or being violent', it was how they talked, adding: 'just because it's ghetto does not mean that it is bad'. While giving me a tour, we pass Brandon, a tall, black young man wearing a puffy black parka. Tameka points out that someone like Brandon is seen as a troublemaker because of how he looks, even though he is well-behaved. We walked down a corridor and Tameka pointed to Bridget, a white girl in her year, and said she was naughty too. Bridget found this funny and started pulling faces before a teacher reprimanded us. Despite her blond whiteness, Bridget was clearly not part of the 'blond nerd' group. The reading of bodies as 'bad' is formed through complex mutually produced amalgamations of raced and classed hierarchies that persist in hyper-diverse spaces. Tameka thinks Dreamfields has stereotypical ideas of Urbanderry as a ghetto where 'all the women are walking around pregnant with prams' and 'every young man has been in prison'. These bodies become the origin of bad feeling and serve as representations of deviance, regardless of actual action or intent.

Unsurprisingly Tameka does not identify with any class grouping, as this would align her with a devalued position (Skeggs, 1997). Instead Tameka proudly says she is 'ghetto' because she speaks 'bare slang', but also emphasises that she is just a 'normal teenager' who has everything she needs – a family, an i-Pod, trainers, brand-name clothes. Tameka draws value from being a 'Urbanderry girl' by fashioning negative raced and classed notions of Urbanderry into an authentic coolness that she feels is emulated by some 'posher' students. Manthia Diawara discusses how John Travolta 'wears' blackness and achieves transcendence in the film *Pulp Fiction*, whereas Samuel Jackson's coolness is innate; he's not acting and he cannot take it off – it's just who he is (1998: 51). While posh students may try on a 'black esthétique du cool' and deploy blackness as cultural capital, Tameka's body is immanently cool. Although she receives approval from her peers, it is not the institutional authorisation that has purchase in the wider 'legitimate' world. Yet Joshua, Samuel and Isaac have achieved partial transcendence within Dreamfields, signalling that a mobile subject position is not universally available, but a privileged identity position which creates new forms of power and may be more readily accessible to men (Adkins, 2002).

Tameka occupies a complex and contradictory position. She actively points out racialised judgements while simultaneously conceding to Dreamfields' demands. When talking about the formal sixth-form dress code, Tameka professes that she probably needs to be 'less street' and wearing heels and skirts would be 'good practice' to make her more 'ladylike'. Tameka is unsure that she could handle the formality and needs to save money for a whole new wardrobe. While Tameka feels a need to change herself, she also resists the idea that her practices are innately wrong and accrues some capital through being an 'Urbanderry girl'. Like Ahmed's 'melancholy migrant' whose 'fixation with injury is read as an obstacle' to their own happiness and where the 'moral task is thus "to get over it"' (2010: 143–4), Tameka refuses to accept her pathologisation or an easy vision of happy multiculturalism. Her position is precarious; while she does not fully dispense with her ways of being, she is willing to 'practise' alterations perceived as beneficial to her future.

Unspeakable structures

While Tameka referenced class and race through the language of place and style, many students and parents struggled to discuss difference. Social class is rarely discussed by young people, but is deeply ingrained and threaded through their lives where the affective politics of class is a felt practice (Nayak, 2006b). A series of interactions illustrates the difficulty of talking about these topics when national and institutional narratives uncritically celebrate diversity and position racism as past-tense. Eve described the complex position her mixed-race daughter Lorna occupied: 'I mean, Lorna's classified as white middle-class, but we are a one-parent family, working-class, but I suppose it's classified on the lifestyle you live.' Eve did not see herself as middle-class, but understood why Lorna did due to a lifestyle that had 'whitened' her. Eve adds:

> It's just such an awful saying, you hear it every day now, 'white middle-class parents, white middle-class parents'. Um, I don't see the need for it, to be honest

with you – hard-working parents. It doesn't need to be put in classes at all. Especially, why do you have to be white to be middle-class? I don't understand it.

While Eve picks up on the inconsistency and fluidity of race and class, there is no critical vocabulary to draw upon to articulate her frustration, ending in a refutation that ignores power dynamics.

Several participants were worried about what they could say. Before describing the group that had excluded her daughter, Sarah said: 'See, I feel really nervous about saying anything like this', before adding: 'But it is the white middle-class kids.' Turkish sixth-former Alara also paused when describing social groupings, saying: 'The white people – am I allowed to say that? I don't know how PC we are going here!' As Joshua described social divisions in the playground he paused, asking me if he could say 'black'. I found it extremely awkward that a black student was asking a white person for permission on how he could define himself and other black students. I mentioned this, and Joshua paused quizzically before continuing. Lorna also debated whether or not to tell me that her group of friends were overlooked by the police who were called by a security guard because they were sitting on the roof of a local building. She described how the police car did not stop them because not enough of them looked like her; they drove past because the group was mostly white. Lorna feared that pointing this out might make her sound like a racist. In the face of our supposed colour-blind happiness, calling attention to the presence of racism becomes synonymous with resurrecting and reinstating it; the exposure of violence is therefore equated with its origin (Ahmed, 2012).

However, it is important to also note that participants' wariness of invoking race or class is not simply a negative, regressive impulse. As Les Back (1996: 66) describes through the concept of 'neighbourhood nationalism', the idea that talking about people's colour is 'out of order' is 'not an empty gesture but the product of a long struggle over the inclusion of black people within this parochial identity'. This neighbourhood nationalism produced out of lived struggles over belonging is arguably present in Urbanderry, yet it is particularly amenable to being co-opted and obfuscated by the colour-blind policy rhetoric used by the DfE and the academies programme. This aspirational rhetoric draws on this neighbourhood feeling, inverting it to cover over and forget these struggles while precluding current struggles from being named or discussed. Despite the willingness of many young people to cross borders, institutional structures and practices work to make equality and mixing more and more difficult to achieve. There are sound reasons for students' attempts to move away from race talk; there are good intentions in these moves, yet this goodwill is subverted by institutional structures that work hand in hand with narratives of meritocracy and neoliberal fantasy.

Unsurprisingly, only middle-class students and parents confidently placed themselves into a class grouping, as this was a valued identification. Contrastingly, parents who did not fit into this group emphasised their ordinariness and frequently rejected class as something they did not believe in. Gazi's mum Laila says: 'I'm a human being, a normal person. I would not even put myself into a class … I work my backside off, yeah, and whatever I eat or drink, I pay for it very hard. But I'm just an average person.' While parent Marie says:

> I would just say I am working-class, I've always been working-class, I'd say. Or should I be middle-class by now? [*laughs*] But I don't really believe in class. I don't believe in class at all, because I believe in humanity. I believe we are all the same, no matter what job you've got.

Marie references the idea that there should be some sort of progression to middle-classness, yet goes on to evoke a universal humanity, drawing on her spirituality to do this. Bernadette, Charlie's mother, abruptly responds to class: 'I don't have nothing to do with that, I will go and talk to whomever I want to', yet later adds that she is 'definitely not posh'. The difficulty of discussing difference or power dynamics was a recurring phenomenon, attesting to the successful silencing of these issues after over thirty years of meritocratic aspirational narratives. There is little language left to speak of race- and class-based inequity that is continually positioned as past tense, highlighting how power escapes description.

Searching for explanations

Finally, I would like to reflect on a group discussion with seven students that shows how young people grapple with the murky hierarchies running through Dreamfields' institutional structure. The participants included Daniel, Lorna and Poppy, who were all in set one, and also friends outside school; Afra, who is also in set one, but did not socialise with anyone else in the group and only spoke once during the session; Abisola, who is in set three; and Gazi and Charlie, who are in sets three and four.

I ask them to imagine the then-education minister Michael Gove wanted to know what they thought schools should be like – what would they say? Abisola pipes up, saying: 'I know, I know!' She feels Dreamfields 'should be more fair because certain kids get more opportunities when they are doing things; like right now if they were to choose four people to go on a trip, it would be one, two, three, four'. She points to Daniel, Afra, Poppy and Lorna. There is an uncomfortable silence. Lorna's jaw drops until Gazi finally cuts in, asserting: 'This is because they are smart and get good grades.' Abisola quickly retorts: 'It doesn't have to be the smartest lot, that's the thing, they should have like different kinds of people for.' Poppy finishes Abisola's thought with 'opportunities for everyone'. Charlie adds 'Exactly, exactly.' I ask Daniel, Poppy, Lorna and Afra if they think that Abisola's statement is fair – would they be the ones chosen for the trip? They unanimously agree before Lorna attempts to explain their exclusion:

> *Lorna*: Yeah, but I think it is just because we're … wait … how to put this? *(She pauses)*
> *Abisola*: Smarter?
> *Lorna*: No.

> *Abisola*: Better? More experienced? Politer?
> *Lorna*: No. *(tentatively)* Better behaved?
> *Daniel*: Not really!
> *Poppy*: No.
> *Abisola*: Not all of us are actually –
> *Lorna (cutting her off)*: Wait, how many merits do you have?

When Lorna's suggestion of better behaviour is rejected by both Daniel and Poppy, she turns the discussion to merits, asking Charlie, Gazi and Abisola how many they have. Gazi and Charlie had 12 and 18, respectively. Abisola sharply retorts: 'I don't get merits, I get notes in my planner', adding that even when she got 183 merits two years before she did not get anything. Lorna then asks Poppy, probably one of the highest achievers in her year group. Gazi bets she has 'like 100' merits. With an air of blasé lethargy, Poppy announces she has none. Gazi asks: 'Seriously?!' No one believes her. We all wait while Poppy irreverently flips through her planner, finally getting to the back where merits are affixed. Each page is blank. We gasp in unison. Gazi laughs loudly in disbelief, slapping his hand on the table, while Charlie exclaims: 'Jeee-sus!' Clearly, preferential treatment is not determined by merits.

Momentarily defeated, Lorna returns to her original idea that they are chosen for trips because of good behaviour, not cleverness. Slumped in his chair, Daniel sarcastically mutters: 'Yeah, sure' under his breath. Gazi points out they are also placed in sets according to their behaviour, not simply their intelligence – something he has experienced first-hand after being moved down from set three to four in his science lessons for poor behaviour, not poor achievement. Setting practices have been shown to disproportionately disadvantage ethnic-minority and working-class pupils, creating institutional landscapes which reinforce social hierarchies, even in mixed settings[5] (Troyna, 1993; 1991). Meanwhile, Daniel and Abisola talk inaudibly at the end of the table until I ask them to feed into the discussion:

> *Abisola*: He knows I'm right.
> *Daniel*: Yeah, Abisola is right.
> *Abisola*: Thank you!
> *Daniel*: If you are in set one, you get treated better. You can get away with a lot more when you are in set one.
> *Poppy*: Yeah, you can.
> *Charlie, Gazi*: Thank you.
> *Abisola*: Because they believe that you are more responsible.
> *Charlie*: I'm responsible!
> *Daniel*: 'Cause they don't want to, like, give you a detention and then you throw a fit and then fail your GCSEs.
> *Lorna*: It's because they work us hard, they have to pay us back ...
> *Daniel*: They don't want to, like, upset us because we have to, like, do well or they don't look good.

This debate over why certain students are treated better than others highlights the ambiguous criteria constituting hierarchies of student value. If, as Abisola asks, superior treatment is not down to being smarter or better behaved or politer, then what determines it? What lies in this grey area of subtle yet repetitive and compounding judgements and classifications that steadily create and sustain hierarchies? While Lorna earnestly attempts to defend Dreamfields as a meritocracy, Poppy and Daniel more cynically attribute their preferential treatment to their set-one position. They recognise themselves as valuable assets that produce good results with minimal teacher labour; they literally carry and produce value for Dreamfields. Yet, as Gazi points out, set position is not solely determined by intelligence, but by displaying 'appropriate' behaviours, or as Ms Austin mentioned, how students 'show themselves'. The heightened surveillance and negative expectations of ethnic-minority and working-class students and the promotion of speech and comportment more readily embodied by white middle-class students all work together to mark 'other' students as pathological from the outset. But, at the same time, ethnic-minority students like Daniel, Lorna and Afra, as well as Joshua, Samuel and Isaac, come to form part of the 'buffer zone', gaining access to a highly favoured status because they visually enact the correct bodily dispositions and generate results. They also gain value, at least within Dreamfields' parameters, through projecting an image of racial equality and progressive cosmopolitanism.

Conclusion

This chapter began to unpick the inherent normality and 'innocence' of the middle classes embedded within Dreamfields' institutional perspective (Savage, 2003: 537). It examined how this preferred normality intersects with race and is compounded by the education marketplace's demand for results. It also explores how these parameters shape teacher and student negotiations. While multiculturalism once served as a happy object, it now frequently features as a source of anxiety that can be made happy once again by reformulating it around integration (Ahmed, 2008). Dreamfields does this, promoting integration through the forced uptake of norms. As Essed and Goldberg point out: 'Cultural cloning is predicated on the taken-for-granted desirability of certain types, the often-unconscious tendency to comply with normative standards, the easiness with the familiar and the subsequent rejection of those who are perceived as deviant' (2002: 1070). Students' social groupings are structured by these institutional norms which they navigate and circumvent from various positions within Dreamfields' hierarchy. Possessing mobility means possessing value, but mixing for mobility is only a necessary strategy for those who do not inhabit the classed, raced position of ideal student. Supposedly more expressive black bodies like Tameka's are consistently more heavily policed in the playground, while Joshua and others can and do consciously perform 'whiter' forms of comportment – a tactic that reduces their surveillance. This allows them to move with greater ease and also highlights the ontological impossibility and elasticity of race. These adjustments problematise the notion of mobility; rather than being depicted as an upward liberation, mobility has deeply defensive aspects, gendered boundaries and requires sacrifice (Walkerdine, 2003).

The academy structures the ideal subject through creating distinctions that attribute judgements and values through bodily and social orientations. These orientations form the basis of a moral economy, as Dreamfields' moral distinctions of worth become social distinctions of value negotiated out in the playground (Skeggs, 2004). Culford demands a 'no-excuses culture', claiming that mentioning social factors only 'entrenches mediocrity'. Yet this 'no-excuses' mantra divorces students from their social positioning, trivialising continued hardship, institutionalised racism and moral value judgements. Dreamfields' 'structures' seek to 'liberate' children from pathological raced, classed identities, but in ignoring the power of inequitable structures they simultaneously reify them. The sanctioned inequality Bourdieu described is heightened through these practices. Not only are disadvantaged students further disadvantaged through formalised equality, but the heavy policing of ethnic-minority and working-class bodies compound this disadvantage.

Notes

1 Mary struggled with her attendance at Dreamfields and periodically refused to go to school.
2 Marijuana.
3 I have not had the space to address how accusations of 'racism' can be used and played with by students – sometimes opportunistically – whereby 'racism' becomes shorthand for something they perceive to be unfair and takes on a variation of meanings.
4 Greeting one another by touching fists.
5 Several students also described the role of setting in the formation or separation of friendship groupings.

6

Students navigating and negotiating the conveyor belt: aspiration, loss, endurance and fantasy

> People born into unwelcoming worlds and unreliable environments have a different response to the new precarities than do people who presumed they would be protected. (Berlant 2011: 20)

While the previous chapter established the normative position of the white middle classes and the resultant variations in how students were policed and valued, this chapter will examine how young people negotiate the landscape from a variety of positions, where the social world is not a fair game of chance offering equal opportunities (Bourdieu, 2000: 214–15). In Chapter 4 teachers discussed balancing the benefits and drawbacks of working at Dreamfields; similarly, students also make a contract with the institution that is continually negotiated. This contract is easier or more difficult to make and maintain, depending on their relationship to the unevenly structured terrain explored in the previous chapter. This chapter explores how students navigate Dreamfields' conveyor belt while learning how to imagine themselves and their future in particular ways. The numerous paradoxes and contradictions found in their accounts reflect the inherent ambiguities of the belief-generating tales offered by Mr Culford in Chapter 4. Despite students' concerns over a disciplinarian environment where their opinions are largely irrelevant, Dreamfields' production of good results ultimately quells most misgivings to move them along the conveyor belt. Yet some young people cannot submit to Dreamfields' logic and are pushed to its periphery, spending large amounts of time in the LSU.

'The Child-Catcher'

The shifting reflections of Isaac, a 15-year-old black British student, exemplify the continual project of becoming both subject and subjectified. While both his parents were born in the UK, Isaac's grandparents are from Jamaica and of mixed Jamaican and European heritage. At the outset of our meetings in September, Isaac declared there was 'no way' he was attending the Dreamfields sixth form, but added he was 'keeping his options open'. He felt it was not a 'real' sixth form, but a continuation of lower school, with a different outfit and slightly more responsibility. Like most Year 11 students, he was nervous about the impending workload culminating in GCSE results.

Walking around the deserted playground after school in October, Isaac glanced sentimentally across the tarmac. Admittedly, he already felt nostalgic, but maintained that he could not handle another two years at Dreamfields – it was 'too much'. He wanted to go somewhere new. Isaac described how he frequently misbehaved in lessons, transgressing rules in a crafty way. Instead of open defiance, Isaac showed me a hilarious array of lethargic faces and decrepit poses he enacted, moving in slow motion so that a simple task took ages to complete. When threatened with a detention, Isaac would speed up and finish the task to avoid punishment. This deviance 'really wound teachers up' because it was difficult to manage. While Chapter 3 showed how Dreamfields employs strategies which 'pin their hopes on the resistance that the *establishment of a place* offers to the erosion of time', de Certeau describes how tactics as 'an art of the weak' rely 'on a clever *utilization of time*, of the opportunities it presents and also of the play that it introduces into the foundations of power' (1988: 38–9; emphasis added). This playing with time through slowing it down is one tactic frequently employed by students to subvert authority.

Isaac's friend Patricia joined us and they reminisced about their primary-school years, agreeing 'it was the best time ever'. Unlike at secondary school, learning was more fun and stress-free. Patricia thought the Year 7 students who were eagerly joining every club and sporting group would soon lose their enthusiasm; unlike Isaac, Patricia would not miss Dreamfields. They both recalled their initial shock when they arrived. Watching senior teacher Ms Morrison shout at another teacher in front of the students in the playground was an eye-opener for Isaac, who suddenly realised: 'Oh, so this is what the real world is all about!' Observing how teachers, like students, were openly excoriated had shaped his idea of the future workplace.

Two months later Isaac discussed his ambitious future plans. Initially he had wanted to study medicine like his mother, but now he wanted to pursue theology. Most importantly, he wanted to be rich. Isaac felt Dreamfields fit with Urbanderry, calling it a metaphorical Chitty-Chitty-Bang-Bang child-catching machine – but, he quickly exclaimed, while chuckling, 'in a good way!' Roald Dahl's Child-Catcher is a sinister villain employed by the story's central antagonists to capture children by driving a brightly coloured carriage into village squares, ringing a bell and singing to children that he has free cakes, ice cream and lollipops. After the children are lured into his carriage, the cheerful trappings disappear to reveal that the children are locked in a steel cage. I laughed at this metaphor as Isaac reiterated the positive aspects of taming and training some kids from the area who were 'quite wild and a bit rough'. He felt this wildness was often no fault of their own, but due to extenuating circumstances, and Dreamfields trained them to get along. Isaac thought this training was about making people equal, where it was not about where you came from or what you were like, but each student's 'physical capacity' for intelligence, so not only middle-class kids succeeded. Despite teachers saying he was lazy, Isaac thought he was still doing much better than he would have done elsewhere because he needed pushing. Isaac felt some students had a natural inner drive to work, but he lacked this quality.

Isaac had been firmly 'caught' by the Child-Catcher by the time May arrived, announcing that he had stopped 'messing about' and decided to stay on in the sixth form in order to get better grades. He described wanting to leave Dreamfields as a phase he had passed through. With vigour, Isaac produced a paper outlining his predicted GCSE grades, all As and Bs, which he thought could be substantially higher because he was working harder. He talked with animation about his 'life plan' that he had 'all mapped out', musing about attending Oxbridge, the route to becoming a theologian, and his changing friendship group touched on in Chapter 5. Walking him back to his class, I mentioned that I had included his metaphorical child-catching machine in a presentation. He chuckled and merrily replied: 'But it's a good child-catching machine – you don't want to be caught, but once you are it's not that bad!' Isaac's deliberations introduce some of the key themes discussed by other students, although many could not access Isaac's store of middle-class cultural capital. While being 'caught' by the machine was initially undesirable, Isaac came to see it as ultimately beneficial to his future. At the point of catching, the logic of the machine and the benefits it generates start to make sense.

Learning to live within imagined futures

Isaac's colourful metaphor of Dreamfields-as-Child-Catcher seducing Urbanderry parents and students into a shiny new building with promises of a brighter future lingered in my mind. Yet the institution's position and the contract students make was more complex and mutually beneficial than an evil cartoon villain trapping children without any promise of future compensation. Rather than being tricked, many Urbanderry parents are desperate to get their children into Dreamfields and most children are keen to stay once there. Dreamfields is vastly oversubscribed, with over 1,500 applications for just 200 places. Excellent GCSE scores and offers from elite universities have provided solid 'proof' of Dreamfields' potential rewards, persuading students like Isaac to continue and, crucially, attracting high-achieving external sixth-form candidates. Isaac's father Franklin felt Isaac had 'seen for himself the school's attitude to certain students, and I think now he wants to be part of that inner circle to the top-flight students in the school', for Dreamfields would 'naturally start grooming the next batch if you like to get them applying to Cambridge and Oxford and the Russell Group universities'. Samuel was also in awe of Dreamfields' association with prestigious universities, predicting Dreamfields would become renowned, mimicking someone saying: 'Oh, you got into Dreamfields, that's great.' Eight of the ten Year 11 students wanted to attend the sixth form, although most had initially considered leaving. Isaac's realisation that this was the beginning of the onerous 'real world' pushed him to conclude that Dreamfields offered him the best chance of success in this competitive landscape.

Dreamfields' employment conditions come to represent all future workplaces.

Several teachers referenced the similar position teachers and students occupied when meting out punishments. The following exchange occurred outside a classroom:

> *Teacher:* So do you understand why if you do not follow instructions you get in trouble?
> *Student:* Yes, sir.
> *Teacher:* What do you think happens when you're an adult and you have a job and you don't follow instructions? What if I turned up for work late each day?
> *Student:* You'd *(inaudible, very quiet whisper)*
> *Teacher:* I'd get in trouble. And what if I turned up late a lot?
> *Student: (inaudible)*
> *Teacher:* I'd get fired. And if I get fired what happens?
> *Student: (inaudible)*
> *Teacher:* I don't have a job. And if I don't have a job I don't have any what?
> *Student:* Money?
> *Teacher:* Any money. And if I don't have any money I can't buy food, pay for a house. Do you understand this?
> *(She nods)*
> Right. Go.

Another teacher employed a similar comparison during a meeting with a student and his mother:

> *Teacher:* It's not all about you. Everyone is treated the same, everyone gets told off. Sometimes Mr Culford tells me off – do you think I go *(makes a sound of kissing her teeth and sulky body language)* 'It's not fair, you're picking on me!' Do I do that?
> *Student:* No.
> *Teacher:* Why not?
> *Student:* 'Cause you'll get sacked.
> *Teacher:* 'Cause I'll get sacked.

As this teacher added in a later meeting with the same boy, the school trains you to get used to a job, where jobs require following instructions without contestation; to underperform or complain is to risk destitution. The unforgivingly narrow requirements of employment portrayed by teachers and projected onto students reflect the dilemmas of teachers' own working lives explored in Chapter 4, where they must either conform and perform – or leave. Many students like Isaac embraced this approach. He describes how he could think of several teachers who just were not around any more without any explanation given. His brother Steven, a sixth-former, joined one of our discussions, adding that there were 'loads of conspiracy theories' circulating regarding vanishing teachers. Steven described how in other schools it 'took ages to get rid of a teacher', but at Dreamfields they 'just disappeared'. They surmised that either teachers could not take it and left, or were forced out because they disagreed with the ethos; these were common student speculations. Isaac pitied infantilised teachers, yet adopted

Dreamfields' deregulated approach to labour, adding: 'If they are underperforming, they are out the door and there will be another teacher to replace them –
tough!'

However Daniel, a black British Year 9 student, more critically assessed
how Dreamfields' authoritarian training could prove detrimental in adulthood.
Although he usually understood why he was being reprimanded, Daniel questioned the harsh methods teachers sometimes employed, suggesting that while
this might be appropriate for students with high self-esteem, shouting at students
with low to medium self-esteem was 'not very nice' and 'can make you feel bad'.
Daniel referred to a diagram frequently shown on the flat-screen monitors around
the school depicting Dreamfields as a series of concentric circles, with staff, the
PTA and students represented as equals. He contested this representation, tracing
an oblong shape on the table with his finger that placed teachers and PTA at the
top and students at the bottom. Daniel felt like he was 'at the bottom of the food
chain'; students had to respect and obey everyone, but no one had to respect them.
Clearly aware of staff hierarchies, Daniel outlined Dreamfields' management
structure running from heads of year to heads of learning areas, down to heads
of department and class teachers who could not contest their line managers. He
thought this feeling of being at the bottom could have adverse effects on students
when they entered the workplace; they might become downtrodden employees.
While Isaac does not challenge the institutional structure, but attempts to excel
within it, Daniel is more apprehensive about his position.

Like Daniel, black British sixth-former Florence felt the discipline sometimes
took advantage of her cooperative disposition. Although her feelings vacillated,
she justified discipline through an imagined future workplace:

> During my first year, I was just like 'this is really ridiculous' sort of thing … I
> understand the idea of discipline, but I just think that they took it a bit far. And
> then some years it would not be that bad … I'd just think, 'oh, you are just over-
> reacting', and then I'd think, 'oh, it's a good thing', when you see people in your
> class who are just playing up and stuff like that and you are like, 'oh, they need
> the discipline', but when you are someone who doesn't need that much disci-
> pline, you kind of feel they are taking advantage … Like, you are a good person,
> why are they kind of being so set and orderly? We used to call here the prison
> because it actually did seem like that sometimes. But … they are a lot more
> lenient with us because we are in the older year.

Despite objecting to 'really strange and strict' rules like banning hugging, Florence
answers her own theoretical question, 'Would I send my child here?' with 'yes'.
Discipline is beneficial, 'because I think some people take advantage and then
when they get to the workplace they will not understand the whole order … And
we have had that order so we are growing up with it, so it's good.' Students grow
up and into an order presented as inevitable and positive. Instead of perceiving
Dreamfields' disciplinarian environment as a response to its ethnic minority and
working-class student population, this securitised stance becomes tied to helping
its students prepare for work.

Reservations and promises

This disciplinarian order is reflexively recognised by several students and parents as potentially negative. Shazia, a 16-year-old Bangladeshi student, described how many of the rules were ultimately irrelevant to education and more about Dreamfields having control over the student's body. Shazia thought Dreamfields rationalised these rules by connecting good behaviour to better learning outcomes. Although Shazia now attested to using longer words, she felt intrinsically unaltered by Dreamfields and would continue into the sixth form to ensure she achieved good A-levels. Poppy thought Dreamfields attempted to control students' minds, comparing Culford's rhetoric to a graphic novel she had recently read featuring a character who was fighting against the government's attempts to brainwash everyone. Poppy described how this government said: 'give them rules in order to free them'. This phrase triggered a flashback in her mind to an assembly where Culford said rules freed students to learn – a connection she felt was 'really creepy'.

Alexander, a black middle-class parent, comments on how Dreamfields' physical regulation affects his son Daniel's comportment:

> *Alexander:* But I look at my son, and if he is being talked to, he sits like that *(sits bolt upright)* – he sits rigid. Kids are walking through – 'Straighten your tie!' – and they are rigid, and I'm thinking, oh – I wasn't like that at school. And I went to school in south Urbanderry … But I enjoyed school. When teachers spoke to me, I was not scared. I was relaxed.
>
> *CK:* And you think here they are scared here?
>
> *Alexander:* I just look at their mannerisms and, they are just like that *(affecting rigidity and looking frightened)*.

Several students attested to feeling afraid upon arriving at Dreamfields. Derek, Emily and Florence used the word 'scary' to describe their initial days, while Lawrence, a black Caribbean working-class sixth-former, describes how his compliance was gained:

> To be honest, first coming, because I was a bit nervous and scared, like I kinda had no choice but to follow [the rules]. Not that I would go against it now, but the situation as I become older – the way I am basically, obviously I didn't get in trouble that much and it's a situation where I just say if you just behave yourself and do what you're supposed to do, then you won't have to worry about getting into trouble or anything … it just doesn't really bother me now, basically, because I know that certain things don't apply to me because I'm not getting into trouble and stuff like that.

Although Lawrence was too scared to do anything but follow the rules, he recognises that this ensured he avoided trouble and eventually the rules applied to him less. As a working-class black boy, Lawrence could easily be branded as a potentially dangerous 'urban child' in need of reformation, making it imperative that he tows the line.

Veronica, a white middle-class parent, also mentions an atmosphere of fear. While in Chapter 3 I described Veronica's concerns over Dreamfields' architecture and a 'culture of fear', she struggles with these inconsistent feelings later in our interview: 'The whole rubric surrounding the school – the unit [the LSU], and the detentions and the guard-like kind of mentality *(sighs)* I find it – I don't want to embrace it, but it seems to work.' Yet it is important to remember that Veronica's daughter does not endure the same level of surveillance or assumptions tied to darker, more working-class bodies. Pragmatically Dreamfields 'works', although she adds that she has a 'residual feeling about how will this very structured environment actually affect her [daughter]'. While students receive good grades in the present, how might students be shaped by this environment in ways that are not immediately evident? A few minutes later, Veronica expresses relief at Dreamfields' involvement in her daughter's upbringing before laughing and adding: 'I suppose I'm totally contradicting myself now! Isn't it just the way with these interview participants? Contractions left, right and centre.' Veronica sums up this ambiguity with the following comments: 'Yes, just live with the contradictions. Live with the paradox of being pleased that she has all these structures and unhappy in an intellectual sense, but pleased in the personal sense and, oh God! What can you do?' These comments mirror the ambiguous feelings expressed by many teachers in Chapter 4, where most doubts are subsumed by the delivery of results.

Alexander was one of the few parents to actively critique how an exam-driven focus could negatively shape students:

> Well I think this, I think we are not producing kids – even though I want my kids to do really well in terms of exams – what we are really doing is we are producing children to go into the world and take their part. It's not just a matter of getting eleven GCSEs and all of them are A-star. It's about being able to cope with society when you get in there, it's about being able to mix in the workplace when you get there. We want to produce rounded people, people who can see both sides of the argument, you know what I mean? And understand things properly. I am not sure if we are going to get that if there is not a bit of warmth or flair coming out of the kids. Now it gets better as they go through, don't get me wrong.

Alexander is not convinced that understanding or taking part in a diverse society can be achieved through testing regimes and discipline. He describes how his younger daughter Molly was 'petrified' of getting a detention. Alexander tried to assuage her fears by presenting detention as good life experience, but Molly rejected this idea and needed encouragement more than draconian rules. Despite his reservations, it is important to note that Alexander does not consider sending his children elsewhere.

Ambivalent feelings rest at the heart of Dreamfields' project as future fantasies promising happiness and enjoyment are allied to the present-day endurance of heightened control, discipline and securitisation. Dreamfields blends numerous techniques to mould impressionable youngsters into self-structuring individuals invested in obtaining value through market participation. This training encourages the production of subjects willing to fit within increasingly casualised, unstable and often exploitative positions whilst simultaneously understanding themselves as individuals who are authoring their own biographies. This individualisation makes it very difficult to actively recognise how raced and classed inequality both relates to and reinforces the militarisation of schooling (see Chadderton, 2014). With young people three times more likely to be unemployed than the rest of the population in 2015, students are understandably anxious to secure employment (Boffey, 2015). Jodi Dean discusses how neoliberalism as an ideological formation must offer something to people whose lives it shapes in order to maintain its dominant position: 'It has to structure their expectations and desires so that it *feels right, like the way things just are*' (2009: 50; emphasis added). The desire to 'reach my true potential' bears an irrefutable rightness for many students, most of whom adapt to institutional demands which become normalised. Readiness to be consumed by the market becomes the central concern for many students, who learn that compliance is what employment requires. By shaping expectations and desires from a young age, Dreamfields' structures become the way things are; as 13-year-old Lorna reminded me, she had nothing to compare Dreamfields to – 'it is all I know'.

'Structure liberates' promises future enjoyment and happiness. Drawing on Slavoj Žižek's reworking of Lacanian psychoanalysis, Jodi Dean discusses how ideological formations draw together a host of often antagonistic, contrary promises of enjoyment and accounts for why enjoyment has not occurred, where 'Ideological formations, then, work as economies of enjoyment to forbid, permit, direct and command enjoyment' (2009: 50). She argues that the addition of enjoyment to the theory of ideology makes ideology about more than sets of meanings, images or accumulated effects, but highlights the role of fantasy, where fantasies 'bind subjects to certain sets of relations, structuring and confining their thinking and acting so as to attach them to seemingly inescapable patterns of domination, patterns they may well recognise as domination but keep following, nevertheless' (2009: 50). While Foucault illuminates how Dreamfields' ethos incorporates liberalism's paradoxical contractions where freedom is accessed through submission, he does not touch on the more affective dimensions of why subjects stay attached to ostensibly damaging positions – including how fantasies of future fulfilment can act as a powerful adhesive bonding subjects to neoliberal ideological formations. The structuring of teachers and pupils is a creative process where Dreamfields proffers both the problem and the solution; it is not surprising that parents continue to send their children to Dreamfields and students willingly attend. Culford's inspirational tales frame the orientations of many students and teachers. Rather than preparing students for some inevitable 'real world' awaiting them, Dreamfields' practices help create the parameters of this world to come by imagining and rehearsing an order with children so they grow up and into it.

Becoming 'little robots'

As Chapter 5 outlined through students' approaches to mixing, growing into these structures often requires work and adjustment. For many students, learning to accept authority was a prerequisite for self-advancement and framed as an important realisation of their school career. Nearly every student commented on Dreamfields' high expectations that produced good results and provided a valuable incentive to tolerate discipline. Lawrence describes adjusting to Dreamfields after primary school:

> It was a big step, but after a while I did get used to it and, like, now, I don't really mind that much, like going through what I did go through, with all the rules and stuff. I know it's for a reason and obviously it's, like, helped to shape me and form me into something great, innit.

Lawrence adjusts to the rules because there is a rationale behind them and he feels they ultimately benefit his future. Even when he did not agree with certain things, he realised open contestation was not only futile, but might 'make me seem much like a bad person basically'. Like Florence's dismay over such rigidity despite being a 'good person', Lawrence describes cooperating to avoid being labelled as 'bad'. He conscientiously avoids acquiring the bad reputation now following students like Gazi and Tameka. Lawrence feels that 'overall it is a really great school', and although he has 'a sceptical view' towards some rules, he feels he is in no position to criticise them due to Dreamfields' enormous success. Instead, 'I follow the rules and I do what I am supposed to do, basically.' Unlike white middle-class Poppy, it was too dangerous for Lawrence to contravene the rules, as falling into the category of troublesome black boy could severely jeopardise his future chances.

Unlike Lawrence, Derek was not obedient from the outset and found himself saddled with detentions until Year 10. Derek, a black British working-class sixth-former, advises new students to 'just follow the rules to the best of your ability' and related the most unequivocally positive transformation story I heard during the research, describing how Dreamfields had 'changed' him:

> All the detentions and everything, you just sort of realise it is pointless after a while. You get to a point where you just realise that you have got to grow up. Otherwise you won't get the work done. It sort of moulds you into, preparing you for when you leave school and the way you are supposed to act in the outside world.

Derek described how he was not as loud as he used to be. Instead of talking back immediately, he could now 'hold it in'; he has adopted the quiet restraint that Joshua termed the three C's in Chapter 5. Although sometimes Derek wants to talk back, he realises this would only exacerbate his situation. The school 'makes you think about things before you actually do it, that's what I've learned – to just think before I actually speak or do an action', attesting to an enhanced ability to delay gratification. Derek describes how Dreamfields' parameters have become habitual:

> Because the principles have been – I have been here for seven years now. *(laughs)* That's a long time, so yeah, it is sort of installed in me. But I think it does help me outside school in certain situations where you just learn to keep your cool and go along with other people and being able to accept authority, really.

Derek can 'accept authority' and feels friends at other schools 'are now completely different to the way me and other people that went here are'. Yet he attributes his old friends' different behaviour to teachers allowing mischievousness – not urban chaos or their unstructured families. He suspects that if he had attended another school he would still be loud, talk back to everyone and not care about school. Derek feels 'there is something about this school that just makes you different to everyone else, really'. While his old friends think 'they turn us into little robots', Derek laughed, adding: 'but it's a good thing, really'. While his friends may laugh at the fact he has to wear a suit every day, Derek describes how 'There is a sense of pride really when you are walking out in a suit. It's not that bad, really. You start to feel good about it.'

Dreamfields has marked Derek out as different from his friends. Instead of 'not really caring', he has invested in a future-orientated version of the self with enhanced capital due to his adoption of 'appropriate' dispositions, professional dress, and qualifications – all of which carry value in the eyes of legitimate society. It is unknown if Derek's acquired capital will be symbolically recognised beyond Dreamfields, and this grafting on of capital is not wholly liberating. Derek is normalised through Foucauldian institutional discipline, and Bourdieu urges us to recognise the continuous and often unnoticed pressure of oppression through normalisation, as 'the conditioning imposed by the material conditions of existence' fit Derek into the dominant symbolic (2000: 141). These transformations also require submission and loss.

The 'care' provided by Dreamfields' teachers makes 'caring' worthwhile for students; investing in narratives of future success and an 'ideal student' identity becomes worthwhile. Yet the differences Derek describes between him and his friends are not explained in terms of exam results, but through different orientations towards the future, ways of speaking, being and interacting with others. Louise Archer and her colleagues concluded: '"Being good" and the achievement of a "good" pupil identity was as much bound up with compliance to educational and social gendered and class norms and expectations, as it was to the achievement of academic results and grades' (2007: 565). Being 'good' is also a racialised position: it involves ethnic-minority students making it unequivocally clear that they are not aligned with Urbanderry's alleged 'gangster' culture by showing an unswerving respect for institutional rules. While Lawrence, Derek and Florence connect breaking the rules with being perceived as a 'bad person', students who occupy an ideal status like Poppy do not worry that their misbehaviour would lead to being labelled as 'bad'. Her value as a white, middle-class student is not in

jeopardy, unlike Lawrence, who realises he could easily be designated as immanently 'bad'.

Accepting authority is viewed as an essential component of maximising one's
future potential. Sixth-former Alara describes herself as being 'a bit cheeky' and
rebellious during Years 7 and 8. Her parents were called in for meetings each
week, but after two years and much to her mother's relief, she was now 'a lot more
tamed'. Alara, the daughter of two Turkish immigrants who describes herself as
working-class, traces her epiphany:

> I remember doing SATs [statutory assessment tests] in Year 9, and I remem-
> ber thinking, well – it was just all then that I just realised that, uh, I want to do
> something with my life. And I might want to go into law. And I have to get really
> high grades for this. And it just kind of dawned on me, being like what, fourteen?
> *(laughs)* Yeah, I just remember thinking that I cannot not carry on like this if I
> actually want to go somewhere and get really good grades. So I stopped – or I
> tried to stop. And then, yeah, I got really good GCSE grades; now I'm hopefully
> going to study law.

Although Alara critiques several aspects of the school, she thinks Dreamfields is
essentially good, professing: 'I think it worked out really well for me, personally.'
She describes how the strictness meant less time was wasted in lessons, while
teachers were constantly available to help. Alara attributes her transformation
from rebel to compliant student both to maturity and repetition:

> But I think you just kind of get used to it. And it's kind of maturing as well – and
> you come to the realisation that you need to kind of go along with the system if
> you want to make sure you get the best outcome for yourself.

A particular, submissive maturity is cultivated through repetition. Like in Chapter
5 where Isaac decided to stop misbehaving to 'get on top', Alara feels that conceding to 'the system' is necessary to achieve the best personal position. Alara
recounts being angry and crying after two teachers discouraged her from applying
to elite law schools because they were 'not my kind of uni'. Less prestigious universities were described as 'a better choice', although she ignored this advice and
gained entry to an elite institution. Alara felt it was assumed that attending a top
university was not for the likes of her; despite conceding to Dreamfields' parameters, teachers still attempt to limit Alara's aspirations, despite their validity.

La perruque, or 'the wig,' is described by de Certeau as a popular diversionary tactic where workers disguised their own work as work for their employers.
While the worker remained present and nothing was stolen, time was diverted
'from the factory for work that is free, creative, and precisely not directed toward
profit' (1988: 25). Within Dreamfields' setting, this free, creative and profitless
activity can be found in Isaac's lethargic slowing-down of time, in Tameka's
'spudding', or in Gazi's spontaneous backflips off rubbish bins at break time. It
rests in the 'swagger' perfected by many young men or the 'winding' of young
women like Abisola in the playground. De Certeau asserts that these practices

entail cunningly taking pleasure in self-directed making, while forging solidarity with fellow workers, arguing that these practices continue in the 'most ordered spheres of modern life' (1988: 26). Although these creative diversionary practices continue within Dreamfields' borders, there is limited space and time for *la perruque*. 'Putting one over' comes to be seen by many students as not hurting 'the system', but only hurting one's self, as this self must be realised through Dreamfields' parameters. This connects to Lauren Berlant's inverted reading of de Certeau: 'Instead of the vision of the everyday *organised* by capitalism that we find in Lefebvre and de Certeau, among others, I am interested in the overwhelming ordinary that is *disorganised* by it, and by many other forces besides. This is a matter of a different emphasis, not of a theoretical negation' (2011:8; emphasis added). Here seemingly timeless, ordinary school high jinks are disrupted, as many students like Derek or Isaac curtail misbehaviour and rebellion in exchange for the promise of future rewards. The orientation between ruler and ruled is disorganised, whereby there is not an attitude of complete rebellion, but muted compliance in order to access individualised success.

Performing compliance

Several students discussed how they coped with Dreamfields' disciplinary structures by feigning compliance. Like Lawrence, Florence gauged early on that 'letting the teacher be right' was the easiest option, but more reflexively explains her acquiescence:

> If the teacher is shouting at you, just accept it. Don't retaliate, because that's not the way in life or in this school either. I know it sounds really bad, but just let the teachers have their way. You won't be here forever; make the best out of the situation … just get on with your work and don't be disruptive.

As fighting the rules gets you nowhere, Florence recommends displaying obedience. Although she acknowledges that advising students to accept all punishments without question sounds 'bad', students should accept the confines of the institution. Florence recalls her annoyance at students not taking this approach:

> Sometimes when people argue back it's like, just, like, shut up, just let the teacher be right. The teacher wants to be right, the teacher's not going to go, 'Okay, I'm wrong now.' Because I had a few troubles with one of my maths teachers and I found that just by being submissive that she just got over whatever issues she had. You just need to make the teachers feel like they have the authority. So it's the best way to go.

Through performing submission, Florence reassures the teacher of her authority and she can get on with her work – even if her compliance is feigned. Although Florence resigns herself to this performance, there is an underlying cynicism to her assent that ultimately questions the legitimacy of her teacher's authority. Tameka also relates how she used to 'get hyped up', but is now 'cool' with teachers, responding with the cooperative attitude of 'okay, great stuff' when corrected and carries on with her work. She feels her submission 'pisses them off' more than anything because they want her to retaliate; with satisfaction, Tameka describes how she can see it 'hurting them inside'.

Daniel also told teachers what they wanted to hear as a means of escaping the LSU. Daniel described the LSU as a place created 'to bore students out of their heads', so eventually they admitted they did not intend to do whatever they were in trouble for; it was 'pretty much hell on earth'. Daniel explained being sent there for retaliating against a group of boys in the playground who had attacked him. He used his fingers to put quotation marks around 'retaliated', rhetorically asking: 'What else was I supposed to do? Let myself get beaten up? That would have been worse.' Daniel describes how he dutifully conceded to the teacher that the next time he was attacked by a group of boys, he would just stand there and do nothing. Related with much sarcasm, Daniel's performance of compliance was necessary for his release.

For Florence, Tameka, Daniel and other students, performing compliance is one possible line of action, yet not a particularly rebellious one. De Certeau describes how '*power relationships* define the networks in which they are inscribed and delimit the circumstances from which they can profit ... We are concerned with battles or games between the strong and the weak, and with the "actions" which remain possible for the latter' (1988: 34; emphasis added). The idea of a pitched battle between weak and strong is disordered and rearranged through students' concern for their futures and the necessity of conceding to the institution in order to flourish. This narrows the range of games deemed possible or desirable to play, as they are symbiotically bound to the institution through the benefits accrued.

'Becoming more white'

Loss and gain becomes a raced and classed process, where students must move away from essentialised representations of blackness and working-classness to better fit into the Dreamfields landscape. Sixth-former Olivia describes how Dreamfields has 'widened the possibilities' of what she could become. During primary school Olivia had 'morphed' herself into the 'perfect Urbanderry princess' to fit in. Most of her friends were 'Urbanderry kids', which Olivia describes as portraying oneself as laid-back, walking a bit too slowly, with a swagger, not conceding to authority, and not appearing to try too hard – all actions that arguably seek to disrupt the conveyor belt's relentless speed. Olivia describes how wearing Kickers shoes or having a Nike bag is the accompanying aesthetic – styles Olivia asserts are most commonly worn by black students. Olivia, half white and half black African, speculates that if she had attended another Urbanderry secondary school, she probably would have red weave in her hair right now. Yet upon her arrival at Dreamfields Olivia felt there was nothing to be gained from dropping her T's; getting good grades was acceptable. Olivia asserts: 'I have ended up becoming more white', laughing and acknowledging this was clearly ridiculous because she was obviously still half black! She reminisces about growing up on an estate before moving to a Victorian house, adding that her mother is a teacher so she was always 'well-spoken'. Yet this 'becoming' entailed difficult compromises which Olivia says required her to ignore or lose certain parts of herself and allegiances along the way. These losses and gains link to how Olivia has orientated herself away from a more black and working-class position towards a more white, middle-class one as she became an 'ideal' pupil.

Olivia describes being mixed-race as difficult to negotiate because people always wanted to force you to choose between being black or white. She also felt she was 'in the middle' when it came to class, referencing her father as a 'contradictory character'. Although he worked as a sports coach and had a 'definite street vibe' going on, he had attended private school in Zimbabwe – something he 'kept quiet about'. She describes trying to 'tread a fine line and strike a balance' between these various positions. Olivia's experience draws out the messiness inherent in essentialised categories and how these categories are made 'real' through reiteration. Drawing on Frantz Fanon, Nayak describes how race's fictitious status is given substance 'through the illusion of performance, action and utterance, where repetition makes it appear as-if-real' (2006a: 419, 416).

These complex negotiations of personhood relate to perceptions of who does or does not achieve in educational institutions. Olivia describes how being white is aligned with doing well in school, while being black is still not granted this association. Whereas smart white kids are just called nerds, smart black kids are called 'bounties', which infers that being black and working hard means you are 'white' on the inside (see Fordham, 1995). The conflict between being an 'Urbanderry kid' and being an ideal student is premised on the idea that there is an integral compatibility between learning or knowledge and respect for authority. This false confluence is normalised, highlighting how Dreamfields' job is not simply to provide children with access to knowledge, but to govern a population and create compliant bodies with respect for the status quo. The acquisition of knowledge is intertwined with submitting to authority; you cannot succeed, or at least will have great difficulty succeeding, as an aspirational subject without conceding to a barrage of seemingly superfluous, yet essential institutional demands. Learning and governance merge together into one package and students must sign up to both.

Despite numerous compromises, Olivia liked Dreamfields from the start. She acknowledges the rigidity was 'to try and stamp out any tendencies people have towards not being a model Dreamfields student. And I think individuality is stamped out with that too, but that's just the price you pay for being within a disciplinarian environment.' Olivia thinks Dreamfields has loosened up as they grew older: 'It's like as you grow, the school sort of opens up for you.' Yet Olivia admits that the school does not open up for everyone:

> What you give, you sort of get back. So you develop a bit of trust with some teachers and they're willing to … give you more freedom. And people who were less willing to cooperate are the ones that get stuffed in the LSU all the time. I'm

not sure that did them any good. It probably just leads to loads of resentment and even more sort of hate for the system.

Olivia consigned her 'Urbanderry princess' primary-school ways to the past, as assuming the position of high-achieving pupil connected to her becoming 'whiter'. Although this movement required sacrifice, Olivia was not required to adopt completely alien ways, but could resurrect already familiar ways of being, like her 'well-spoken' accent temporarily discarded during primary school.

As a working-class black girl, Tameka's journey discussed in Chapter 5 differs substantially from Olivia's. Unlike Olivia, she does not have a 'well-spoken accent' to recall, but must try to acquire and apply unfamiliar ways of being. Working-class female educational subjects must reflexively produce themselves through self-surveillance and the internal incorporation of discourses of authority that highlight gendered and classed inequalities – making schools 'alien spaces for "other" femininities' (Archer et al., 2007: 552–3, 558). These othered femininities are associated with historic representations of the working-class female's embodied excess, while the possession of a middle-class femininity is tied to modesty, restraint, repression, reasonableness and denial (Skeggs, 2004: 99). Stereotypical representations of black women as angry, aggressive, unfeminine and attitudinal are folded into how girls like Tameka, Abisola and Clarice are perceived by Dreamfields, as racial identities are highly gendered (see Morgan and Bennett, 2006; Wright et al., 1998). Dreamfields makes the adoption of raced, classed and gendered ideals of success mandatory for continuation. As Olivia relates, there is 'a price to pay', and the cost is higher for some students than others. Despite the huge amount of ethnic and social diversity at Dreamfields, white middle-class norms are the standard that holds cultural capital. Meanwhile the cultural wealth possessed by ethnic-minority and working-class students is devalued (Carter, 2003; Lareau and Horvat, 1999; Yosso, 2005).

Problematic bodies: 'stuffed in the LSU'

Bourdieu discusses how institutional rites 'guarantee a durable social status in exchange for the durable commitment', where this commitment is symbolised by rituals of incorporation in a variety of senses that require assuming 'in a worthy fashion the explicit and often implicit obligations of that status' (2000: 236). While those possessing the appropriate habitus from the outset have the best guarantee of attaining social status, others can potentially – although often only partially – occupy this space. As we saw in Chapter 5, many students like Joshua, Samuel and Isaac make this contract and symbolically show their commitment and incorporation by displaying dispositions that mark their habitus as appropriate. Yet Osman, Shante and Clarice were located outside the 'buffer zone' and found it remarkably more difficult or even undesirable to acquire and display the dispositions required. As Olivia describes, these students were frequently 'stuffed in the LSU'.

Opting out

Multi-ethnic Year 11 student Shante started truanting in Year 9 after being a straight-A student in Years 7 and 8. She lives on a nearby estate with her mother and siblings and describes how during Year 10 she barely attended school at all, resulting in her mother being fined.[1] Shante attempted to move to a school where they would not continually push her, describing how Dreamfields teachers constantly demanded students learn. Most students referenced this continual pushing. Olivia comments: 'I am not like a naturally dedicated person ... I'm kind of the worst student ... I have ability, but I just don't exploit it. And I think here it's been kind of dragged out of me, whereas other places I would have sort of slipped away unnoticed.' Although Shante tries to 'slip away unnoticed', this is not possible. Unlike Olivia, Shante finds it difficult to cope with having her ability continually 'dragged' out of her, despite being academically gifted. Unable to leave Dreamfields, Shante approached her final year with hopeful optimism, repeatedly emphasising the significance of good GCSEs and describing how teachers 'have really tried to impress upon me how important it is to get good grades now because it will determine what sort of job I can get'. Repeatedly Shante said she wanted to do well in order to 'have a good life' and 'make something' of herself. Although she put her previous truancy down to 'laziness', Shante later admitted that the pressure was too much. As the year proceeded, it became increasingly evident that Shante was unwell. This culminated in a suicide attempt, yet despite ongoing turbulence Shante frequently talked about needing to 'do well'.

Numerous pressures were bearing down on Shante: she described being continually bullied by a group of girls at Dreamfields and felt guilty about the emotional and financial trouble she had caused her beloved mother Beatrice by truanting. She was also extremely worried about her younger brother who was hanging out with a group of older boys on their estate. Shante related how 'every single day I worry about my brother Peter and what is going to happen to him – is he going to get stabbed or arrested?' There had been violence on their estate and Shante was always afraid she would go home to find he had been stabbed. Her eldest brother was already incarcerated and Shante described how her mother was guilt-ridden and desperate to prevent Peter from suffering a similar fate. Shante had a very close relationship with Beatrice; although her father still lived locally, her parents' marriage had broken down after moving to the UK from Nigeria, leaving Beatrice to raise their children while struggling to find part-time work without any qualifications.

Shante half-jokingly said she had spent more time in the LSU than anyone else during the previous year, describing it as an 'endless cycle' where she forced herself to come in, but was invariably placed in the LSU because of her prior truanting. Hating the LSU, she often went home, only to be put back in the LSU when she eventually worked up the nerve to return to Dreamfields. Shante said the LSU was 'really boring', but with only one teacher supervising she could sometimes fall asleep into her book. One teacher questioned how Shante had been treated, commenting that Mr Pierce's tactic of shouting had contributed to Shante spending a lot of time in the LSU – a situation that had not helped her, but only made matters considerably worse. Brandishing Shante's progress report, this teacher described how Shante's teachers had confirmed that she could have achieved As in most subjects if she had been in class, but now would be lucky to get Cs.

Although many of the challenges facing Shante were external to Dreamfields, the 'structure liberates' ethos did not free her from the very real stresses of poverty and life on an often dangerous estate and allow her to fulfil her potential. Instead Dreamfields' hard-line approach appears to have further exacerbated her anxieties and estranged her from education; the effectiveness of shouting at and isolating an extremely vulnerable student merits serious question. Shante is clearly aware of the necessity of achieving and realises the stakes are high, but instead of rising to the intense pressure to perform, she crumbles beneath it. Whereas middle-class students approach this 'project of autonomy' where they are called to become both subject and subjectified from a less perilous position, working-class students like Shante are approaching it from a position of having all the wrong cultural and symbolic capital (Lawler, 2000: 24, 46). Shante's mother Beatrice possessed neither the status nor the confidence to contest Dreamfields' approach. As Mr Dean pointed out in Chapter 5, only some influential middle-class parents have 'a line to the top', while working-class students like Shante have less recourse and occupy a lower-status position within the institution.

Lost in the machine

White English and Afro-Caribbean working-class Year 11 student Clarice was a top-set student who wanted to be a graphic artist; her art teacher confirmed that she was exceptionally talented. Clarice lived with a relative on a nearby estate; her mother Danese experienced frequent bouts of mental illness, but was still actively involved in Clarice's life. Her parents were separated and her father seemed to be sporadically involved. Clarice started off the year professing she wanted to get her head down, do the work, get good grades and stay out of trouble. She professed that she did not enjoy being in trouble and often ended up in trouble even when she did not mean to be. Like Abisola, Clarice did not mind coming to Dreamfields because it was a lot better than other Urbanderry schools. She wanted to attend the sixth form and go to university, describing how Dreamfields was 'a different world' from Urbanderry. She thought this was positive because it showed the world that young people from Urbanderry could succeed, echoing Culford's assembly rhetoric.

Yet by May Clarice had changed her mind, saying: 'I have had a lot of problems at this school.' She wanted a fresh start somewhere she did not have so many issues with her peers and teachers, describing how her mother had initially liked Dreamfields, but had 'had enough of the school too at this point'. Clarice seemed genuinely confused about where 'my problems come from'. Like Shante, she took sole responsibility for her difficulties and talked about being 'bad' as if she were a young child. She looked generally bewildered by the experience and clearly lacked confidence. While she thought some teachers were 'okay', she described how others 'just shouted at you and do not listen to your side of the story … they do not try to understand, but twisted around what you had said'. Others would stop, listen, then explain 'what I have done wrong when I have been bad and help me to correct it, instead of just shouting at me'. Clarice described how shouting only really 'worked' in Years 7 and 8 when children were still scared of teachers. Despite these issues, she felt Dreamfields was fair, and enduring the past five years had been worth it for the grades, plus the structure had benefited her, as without it 'I would be a completely different person.'

Although Clarice's mother Danese had dropped out of school without GCSEs, she wanted Clarice to go to university and passionately attempted to advocate for her daughter who was consistently in the LSU. Danese said: 'Not once have they done anything to support my child ... They labelled the girl from the day she come here.' She goes on to admit that 'I lost it in this room [the board room]', describing a meeting where Mr Richards stood intimidatingly in the corner while three other senior teachers sat around the table, one positioned between her and Clarice, who were prohibited from sitting together.

> *Danese:* Ms Butler was sitting there saying, 'Are you scared, Clarice? What, are they gonna beat you up, Clarice? Are you scared, Clarice, what are they going to do to you?'
> *CK:* Taunting her?
> *Danese:* Yeah. I tell you, I lost it. I jumped up and went, 'Who the fucking hell?' – [*aside to me*] I'm not being funny or nothing, I'm gonna tell you how it was – do you think you are?'

Danese found some teachers empathetic, however:

> Ms Butler makes it obvious that she doesn't like my child. She forgets herself in front of her, like, I said, how can you be sitting there as a parent? What would you do? ... I was like, what? What do you think you are doing? What sort of conduct is that?

Danese felt helpless, saying: 'they are putting me in situations where they are provoking me and my child and sitting there talking and we are not allowed to say anything. And then you've got no one to go to. There's no one you can go to.' Instead of sitting quietly, Danese argues back, but asserting herself gets her labelled as problematic and aggressive. Val Gillies's (2007) work highlights 'the empty nature of entitlement claims without social recognition', where mothers without the 'sanctioned middle-class cultural capital struggle to exert power or influence in such institutional arenas'. Working-class single mothers like Danese who try to assert themselves are often set 'on a collision course with an education system designed to promote and value middle-class attributes' (2007: 92–3). Mixed-race Danese describes her capacity to speak in different registers and move through different spaces:

> I have been brought up with both sides [black Caribbean and white English]. I can speak Patois and I can speak the Queen's English. I know how to behave,

I know how to be taken to any restaurant. Half the teachers don't have a clue. This is what I find difficult; the teachers don't really know about Urbanderry and make unnecessary comments.

Although she has a range of resources at her disposal and understands Urbanderry as a lifelong resident, her capitals are not legitimate within Dreamfields. Danese also highlights how a racialised lens is trained on Clarice's father. After visiting Dreamfields, the school claimed they were intimidating them: 'We're like, "No we're not, it's Clarice's dad. It's not our fault he's six-foot something and wide like that. Where did you think Clarice gets her height from? I'm only five foot five, what did you think her dad would look like?"' Finally Danese describes how Clarice and her take tissues out during meetings to signal to each other that teachers are talking nonsense and they are not listening; this tissue game of passive resistance becomes their only recourse.

Criminal types

Turkish working-class Year 11 student Osman more openly contested rules and subsequently found himself in continuous trouble. Osman referred to the LSU as 'my second home', but started his final year intent 'to get on with it and get through the year' without last year's problems. Osman was in sets two and three, wanted to be an architect and was described by his teachers as bright. He lived on a nearby estate with his mother, who spoke limited English. Although he did not call himself 'working-class', he actively differentiated himself from the white, middle-class group, asserting that it was mostly boys and black people in the LSU. Osman said he had never seen 'English people' like Elisabeth and her friends in there and never spoke to them – this was the same group Mary described as posh and exclusive in Chapter 5. Osman was aware he had a short temper, but described how most teachers knew this and tried to help him manage it. Instead of trying to fight Dreamfields' rules, he wanted to do everything right and 'behave' how he was 'supposed to' to get good GCSEs. As for attending the sixth form, Osman pronounced: 'I can't take another two-year jail sentence', and added that he would rather work in a kebab shop.

After a few months, Osman was in trouble again and it had become known around Dreamfields that he was in a gang. Osman rejected this hearsay during our meetings and instead referred to his friendship group as a 'family'. However he also boasted that he was involved in 'shady' activities outside school and spoke a particular slang with 'his boys'. A male staff member Osman confided in mentioned to me that Osman was upset about his situation. He had got in over his head with this friendship group and did not know how to detach himself from them. He had considered trying to get his mother to move house, but this was difficult as they were social housing tenants. Osman would suffer retribution if he did not comply with his friends' requests, which left him little choice but to remain part of the group.

Meanwhile, Osman's attitude towards Dreamfields had hardened; he 'loved the grades', but hated the rest of it. It made him angry and he had not changed at all because of it, adding: 'I still go out and do what I do.' When I asked him what he thought about Culford's 'structure liberates' ethos, Osman reconfirmed that our conversation was confidential before saying structure did not work for him and 'Culford should shut his mouth because he talks a lot of shit.' Instead Osman thought coming to Dreamfields had been a 'massive problem' for him and 'has not helped my life at all, but only made it worse'. Osman described how Dreamfields 'did not understand the background that we are from in Urbanderry … we're not from a posh area where we're all the same'; Dreamfields 'did not get the area'. Osman's initial desire to conform to Dreamfields' parameters was not working; instead he was becoming increasingly hostile and estranged from a school that he felt did not understand the pressures and realities he faced beyond its gates.

By springtime Osman was being searched upon arriving at Dreamfields each morning. He professed that he had no idea why he had been searched 'every day for weeks and weeks' after being told it was for a day or so. The teacher wielding the metal detector described how Osman had apologised to him for looking cross; he realised he was only doing his job. Osman described how his mother had asked why he was being searched, but Ms Butler 'could not give her a straight answer, saying: "Oh, I am not sure, I will have to check on that."' Osman said he and his mother had reached the point of not arguing because 'there was no point' – plus he did not want to miss taking his exams. Meanwhile Mr Pierce felt there was 'more than enough reason to search Osman' due to the information he had shared with a staff member, concluding: 'Yes, he's a criminal.' Yet Mr Pierce also conceded there was uncertainty regarding the truth of Osman's stories. Police officers had not been able to corroborate any of the events he had described. Although Mr Pierce thought Osman was likeable and did really well when he was given a lot of attention, he 'just revert[ed] to type' when placed in a group.

One June morning I discovered no one could talk to Osman because he had been permanently excluded for bringing a screwdriver to school. After arranging a special meeting, Osman explained how he had brought the screwdriver in by mistake because he had been repairing bikes at his friend's house the day before and left it in his bag. He felt this was 'the biggest excuse ever to exclude me permanently' and Dreamfields 'should use their brains, use their psychology', because if he wanted to bring in a weapon, he would have brought a knife. Plus, he knew he was being searched each day. Exasperated, Osman said he had tried to explain, but 'they were not having it'. Although Osman admits Dreamfields put him off education 'one hundred per cent', he continued to value academic achievement, adding: 'I am smart enough to realise that you cannot class all education as the same and other places will be different', asserting: 'I am clever and deserve a chance in life.' Yet most teachers appeared to feel Osman was unsalvageable and best removed from the landscape.

One teacher cautioned me to 'take anything that he says about anything with a pinch of salt'. When I said we were going to discuss future plans they laughed, adding that those looked 'bleak'. While waiting for him to finish his exam, Ms Butler carefully instructed me that Osman 'needed to get out of the school as soon as possible'; I needed to walk him off the site so he could not roam around. Leaning over, she whispered to me: 'Just write "evil and twisted", "evil and twisted"!' and laughed as she carried on down the corridor. Although certainly angry and overcommitted to a volatile peer group, Osman was also a distressed and confused 16-year-old boy. Treating him as a confirmed 'criminal' arguably led him to further embrace his gang or 'family' as a haven of acceptance. Against the increasingly antagonistic landscape of Dreamfields where Osman lacked value, his external identity becomes a more amenable, plausible source of value – albeit officially illegitimate. As Bourdieu writes: 'there is no worse dispossession, no worse privation, perhaps, than that of the losers in the symbolic struggle for recognition, for access to a socially recognised social being, in a word, to humanity' (2000: 241). Despite the real dangers, his 'family' offers him recognition, while his assertion of 'macho' masculinity is not an alternative system of value, but an extension of already present structures (Alexander, 1996). Osman's masculine bravado does not operate outside Dreamfields' value system, but operates within the same parameters as Culford's lawless urban hero rubric – albeit in an illegitimate form.

Yet for Mr Pierce, Ms Butler and others, Osman had become the irredeemably criminal 'type' that had always-already lingered within, waiting to emerge. Youth like Osman are not seen as children to be helped, but criminals to be purged, as the 'geography of childhood' is 'constructed differently across time and place; where children felt to be in need of protection in one area became a "youth problem" in another' (Nayak, 2003: 311–12). The inevitability of this pronunciation shows how the carceral systems within the school tie to the external prison complex. While prisons punish delinquency, they also produce it in and by incarceration, as 'The prison is merely the natural consequence, no more than a higher degree, of that hierarchy laid down step by step' (Foucault, 1991a: 301). Time in the LSU functions as both a dress rehearsal and guarantee of the 'real thing' for boys like Osman, as internally excluded students become externally excluded criminals, shifted from one cell to another.

Dreamfields does not help Shante, Osman, Clarice and many other students like them who cannot claim or access 'buffer zone' status. These students failed to become the right kind of subjects, highlighting how cultural games are played out and how these matches are seldom fair. Although the difficult circumstances these students must navigate may be more extreme than many of their peers, Dreamfields does not fulfil its promise to act as their saviour. Its structures do not liberate them from their positions, but only compound already difficult situations, ensuring that those born into the 'less welcoming worlds' Berlant (2011) describes remain unwelcome in other worlds like Dreamfields. Rather than 'catching' them, the Child-Catcher drives onward in search of less laborious bodies more amenable to being caught.

The damage of dislocation

Tameka's frustration over Dreamfields' separation from wider Urbanderry corresponds with Osman's more extreme feelings. As explored in Chapter 5, Tameka felt that it was unfair for teachers to judge her to have a dismal future because she and her friends were trying, but she asserts Dreamfields 'cannot expect it to happen overnight'. She feels black students were showing they could achieve, but needed time to move up. While 'it was all well and good making a school like this', Tameka stressed that they needed to realise they had placed it in Urbanderry. Instead of viewing it as a pathological place, Tameka passionately insists there are positive aspects to Urbanderry that should not be dismissed. Tameka said a lot of students could be both 'street' and intelligent, reiterating that they were trying to 'raise themselves' because everyone knew education was important as jobs were scarce. Tameka emphatically exclaimed that they were 'trying to get the grades and all', but 'they have to realise they have built this school in Urbanderry!'

Conversely, Tameka describes how some teachers like Mr Hudson or Mr Adams knew about Urbanderry. They really understood them and knew what they were talking about. These teachers could 'have a laugh and get on with it', but then other teachers simply did not understand. She said if teachers were nice people, if they were funny and just understood, or if they were 'blessed' in talking to them, then they would be 'blessed' back. But if teachers just shouted and screamed the whole time, 'there was going to be trouble'. Tameka and her friends sought respect and understanding, which she felt she received from some teachers. Incidentally, the two teachers she names live near or in Urbanderry. As Clarice mentioned, shouting is an ineffective way of either coercing or communicating with older students.

Florence developed some of the issues Tameka raised regarding Dreamfields' estrangement from the surrounding area. She felt it was unfair that there were so few teachers of her own colour to look up to, recounting how at one time there was only one black teacher, while now there were about five compared to dozens of white teachers. Florence's comments highlight the noticeable absence of ethnic-minority bodies that becomes symbolic of a wider rejection and exclusion of the external environment. She felt the school would fit better with Urbanderry if it were more diverse and included more black, Muslim, Indian and other ethnic-minority teachers.[2] Florence added: 'it's supposed to be a local academy, but it does not reflect this'.

Isolating opinions

Compulsory compliance leads to a silencing of student voices like that experienced by teachers in Chapter 4, albeit of a more absolute nature due to students' subordinate position within the institutional hierarchy. Although prefect Samuel seldom critiqued Dreamfields at the start of Year 11, by July he described how he had seen himself change:

> I think, actually, as I've grown older, I've become more and more rebellious because in my opinion I do think that the education at Dreamfields is just great, but I do think that the rules are just ridiculous, to be honest … I think there are certain teachers that just stretch it, they really do, they just want to take control.

> Maybe that's their personality and now they're being like a senior teacher so they can impose their authority and just make children's life difficult. And if a child reacts, then I think they will just enjoy that and then they know they can punish them even more.

Sometimes Samuel doubted teachers' moral authority, particularly when they visibly relished over-exercising their power; however his rebelliousness remained a largely internal, reflective phenomenon.

Samuel tied his inner rebellion to an incident that occurred on the day of the student tuition fees protest in November 2010. One student had planned via Facebook for students to gather in the playground and walk out, or, more realistically, given Dreamfields' security, for everyone to sit down when the bell rang. Samuel described how everyone had gathered in front of the locked gates, but teachers became aware of the plan and break time was cut short. Samuel was heading towards his lesson when Ms Butler pulled his bag. He recalled politely saying: 'Miss, you don't have to pull my bag.' She looked at him and said something about the protest; Samuel remained expressionless and continued, but Ms Butler pulled his bag again and he repeated: 'Miss, you don't have to pull my bag.' Samuel described standing in the corridor as three successive teachers shouted at him about setting a poor example. Then he was sent to Ms Butler's office, where she too shouted at him. Samuel spent the rest of the day in isolation with a 6.00pm detention for allegedly trying to get out of the gate. After inspecting Samuel's planner, Ms Butler said he would have to miss his rehearsal.

Samuel was particularly upset about missing his rehearsal and related this incident to his mother Celeste, who asked him to honestly relate his story. His mother decided it did not sound right and phoned Dreamfields. Ms Butler argued with Celeste, and Samuel described how this irritated his usually calm mother. Celeste then met with Ms Butler, who professed to be unaware of Samuel's play rehearsal, claiming if she had known, things would have been different. Samuel felt this was not right, as Ms Butler had clearly seen it written in his planner. He also remained confused as to why he was being punished in first place, as he had carefully maintained a polite tone and neutral facial expression. Yet Samuel did not argue back, 'because if I made a point, I know she would have made it even worse, like, "you were answering back" and stuff. I'm not trying to be disrespectful or anything, but if I know something is not right, I will say it in the politest way possible. I'm not trying to be rude, but if I don't think this is right I will say it.'

Although Samuel sensibly points out the difficulties that might have arisen if the entire school had marched, he also felt dissent would never be allowed in an environment like Dreamfields: 'I knew in my head it was not going to happen – not at the school that does not allow students to stand in groups of more than six.' Lorna also felt nothing subversive could occur at Dreamfields, and instead ran to take advantage of the shorter pizza queue during the protest. However Lorna took a quick snapshot beforehand; one of her photo-diary snapshots depicts a dense congregation of students in front of the gates, something Lorna felt was a remarkable scene. Lorna's mother Eve described how she would have been delighted if they had all sat down, relating an exchange with her daughter:

> And I said to Lorna, 'Why didn't it happen?', and she said, 'Mum, all it would have taken is for one person to sit down and the whole school would have followed.' Everyone was waiting for that one to do it, and not one was quite brave enough to sit on the floor. And they'd have all, and I don't know what would have happened then.

Eve marvelled at what would have occurred, adding that it is quite annoying that it did not happen. She adds that sixth-form students even requested permission to protest, laughing at the cowed ridiculousness of this gesture; however Eve points out Dreamfields' controlled environment:

> They have security there, though, the gates were locked, there was no way for the kids to get out. And because of the discipline, they know no child is going to get violent, no child is going to push. The kids – the kids are scared. They are.

The student who orchestrated the sit-down on Facebook was excluded for one week, but later made a painting of a student in a Dreamfields uniform with their mouth taped shut, dangling by chains from the hands of a faceless puppeteer (see Figure 6.1). Eve sympathised with the students' position, adding that she thought all the teachers realised it was restrictive, yet 'they also know unfortunately that it works, so I feel that they are torn a bit too'. Students' limited expectation of and scope for agency and the institution's punitive reaction highlight the narrow, constricted nature of Dreamfields' supposedly liberatory structures. As Bondi and Laurie (2005) discuss, neoliberalism actively works to deplete and constrain activism; Dreamfields' systems teach students the pointlessness of attempting to make their voices heard from the outset. Unsurprisingly, students are more amenable to compliance.

Accordingly, the majority of students complained that Dreamfields did not listen to them or take their opinions into account. Abisola said the one thing she would change about Dreamfields would be to give the students a chance to have a voice in things – to be able to say how they felt, to be listened to, to not have to go it alone and to have someone to talk to. Samuel described how only advice on trivial matters like where benches should go in the playground was heeded:

> You can voice your opinion, but I think the school won't listen or will just put you in isolation or something like that. I don't think … the school is very autocratic, it does not like to listen to suggestions and ideas, it just thinks about what is right for them. Even if you wanted to get your ideas heard, it would only be for minimal things.

Joshua described how the student council was like *The Lord of the Flies*. Although he was initially enthusiastic to alter the hair rules discussed in Chapter 4 by joining the council, it ends up being a performance of hearing without listening.

6.1 Student artwork in response to exclusion

Although Dreamfields provides a formal mechanism for pupil voices to be heard, it does not actually listen to what students are saying.

Some parents are also ignored by Dreamfields. Florence's family sometimes felt the school was too strict, particularly when she felt sick and was not allowed to go to the toilet during a lesson, resulting in her vomiting on the classroom floor. With a sense of smug vindication, she described how this portion of the floor had to be re-carpeted. Her working-class black British father came in to speak to a teacher when Florence was forbidden to attend a medical appointment, however it was made abundantly clear that his opinion was irrelevant. Florence reflects:

> Teachers like to have the whole authority over the student and the parents as well. They don't really listen to what parents say here, I don't think. 'Cause they got a PTA, but I don't think they really listen to the PTA or the PTA that they had was just the selected ones who they liked with the good opinions about the school ... And I think the PTA even complained about something ... and I don't think the school done anything about it. And we even had the school council for this school, obviously – a school council for the students and we were saying how we felt about stuff ... but the school just ignored it ... I just don't think the school listens.

Not only are student voices irrelevant, most parents are ignored unless they are on the PTA, which Florence designates as a repository for those with 'good opinions'.

Conclusion

> I remember saying to a teacher, and I won't mention his name ... I said to him, 'What is important is the ability of kids to think.' He said, 'Well, if you wanted them to think, you sent them to the wrong school.' So in other words, we can teach them, here's Pythagoras, put the numbers in, there's your answer. But don't ask them to derive the equation. They are not thinkers. But we want thinkers, not just to deal with existing problems, but to address new problems. (Alexander, Daniel's father)

Whereas many working-class and ethnic-minority students often disinvest in education and 'know their limits' after repeated experiences of academic failure, Dreamfields presents a limitless landscape where investment is mandatory (Archer and Yamashita, 2003b). Unlike other research which has shown how masculinities are often built on displays of resistance towards school work or an apparent lack of effort (see Francis, 1999; Frosh, Phoenix and Pattman, 2002; Sewell, 1997), where education is framed as an effeminate space (Willis, 1997), Dreamfields makes trying not only acceptable for both boys and girls, but a mandatory requirement. Even Charlie or Gazi, who aligned themselves with 'tough' masculinities, participated in schoolwork and were only, as Charlie described, 'fake bad boys'. Although this limitless horizon is a mirage, the continual pushing of students means that most experience progress in their levels; this degree of success makes trying and moving towards an 'ideal' pupil status appear possible for many – even if it reiterates that they are pathological. These manoeuvres are riddled with contradictory ambiguity. As teachers write efficiency, compliance and skill upon the student body, students take up these inscriptions and learn to write themselves. Yet this self must be written in a certain font; only certain selves are acceptable as Dreamfields attempts to shift the student from a black and white working-class to a more white, middle-class culture. This 'liberation' may bring the benefits of good grades and future success, yet these benefits come with a cost.

Throughout this process students are urged to regard themselves as commodities made better and more valuable through their training. Boltanski and Chiapello reflect on capitalism's expanding and deepening reach post-1968 in comparison to the traditional Taylorisation of work that treated people like machines. They argue that the new spirit of capitalism penetrates 'more profoundly into people's interior being' as they must give themselves over to their work (2007: 465–6). They describe how this places 'the most specific qualities of human beings – their emotions, their moral sense, their honour, and so on – directly in the service of the pursuit of profit', allowing human qualities to be instrumentalised and commodified. Market logic penetrates these young people's lives and their social relationships at an intensely personal level. Dreamfields students and teachers must 'give themselves' to the institution, they must be 'caught', and to be caught is to be, or at least act, uncritical and be a good 'little robot'. There is little space for critical thinking, innovation or creativity in the neoliberal school; instead there is obedient reproduction where students, parents and teachers learn to accept that Dreamfields' approach is the only option.

Notes

1 See www.gov.uk/school-attendance-absence/legal-action-to-enforce-school-attendance regarding the use of fines to compel school attendance.
2 Although see Maylor, 2009 for arguments against 'ethnic matching' of teachers and students.

7

Urban chaos and the imagined other: remaking middle-class hegemony

While Chapters 5 and 6 explored how students navigated and negotiated Dreamfields' conveyor belt, where middle-class and mostly white students were positioned as a buffer zone against urban chaos, this chapter examines parents' orientations to the institution. Responses to the urban chaos discourse show how parents and students conceptualise their positions within this imagined Urbanderry landscape. Discourses of pathology shape the relationships developed between parents and teachers, impacting upon how students and parents are perceived and treated by the school. The urban chaos discourse powerfully reiterates the inequitable positions of the watcher and the watched, the judger and the judged. The white middle-class parent occupies an invisible, normative space, while working-class and ethnic-minority parents feel the potential weight of discipline's reformative hand. These white middle-class parents' habitus is in sync with Dreamfields: 'And when habitus encounters a social world of which it is the product, it is like a "fish in water": it does not feel the weight of the water and it takes the world about itself for granted' (Bourdieu and Wacquant, 1992: 127). White middle-class parents position themselves as buoyant, automatically appropriate subjects, while other parents labour to gain institutional recognition and protect their children from being marked by discipline. Ultimately, rather than students being measured as data like Dreamfields claims, the continued use of types, categories and subjective judgements becomes evident as students are weeded off the conveyor belt as it progresses from the compulsory lower school to sixth-form college.

Whose oasis?

Many middle-class parents recognised their innate 'worth' on the education market, and their ability to manipulate this market. Middle-class students' favoured status connects to their parents' position of value to form a circuitous route of privilege. As Ball (2003) points out, this preferred position must be struggled for; efforts must be made to secure their child's position on the conveyor belt. Veronica described how a group of middle-class parents at her daughter's primary school actively strategised to gain admission:

Veronica: Then I gradually found out that the Laurence Grove[1] parents, who were in a desert of secondary-school provision, were actually trying to entice Mr Culford over into their camp to invite him around for drinks … In order to try to, well basically, to allow their children in. So in whatever way he could.

CK: Because they are out of the catchment area, aren't they?

Veronica: Oh yes, they are certainly out of the catchment area. Yeah, totally, it's [postcode] down there.

When I later asked if their drinks party had succeeded, Veronica replied: 'Ah well, incriminating as it might sound, yes, it did. I don't know if it was that that did it … but I think their plea was heard.' Several other parents described how Dreamfields' much-publicised success had attracted middle-class parents from outside the catchment area. Poppy's father, Stuart, a white middle-class Canadian, asserts:

I mean, I know for a fact that there are kids who go there who only go there because their parents had the wherewithal and the energy to kind of work the system enough to get them in there … 'Cause there are ways of doing it, if you are persistent.

Franklin, Isaac's middle-class black British father, describes how

When schools are successful, or the perception of them is successful, well, what do you think it does? It creates a magnet for – let's face it – the chattering classes. All of the sudden their children want to go and they might not even live in the area, but they will have strategies to get their children in.

Given the pressure to attract and establish a middle-class cohort to prevent Dreamfields from becoming what Ms Wainwright referred to as 'a sink school', these strategies often work, and middle-class parents are very aware of them.

Parents did not necessarily position 'working the system' as problematic. Phil, a middle-class white British parent and PTA member, portrays it as beneficial:

You've got all middle-class parents desperate to get their kids into Dreamfields and doing whatever they can and being as pushy as they can and fiddling the rules … and of course the end result is that you do have a mix. And a mix works.

Phil concludes that pushy middle-class parents edging other parents out of this mix make a more balanced environment, adding that if Dreamfields' intake were only poor kids, it would fail. In these terms, the long-term policy push to fashion parents into consumers has been successful. Reay (2008: 642), referencing Chitty (2007), says: 'Blair's greatest achievement was in ensuring that the marketisation of the public services is now built into the DNA of public service provision.' Not only is marketisation built into the DNA of services, it is part of middle-class parents' DNA as consumers.

The transition to secondary school marks a potential crisis in reproduction for middle-class families, all of whom described undertaking extensive research to ensure their children attended a good school in Urbanderry or elsewhere. Emily, a white British middle-class mother, remarks: 'Yeah, we did a lot of research because it's very scary, secondary schools.' Ball describes how individualist modes of social reproduction entailed by the modern market are riddled with fear, insecurity and potential failure; smooth reproduction is not guaranteed and class boundaries must be continually reproduced and maintained (2003: 149). There were several local schools that these parents automatically dismissed as inadequate. Julia, a middle-class white British mother and PTA member, describes her situation:

> I fought tooth and nail, or my partner and I, fought tooth and nail to get our son in there originally. He was one of those unfortunate kids who was not really offered any kind of viable alternative. He was offered a place at what was the then-failing Glendale school. And we wouldn't, we couldn't have sent him there. It was just horrible.

Yet Bernadette, a working-class white British mother, describes how one of her sons did not get into Dreamfields, 'so he went to another school in Urbanderry which was absolutely crap, rubbish'. Unlike these middle-class parents, Bernadette did not possess the legitimate capital and arsenal of strategies necessary to ensure her son could avoid an inferior school.

As Ms Wainwright described in Chapter 5, although middle-class parents can be 'whiny', they are also supportive through institutions like the PTA. Veronica, who organised the fairs at her daughter's former primary school, describes a conversation with another parent when her daughter was in Year 3:

> She was saying, 'Oh, have you thought about what schools?' I said, 'Oh, I don't really know.' And she was saying, 'Well, you know, Dreamfields, they do want you, you know, they do want you.' She said 'you', i.e. middle-class parents, *they want you*. And I said, 'Oh, what do you mean?' And she said, 'Well, they wouldn't have this, would they?' In other words, the summer fair and that link with the community kind of thing, or something that represents a link with the community anyway.

Veronica comes to realise her 'wanted' status, while both Phil and Julia recalled a boy from another academy telling them during Dreamfields' winter fair that his school did not have fairs because there were no middle-class children there. Phil describes the PTA as 'the same old suspects – it's the white middle-class parents, you know, who are doing that. And there is an issue here – and it's not all, there are certainly non-white middle-class parents on the PTA, but very few of them.' Phil suggests that white middle-class parents are performing their duty while others are not. He describes how Dreamfields responded to Ofsted's instruction to engage with the community by encouraging the PTA, although Veronica recognises this as a symbolic, unrepresentative act because the PTA is composed of primarily white, middle-class parents. Alexander comments: 'If the PTA puts on a function … it's associated with top sets. And I know my kids are in there, but I have not seen much where people have cooked Caribbean food and things like that.' Phil emphasises how important it is for parents to support their children through being 'integrated and involved in the school, because I think it makes the child have a very different attitude towards the school', inferring that working-class and ethnic-minority parents are not supporting their children properly through a failure to integrate. Yet, as Alexander points out, the PTA and Dreamfields, as highlighted by Ofsted, are the entities estranged from and unrepresentative of the majority of the surrounding community.

Bernadette anticipates Phil's critique when she emphasises that she attends all the fairs and drama productions, regardless of whether or not her children are involved, but she is not a PTA member because 'They're not my cup of tea, I'm afraid.' She describes how 'a lot of kids in this school do come from out a little bit … yeah, there is these posher children that stick to their little groups'. She thinks the behaviour of these 'posher children' mirrors their parents:

> Sometimes – this is probably going to sound wrong – but like the way they talk and things like that, you know. They're not, they would not be my first choice of a group of friends, like I probably would not be theirs. 'Cause they seem to have – when you come to the fun days or the fêtes and that, they sort of, they all like *(demonstrates distance)*, they're like their children, they all stick together. I mean, I don't have problems with them, but.

Bernadette is not unsupportive of Dreamfields, but feels alienated by this exclusive group of 'posher' parents and their children who she portrays as coming from outside Urbanderry. Despite the narrow cross-section it represents, the middle-class 'buffer zone' comes to signify Dreamfields' community via the PTA.

Dreamfields' 'oasis in the desert' assumes a dual meaning and purpose. Besides its widely publicised task of saving 'urban children', Dreamfields more covertly invites middle-class parents to colonise this space as they actively seek admission. This suggests that the academy programme's effect within boroughs like Urbanderry is much different than that claimed by policy rhetoric. Veronica hints at these less-publicised effects when discussing school choice, reflecting that even if she could afford private schooling she would 'opt for state somehow', but qualifies this: 'I suppose the question is, would I have left like all the other middle-class parents seemed to do prior to the academy roll-out? Uh, I don't know is the answer to that.' Although New Labour and Culford continually positioned the 'roll-out' of academies as breaking a culture of cyclical underachievement, Veronica points out how academisation has kept middle-class parents in Urbanderry while attracting others from further afield. The Laurence Grove parents outside the catchment area, stranded in 'a desert of secondary school provision', can mobilise their cultural capital to enter this oasis, while parents like Bernadette, who lack the legitimate capital yet live adjacent to Dreamfields, are excluded. This highlights how education markets do not promote equality and calls into question whose children these new academies are actually benefiting.[2]

Efficient business professionals

Many middle-class parents readily compared schools to businesses and positioned the market model as obviously and unproblematically applicable to education. They frequently drew on their own experience as private-sector professionals and managers to praise Culford's leadership. With her human resources background, Julia marvelled at Culford's management skills that she felt made all staff members feel motivated and rewarded accordingly. Julia joked that she should undertake a PhD in effective management, using Dreamfields as a template. Emily, a marketing consultant, recalls meeting Culford several times:

> I liked him because it's all about leadership, so I think he is a very good head and I think people respect him, so it's like any business you are running – the person at the top has to be respected and doing a good job … I think he makes the right decisions.

Miriam, a media professional, also draws this parallel:

> It's like business. It depends who your senior management team is, you know the business might not change, what you do, the rules, but it can make a huge difference to the whole culture of the company, depending on the individuals who are running it.

The complete lack of resistance to marketised education shows how deeply ingrained neoliberal market logic is in the minds of middle-class parents. Despite Urbanderry's longstanding history of leftist politics, there was little resistance or critique of these models from Dreamfields parents; if anything, they were embraced.

Emily was amazed at how Culford has consistently kept Dreamfields running 'like clockwork' for years, relating this story:

> This made me laugh. My son was saying Mr Culford did a tour of the classes yesterday and he said one of the teachers ran over to the other teachers and said, 'Mr Culford is coming down the corridor.' *(laughs)* And he said to me, 'Everyone is scared of him. Why?' And I'm like, 'Well, they're scared.' I thought that was hysterical. Can you imagine? So they are looking out for each other, the teachers. I thought that was quite sweet, actually. Just saying, 'He's coming, he's coming.'

Emily muses at how Culford retains this control, saying: 'It's not shouting, it's just the look, he just gives the look', adding he is 'quite gentle'. Instead of scared teachers being a negative phenomenon, Emily feels this fear 'keeps them on their toes and makes sure they deliver. And a lot of them are quite young, aren't they, so it's great for their CV … I'm just so lucky, you know, for a state school, I'm just like, "thank the Lord!"' Not only is this portrayed as a good CV-building experience for teachers, her son receives a high-quality, free education. Emily and Julia's wonderment at Dreamfields' management structures jars with many teacher accounts explored in Chapter 4, where staff describe labouring for long hours in an atmosphere of distrust, surveillance and fear.

Only Miriam suggests the onerous demands made on teachers:

> There is a very high turnover of staff which I have been very surprised of, and which has been quite challenging to Poppy, that she will have had her favourite science teacher, English teacher, and you know, when we go to that parents' evening there are many goodbyes. And I don't know why that is. I don't know if it's because it's fine for the kids, but all a bit damn tough on the teachers and they've had enough by the end of the first year or two?

While Poppy benefits, Miriam wonders if teachers cannot withstand Dreamfields' demands. Her partner Stuart speculates that teachers might be headhunted, while Miriam adds this high turnover stands in stark contrast to her older son's experience at secondary school where he had the same teachers throughout.

Yet the teacher revamped as dynamic business professional is a popular image with parents. Several parents noted that Dreamfields teachers were youthful and enthusiastic. Phil describes the general teacher profile as 'highly committed, highly energetic', a profile reinforced by aesthetic presentations:

> And again, it's good marketing – because they just look, they look like young business people and you just think, 'I can't believe they're teachers, surely they're not teachers?' You know, they just don't look like teachers because they are all in smart suits and, you know, pretty sexy. Sexy guys, sexy women, and you go, 'Hang on a minute, they can't be teachers!', but of course they are.

As Thatcherite, Blairite and Coalition governments have portrayed education as an engine for economic growth, who better to deliver this service than teachers styled as business professionals? This image of energetic youthfulness sells the Dreamfields brand to professional parents who recognise themselves in its image, yet it is important to highlight that this middle-class grouping is not homogenous, but riven with subtle cleavages (see Ball and Vincent, 2006). Veronica describes teachers as 'terribly committed', adding: 'I mean, I don't know where they find them from. What's the blueprint? I just don't know where they – apart from they are very young, aren't they? … There doesn't seem to be any dead wood.' Veronica congratulates whoever is responsible for recruitment, musing that there must be some 'who can't hack it and just leave', yet she adds that they do not hear or know about these cases, 'so all we are presented with is a bunch of highly enthusiastic, competent, up-for-it energetic teachers'. Several other parents commented on how wonderful it was for teachers to give up their time to patrol the streets after school, assuming this was a voluntary rather than an institutionally required action. Parents' delight as consumers getting a good service is combined with Dreamfields' closed-door secrecy to obscure the labour issues underlining the production of these young, dedicated, yet ultimately disposable teachers.

Disciplinary façades

The privileged status accorded to middle-class parents shapes their relationship to discipline, with several suggesting that although Dreamfields seems heavily disciplined, this is more an impression created than a daily reality. Julia describes being 'hugely' irritated by some rules; however, she is comforted by the teachers' caring and appreciates what Dreamfields has done for the community:

> I can't bear the no-touching rule, any kind of touching. At the transition day when our youngest was there with his friends, one of them high-fived somebody else and got shouted at for no touching. And I think that is over the top, I think it's completely unnecessary ... I don't see the need to terrorise would-be Year sevens, you know. The comparison with the military and breaking your spirit come too easily to the forefront. And I don't like that. But what I know, and what comforts me, and what I was able to say to the children, is that might be the impression they create, but in fact once you are there, very good relationships are formed with teachers and they are very caring.

This idea of discipline as more impression than reality was also developed by Phil. When I asked him how he felt about Dreamfields' ethos, he tied impression-making to impression management and marketing:

> I mean, I think a lot of it is smoke and mirrors. I think you know above all – whether a school is strict or not strict – you want the pupils and above all the parents to think that it is strict. And I think that they have done a good job. I mean the one thing that Dreamfields and Mr Culford are good at is marketing. And I think that you have to market a school, and one of the means with which he markets it is to say that it is a strict school. Now there will be some people, and I know of them, who will say *(imitating a very posh accent)*, 'Oh, well it's just awful, disgraceful. The school is so strict!' Well, you know, so don't send them there, then. You know. It does what it says on the tin. It says it's a strict school. In fact, I do not think it is that strict.

Phil thinks Culford cultivates an aura of strictness as a marketing device to garner parental support, but sees this rigidity as largely illusory, for 'as long as you keep your nose clean and keep a low profile, you'll be all right'. Phil describes how his son Frank dreaded attending Dreamfields and received numerous detentions when he first arrived, but now he loved it because he had learned the rules and acquired more freedom. Unlike Gazi or Tameka, white middle-class Frank is not impeded by a bad reputation, despite his initial misbehaviour. Phil felt the 'trick' or 'key' to Dreamfields' success was that it maintained 'a façade and a belief structure that it is strict', but 'once you know what those rules are and you abide by them, you can go beyond that and have the freedom to develop and mature'. In a similar vein, Emily describes how her son Oscar found the discipline difficult at first, but she felt Oscar could be creative:

> I think once you get used to the rules, you know, as long as you follow the rules, you can always do whatever – express yourself … the school is quite good because it does encourage, and if you are creative or musical it does encourage that.

Yet what is deemed 'creative' occupies a narrow range of forms and times for expression; while the raps produced by Samuel and his friends were prohibited, creativity can legitimately be cultivated through music lessons. Emily and Phil assume their sons' experiences are universal, whereby adjusting to rules and keeping a 'low profile' allows freedom. However, as discussed in Chapter 6, keeping a low profile is much easier for some students than others.

After initial misgivings over Dreamfields' atmosphere, Miriam and Stuart also mentioned the leniency of rules:

> *Stuart:* Yeah, I know, it seemed before we went there, it definitely seemed kind of scary. It did to me. I mean I thought it seemed kind of quite freaky.
> *Miriam:* A bit culty.
> *Stuart:* But I can't at the moment complain, at least in terms of it does not seem to be making anyone unhappy. They also, as far as I can see, it's more – I don't think they actually exercise all those rules, as much as they, I mean they kind of have them, but I don't really think it's as strict as they say it is in practice.
> *Miriam:* Well, it's impossible for us to say.
> *Stuart:* Yeah, we aren't there.

These comments highlight parents' limited first-hand knowledge of education; as Miriam and Stuart acknowledge, their assertions are merely speculative. Stuart feels Dreamfields does not seem to make anyone 'unhappy'; however, they later mention how Poppy's friendship group predominantly comprises other white, middle-class students. While Poppy speaks fondly of ethnic-minority students with whom she is friendly in school, she does not socialise with these children beyond school. Miriam explains: 'You know, there is this terrible expression which is "PLU", so yes, the parents of her friends are "people like us", more than people we wouldn't encounter in any other walk of life.' Other white middle-class parents including Veronica, Phil, Emily and Julia attested to a similar lack of inter-ethnic or cross-class socialising beyond the school gates, reiterating the social divisions explored in Chapter 5. This lack of mixing reduces Stuart and Miriam's vision to the vantage point of a middle-class and predominantly white parental network. They also point out how the large middle-class peer group available to Poppy was not present when her older brother went to secondary school, attesting to Urbanderry's rapid gentrification. Although there is not necessarily a perceived threat at every level, as in Butler and Robson's (2003) study of London's white middle classes, the exclusivity of this group is certainly maintained within Urbanderry.

For many middle-class parents, discipline was depicted as beneficial, albeit not directly necessary for their child. This ties to Ms Carrier's comment from Chapter 4 describing how middle-class parents 'tolerate the behaviour system' because they realise it works on a 'whole school level' and 'allows their child to go to a comprehensive urban school'. Discipline was repeatedly associated with ensuring a safe environment. Miriam describes how Poppy's 'horrific' experience at another secondary school in Year 7 prompted her move to Dreamfields, despite its 'cult status'. Miriam describes Poppy's transition as 'a transformation overnight. I think that the code of conduct and the discipline meant, you know, she felt safe. It was expected to be polite, which is obviously the way she was raised and how she had to behave at primary school, so all the norms that she had kind of grown up with.' Dreamfields is positioned as offering safety and comfort through familiar norms that fitted Poppy.

Veronica similarly relates her daughter's experience: 'You know, she doesn't get detentions and she doesn't really need that level of structure; however I am sure she benefits from it.' When I ask how, Veronica replies: 'Because she feels safe. And because she's allowed to get on. I think she suffered in primary school … she is a high achiever – she suffered from many and various distractions during lessons.' Despite his reservations expressed in the previous chapter about the rigid lack of flair instigated by discipline, Daniel's father, Alexander, voices a similar opinion:

> I tell you what, one of the things that attracted me to this school was that [discipline] because Daniel did not need discipline. He was already disciplined … I did not want Daniel going to a school where people were unruly in school and causing fights and he was being dragged into it. Things like that, so I can't knock it. The discipline was what attracted me here.

Like Veronica and Miriam, Alexander does not think Daniel needs discipline, yet he does not want him to become involved with situations stemming from a disordered environment. Implicitly Dreamfields' discipline targets someone else's children, whilst protecting their children from the mayhem potentially caused by these imagined others.

Cementing affinities

Lorna's mother Eve juxtaposed Dreamfields' daily rigidity to the relaxed atmosphere of school trips:

> From what both girls have told me, it's not like that [strict] at all when they go away on trips. The teachers are a lot more fun, a lot more outgoing, a lot more lax and allow the kids to express themselves a bit more. But not all the kids are able to experience that side of it.

As a single parent, Eve was thankful her mother had helped fund these outings for Lorna, yet she also acknowledges that these more relaxed experiences with teachers were not universally available.

Incidentally, a heated exchange about school trips occurred during the group discussion with Year 9 students, including Eve's daughter Lorna. Abisola felt Mr

Pierce did not like black people and Lorna responded, saying: 'Mr Pierce loves me!' Abisola retorted by saying: 'Yeah, that's because you went on that skiing trip.' Gazi, who was not on the trip, interjects that Mr Pierce allegedly said something like 'Thank God there were no black people on the skiing trip.' Lorna and Poppy interrupted, explaining that what Mr Pierce had actually said was 'The reason that you are here is because you can afford it.' Uproar ensued. Charlie exclaimed: 'That's not nice!' Gazi asserted this was still racist, while Charlie added that many people could not afford skiing holidays. Abisola asked Lorna to explain further; Lorna claimed Mr Pierce was not being rude, but was simply telling the truth when he said he did not think anyone on the trip received free school meals and that most of them were in top sets. Whatever Mr Pierce's motives for highlighting these 'truths', they did not sit comfortably with the group, as they starkly pointed out that skiing trips were the preserve of set one, middle-class and mostly white students. Students like Charlie, Abisola, Gazi and Afra are left to experience the symbolic violence of exclusion as the ones that could not afford it – a violence that often goes unnoticed and unpunished, 'and which is, in the last analysis, the product of the "inert violence" of economic structures and social mechanisms relayed by the active violence of people' (Bourdieu, 2000: 233). Differential access to economic resources becomes naturalised and Dreamfields' social structure is shaped through these exclusions. Centrally, these activities also allowed students who already occupied a normative status to become even more familiar, distinct individuals through sharing informal settings with teachers. These privileged scenes of leisure stand in stark contrast to the dehumanising confinement of the LSU.

While middle-class students may experience school trips, they often have little experience of the LSU. Despite his involvement with Dreamfields, Phil describes how 'I only recently found out what the LSU was, and a very unfortunate name, I have to say ... Why do they call it the LSU? It's solitary confinement, basically.' Yet Phil concludes that it is 'probably just like the naughty step, isn't it, really? It's nothing more than that', and proceeds to speculate that his son 'would thrive in the LSU; I'm sure he'd think the LSU is a treat because he just gets endlessly distracted by all the other kids'. Veronica is also unfamiliar with the LSU and uses prison terminology with regard to this space, saying: 'I don't have much dealings with the unit or whatever it is called. I don't even know, what's it called – the place where they go?' Veronica goes on to describe how her daughter 'does not want to be branded as a unit-goer', because 'if you've done time, you've done time in the unit, you know'. To occupy this space is to be marked by it (see Ferguson, 2001).

Phil's equation of the LSU with a benign 'naughty step' contrasts with the accounts of parents whose children had been marked by 'doing time'. Danese, a working-class Afro-Caribbean and English mother, was very distressed about the amount of teaching time her daughter Clarice had missed due to extensive periods in the LSU. Danese said several teachers were impressed at how much Clarice had caught up, yet Danese notes there was a limit to Clarice's ability to compensate for missed teaching, asserting: 'They have tried to prevent her from having her grades.' She imagines how well her daughter, previously a straight-A student, would have done if she had been in class instead of isolation. She actively questions the LSU's legitimacy. Gazi also felt the LSU damaged his results because he missed valuable lesson time, while Mary, Shante, Daniel, Osman, Tameka and Charlie all described this space using an array of derogatory terms. Lorna calls it 'the worst place in the school', while Patience exclaimed: 'Oh yes, this is prison!' when we walked past it. While Chapters 5 and 6 showed that for many students discipline was more than a temporary impression created, but a continual pressure applied, many middle-class parents felt Dreamfields was not really that strict and had little experience of carceral spaces like the LSU.

Discipline as real

Other parents described how their children either felt the weight of or recognised the real possibility of discipline; however it is important to emphasise how discipline was frequently perceived as positive. While some parents felt Dreamfields was too extreme, many described how strictness was necessary for their children and society. Marie, a working-class Afro-Caribbean mother, describes her son Marcel's complaints: 'He says that he feels a bit oppressed sometimes, like he is not allowed to express himself, because he is coming to me in the house and said, "I just feel oppressed, I can't express myself."' Unlike Emily's son Oscar, Marcel feels his self-expression is stymied by Dreamfields' parameters; however Marie feels Marcel needs discipline. Although she has disagreed with his repetitive exclusion enough to speak with teachers about it, she does not feel Dreamfields is too strict:

> I know that a lot of people say that it is overly strict, but I don't really think it's overly strict. In some ways maybe it has got, you know, some strict rules, like with hairstyles and stuff like that – maybe I think there could be some kind of limitations on that. But I think the school is a very, very good school, especially if you want your child to come out with, like, good grades.

Marie feels Dreamfields is academically superior to other nearby schools, offering her son the best chance for future success. Like Marie, Bernadette feels Dreamfields is 'a good place', but also mentioned speaking to teachers about disproportionate punishments, saying: 'Sometimes I think they go to the extreme, and I do make my voice heard when I think that.' Shante's working-class Nigerian and white English mother Beatrice also feels Dreamfields is a 'good school, they have good grades', and thinks children need discipline, but also thinks some of the rules – like students lining up outside without jackets in the winter – are 'silly' or 'too rigid'. Recalling a time when Shante was excluded for something relatively minor, Beatrice said: 'Sometimes I think crime does not suit the punishment … it was a bit extreme.'

Isaac's father Franklin, a black British middle-class parent, also recognises Dreamfields' potentially extreme tactics, describing it as 'absolutely outstanding', but adds: 'having said that, it does not suit everybody and it doesn't suit every parent'. He explains why some parents might be critical:

They probably go beyond what is reasonable in terms of managing the behaviour of the children. But that's their policy, and if you don't like it, then you know you can always move your children, really. But at the end of the day, if you want your child to succeed, then that is as good as an environment as almost anywhere else, I think.

Franklin and Marie's stance is similar to that adopted by students in Chapter 6; although Franklin says Dreamfields may 'rub up parents the wrong way', the institution guarantees good results.

Danese criticises Dreamfields' treatment of Clarice; however she did not send her elsewhere because of its results. She derides Dreamfields' preoccupation with 'being military' and felt their techniques broke students' trust in adults:

It's all intimidation; they use that all the time in this school ... and I think that that form of communication needs to be addressed, because they might not be physically touching our children but they are mentally bullying them.

Yet the test results were clear. Danese describes how 'a lot of people put up with it [discipline] for the grades', yet she felt guilty about making Clarice continue: 'I am sorry in one breath that I have kept her here because I feel like I have tortured my own child and put her through hell just to get an education.' She describes how Clarice suffers from depression and begged her to move schools, but Danese did not want to give Dreamfields the satisfaction. Danese was adamant that Clarice take her exams, adding: 'You've done five years, for Christ's sake, get something out of it. Man – you walk out of there with nothing, you'll regret it for the rest of your life.' After dropping out of school without qualifications, Danese was determined her daughter would not have similar regrets.

Meanwhile Laila, a Turkish and Welsh working-class mother, feels that hard discipline helps her son Gazi. Despite his claims that other students' parents 'stick up for them', Laila firmly dismisses Gazi's complaints. She says: 'Yeah, obviously sometimes they are a bit OTT (over the top) detention-wise, as my son keeps telling me, but at the end of the day it's just a different, it's just a process for them to teach the children discipline.' Mayifa, a black African working-class mother, also thinks Dreamfields' discipline has been positive for her daughter Tameka: 'I said, Tameka, "Now, you are straight now." Yeah, yeah, Tameka is straight now ... Before she talked too much ... she is not a quiet girl, but now this is changing.' Although Tameka and Gazi described enduring bad reputations and criticised its racist practices in Chapter 5, their mothers felt Dreamfields was a positive influence. Teacher Mr Arkanel described how students like Tameka and Gazi are placed in a double bind:

Because your family says Dreamfields is known to be the best school in Urbanderry, plus you are pushed from your family. You have to stay there, you can't mess about. So the family supports the school ethos, supports the school rules and behaviour policy, so the kids are pressured from that. On top of that if the kids – what are they going to say? If they say no to me, that's it – that's an hour [detention].

Students are bound by their parents' support for Dreamfields as the 'best' school in Urbanderry and the non-negotiable discipline of the institution.

Celeste and Esther, from Cameroon and Nigeria, respectively, both recognised Dreamfields' discipline as positive and corresponding to their idea of African values, like respecting elders and not using profanities. They both described carefully directing, protecting and monitoring their sons' development and referenced the permissiveness of Western culture compared to the strictness of their homes. Celeste describes how Samuel benefits from being both British and African:

> I think with Samuel, they have got the advantage in this country, that they were born here, but I was born in Africa and they have dual upbringing and culture in this country. So when the school – and I think it's really helping most kids from an African background because we still try to balance our children to make them know that look, despite that you were born here, we still say things are done this way as well. You don't have to talk to people rudely, you can't just make decisions. I told him, I said, 'The only time I will look at you as an adult is when you are twenty-five years old.'

While English teenagers believe they have rights and can make key decisions, Celeste questions the quality of these decisions. Joshua's mother Esther emphasised how an orderly household curbed permissiveness:

> You have to be strong as a parent and establish that authority because the children nowadays – there is freedom of speech and everything – and especially when you have children who are very good academically and feel they are very sensible.

In stark contrast to the urban chaos discourse that associates ethnic-minority students with disorder, Celeste, Esther, Joshua and Samuel more readily tied deviant behaviour to the white, middle-class student, similarly to Mary and Phil in Chapter 5.

Like Culford's response to the riots, Esther designates discipline as the remedy for societal disorder. Esther comments: 'If they could even go stricter, I'm for it. Because in Urbanderry, we can see the whole world is getting, God help us, it's getting – we are hearing so many atrocities every day', adding: 'where they [Dreamfields] are putting in structure, it is very good because Urbanderry needs a stronger hand'. Afra's mother Nazia, who is Pakistani-British working-class, is also happy with Dreamfields and emphasises the strictness of her household, linking hard discipline to the prevention of societal breakdown: 'Without discipline, no – then you will have, I don't know, mad kids. Mad generation.' Emphasising a disciplined domestic sphere that protects their children from surrounding chaos serves to differentiate and demarcate Esther, Nazia and Celeste's families as respectable. Despite residing on estates, they distance themselves from Urbanderry's 'rough' elements. Gillies writes about how middle-class parenting practices that often highlight democracy and negotiation 'are risky in a context where choice and power are limited, hazards are many and consequences severe'

(2007: 146). These risks and dangers were recognised by ethnic-minority parents who often used more authoritarian parenting techniques to ensure their children were protected not only from Urbanderry's streets, but also from being marked out as troublemakers at school.

Model student protection

While middle-class parents were less likely to feel the weight of discipline, working-class and ethnic-minority parents were more alive to this possibility and assiduously prevented their children from being marked by discipline's moral judgements by cultivating model pupils in step with institutional ideals. Nazia, Esther and Celeste all proudly describe how their children are perceived as ideal students by Dreamfields and their peers. Not only are they clearly proud of them, but the production of an 'ideal student' testifies to their capability as mothers. As Walkerdine and Lucey (1989: 15) highlight, the mother becomes 'the guarantor of the liberal [democratic] order', responsible for producing not only good students, but good selves. Celeste says: 'Most of my neighbours, they will say that these two boys – it's as if they don't live in this estate, the way they comport and carry themselves.' Her sons' behaviour works to distance the family from their vilified estate. Nazia emphasises her duty to produce good children and the huge amount of labour this involved, quoting a Pakistani leader who said: 'Give me good mothers and I will give you a good nation'. She describes the fruits of her labour:

> Even if you ask any of the teachers that have taught Omar, Tariq or Afra, they will all say, 'Yeah, they are good kids, well-behaved, role model.' When people come to me and they say, 'Oh, you've got lovely kids', or 'We know Omar, we know Tariq.' That makes me really happy … That's what I tell them, I said, 'I have done what I needed to do.' Whenever you go around my friends, teachers, people who know me, they say, 'Yeah, she has done a good job. She gave them one hundred per cent.' And I said, 'It's up to you now.'

Esther also gave her children 'one hundred per cent' by sacrificing her own career to cultivate them, and positions motherhood as an obligation to God:

> Although it has taken a lot from me, not going to work and having my own salary money and everything, but one needed to have been in the house twenty-four seven then … you have to really be there to correct them and mould them fast.

Esther feels she has not experienced discrimination within the education system, and suggests her children's behaviour might have affected this: 'maybe because most of the time my children were well behaved, so the teachers were always proud … And my children were always one of the students they could rely on to help them with the class, or to be good role models for the class.' Single mother Celeste is aware of the stigma attached to her position, relating: 'If he was a troubled kid, then that's when it [single motherhood] would have been noticeable', but, like Esther, she suggests Samuel's ideal status has prevented this:

> From primary school, 'Oh Samuel is a wonderful kid, he is so this, he is so honest, he is so mature, and da, da, da, he is doing so well, okay nice to meet you.' That's it, you know … I think the teachers, they like writing letters like, 'Oh this is a perfect student', and so on, so yeah – I don't really have any, I think that's why I am okay with the school.

These mothers are aware of potential pathologisation and take great pains to defend against it by cultivating model pupils. Skeggs (1997: 1) writes:

> Respectability is one of the most ubiquitous signifiers of class. It informs how we speak, who we speak to, how we classify others, what we study and how we know who we are (or are not). Respectability is usually the concern of those who are not seen to have it. Respectability would not be of concern here, if the working classes (Black and White) had not consistently been classified as dangerous, polluting, threatening, revolutionary, pathological and without respect.

Unlike white middle-class parents, these mothers do not assume they will occupy a privileged position within the institution. Quite the contrary, they work overtime to ensure their children will escape raced and classed visions to flourish. Their model status must be achieved and continually maintained. While anxiety over school choice was continuously present within the narratives of middle-class parents, there was little discussion about continuously moulding and monitoring their children to protect them from surrounding dangers and potential pathology. Middle-class parents took more of a laissez-faire approach, assuming their children would be desired by Dreamfields while fighting to ensure their reproduction of privilege through the education market. They did not have to protect their children from pathologisation or continually struggle to assert their value, as respectability 'is rarely recognised as an issue by those who are positioned with it, who are normalized by it, and who do not have to prove it' (Skeggs, 1997:1). In this neoliberal landscape, individuals must fight for their own corner.

Rewriting fantasies of the 'other'

Responses to Culford's urban chaos discourse show the work this narrative does. Respondents position themselves within this version of Urbanderry through actively rejecting, deflecting or augmenting these representations, or discussing them in reference to an imagined other. This discourse lends the urban 'other' a shape, a colour and a voice as fantasies of a chaotic 'other' are perpetuated. Veronica's reflections highlight the creative power of Culford's narrative. She describes how he has made it clear why 'draconian' rules were in place, yet she adds a moment later:

> Yes, the rules are in place and we know why – or we are told why – and that seems to work. And I can understand how those kinds of rules are successful, given the location of the school. I can only reiterate what I have heard Mr Culford say many times, you know.

Veronica acknowledges that her 'knowing' is based on Culford's repeated rationale:

> It might be that the structure works, but for entirely other reasons. It might be they are not so chaotic – you only really know what you have been told. And the likes of Mr Culford saying that on national telly adds another kind of weight to that argument. But no, I have not seen any evidence of it, well how would I? I don't know.

Veronica admits that although she has not seen 'evidence' of urban chaos herself, she has adopted this vision. Crucially, she points out how an influential head-teacher reiterating this viewpoint through the media carries 'weight'. As Chapter 4 examined, Culford makes this discourse ring true through the power of ambiguity and repetition.

Julia felt Culford's rhetoric was accurate to an extent, admitting she never thought she would agree with this viewpoint. Julia describes a conversation between her son Jack and his friend that shaped her perceptions:

> They were moaning about this rigid discipline and then one said to the other, 'Yeah, but you know that the school was not really designed for the likes of us.' And the other one turned around and said, 'No, you're absolutely right.' And when I spoke to them, they had a very strong feeling that the school was designed for the kids on the Turner Estate, you know, that that was the target audience, you know. And that – so that these nice middle-class kids with two graduate parents who would support them with their homework and, you know. They know they have a head start over lots of other kids, they know they do, they are not blind to that. So they felt very strongly that they had to fit in. Well, my son always refused to, but that was the way, that the Dreamfields way was to help the wider population.

Julia's son imagines the school targets children from the Turner Estate, recognising his middle-class privilege and the advantage he has over many of his classmates. Despite Jack being perpetually in trouble, he still feels Dreamfields' discipline is not targeted at him and, notably, he is not pushed off the conveyor belt like Shante, Osman or Clarice who we met in Chapter 6.

Emily also agrees with Culford's diagnosis, tying estates to a lack of structure:

> I think obviously the catchment area of the school is, you've got loads of estates and I can imagine, you know, that a lot of children can't do homework or anything because they've got young children to look after. A lot of families don't have much money, so the school is really supportive. And the fact that you can do homework in school is really good for children who don't have that structure at home.

Although Emily sympathetically attempts to envision the issues faced by parents on estates, her comments belie how middle-class portraits of working-class lives are pieced together with very little first-hand knowledge or contact with actual people. As Emily says, she can only 'imagine' this urban other, despite living in close proximity to them – a disconnect that relates to the lack of mixing between students outlined in Chapter 5. Ball shows how middle-class parents produce boundaries by making judgements that do not centre around knowledge, but were a means to gain power and reproduce their class position where struggle is based on 'a playing out of affinities and aversions' that becomes 'in a sense symbolic' (2003: 76–7). How Emily comes to symbolically define these affinities and aversions in practice will be explored below.

Several mothers living on estates worked within the urban chaos discourse's parameters to deflect the wholesale demonisation of their families. Celeste describes how her estate is considered 'rough', yet she feels disorder is not unique to Urbanderry, but happens across Goldport. Celeste's sons are 'aware of the dangers' and she drives them elsewhere to play outside, asserting: 'Some of us are living here because we've got no choice … if the council offer you a place, what can you do? Just teach your children to make the best of it.' Laila describes how a drug dealer used to live in her block, which made entering and leaving her flat 'a really horrible experience'. Although her block 'has quieted down', she also tells me 'No one likes living on an estate, babes, you know what I mean?', explaining:

> I don't like living on the estate, no, that's why I am working so hard to get my career up and running so I can one day afford a mortgage and actually move my kids out of there. Everyone's dream is that, but I just think as long as you got a roof over your head and keep yourself to yourself, you know. You can live in a house and still get grief. It doesn't just mean to say that just because you are living in an estate that it's why it's like that.

Both Celeste and Laila realise they live in denigrated spaces, yet financially there is no alternative, despite both of them working full-time. Celeste's use of 'some of us' distances and differentiates her family from the roughness of the estate, once again asserting respectability.

Bernadette rejects the urban chaos discourse entirely. She was born on the Turner Estate and has lived there for 35 years: 'We knew, well we know what the estate's like, but to us it's just the estate and where we lived.' The Turner Estate is her matter-of-fact reality, and Bernadette describes her long-term ties with it as both positive and negative:

> So still a lot of the old neighbours was there that knew us when we was little and then I had all three of my children on there, so everybody knew everybody. But Charlie did get beat up there the other week and that made us more determined that we was gonna move away.

Although violence against her son highlights the real dangers and strengthened her resolve to relocate, Bernadette repudiates Culford's idea of unstructured homes as 'wrong':

> All the school is here to do is, when the children come in at, I don't know, half-past eight, lessons start, is to look after them in the school, make sure they are

safe, they do their work and then they go home afterwards. What goes on at home, behind closed doors, it's not for him to say that.

Bernadette renounces the demonisation of her home, anticipating and refuting Dreamfields' implicit critique of single parents, adding: 'I've got friends who are bringing up children on their own and discipline is top priority.' Bernadette feels that once her children have done their homework, the rest of the day is their time and none of Dreamfields' business, asserting: 'And you're not gonna let your children run around and cause mayhem – even though some people do, but there is some of us that don't do that, they give their kids kid's time to do what they want and be a child.' Like Celeste, Bernadette uses the phrase 'some of us', clearly aware her family is implicated in this discourse, while simultaneously differentiating herself from parents who permit mayhem. Bernadette rejects interventions into her home as a space she has jurisdiction over and where she can construct a home–school boundary 'to create a nurturing space in which to soothe the injuries and injustices of class' (Gillies, 2007: 144). Bernadette asserts that although everybody puts Urbanderry down, 'There's places worse than this, you know so. I think they should – them kind of things they should keep as opinion to his self.' Marie also refutes ideas of unstructured families as stereotypical, admitting that Urbanderry has problems, but these problems happen everywhere:

> I think as a community it's actually quite close-knit. I have lived in Urbanderry all my life … So for me, this is the way the community is. And I don't think that – you would be surprised how many parents have got a stable and structured home.

Beatrice, Danese and Fatima also reject Culford's assessment of Urbanderry. These mothers are directly implicated in tales of pathology, while middle-class parents speak of unknown others from afar. Although parents welcomed a good quality local school, they did not need a masculine 'hero' to save their children; however these media-worthy stories are essential ingredients of success in a competitive education market.

Through the lens of urban chaos

The juxtaposition of Emily and Celeste's respective accounts of parents' evening examined below illustrates how the white middle-class parent acts as a person of value casting judgements on others. Reay and her colleagues write:

> In a class-ridden, racist society, to embody both whiteness and middle classness is to be a person of value. It is also to be a person who makes value judgments that carry symbolic power; a valuer of others. And despite the rhetorical flourishes around difference and diversity, it is sameness that routinely gets valued. (2007: 1042)

Class's relational aspects are foregrounded as black and white working-class children deal with the punitive consequences of being positioned within middle-class imaginaries as 'others' to a middle-class norm. Celeste recognises her marginalised position as a single black mother and justifies her approach to parenting. Celeste describes how she supports Samuel before exams by helping him make a timetable and shopping during the week so she can stay home at the weekend, cooking and cultivating a studious atmosphere for Samuel so he can take advantage of the chances Dreamfields provides. While she does not feel Dreamfields has 'transformed' Samuel, she feels it pushes him. Celeste describes how she furthered her own education and moulded her children while receiving benefits:

> Because when I was on benefit, I still gave time to my children. In fact that was the time that I gave them the foundation of what they are today … that's because I sacrificed that time as a single parent. I could not handle work and two children, so I said okay, I will bring them up to a certain age. But while I was doing that I was studying, until, you know I only graduated in 2008. And they saw me studying … and that is the same thing Samuel is doing now.

Celeste serves as an example to her children, but also worries about how a single-parent upbringing might negatively affect them. She recalls a debate she had with Samuel about single versus two-parent families. Samuel was against two parents, as they might disagree on parenting, while Celeste was in favour of two parents:

> I said, 'Well, you know, if you have a dad in the house, a dad and a mum, then you kind of have a steady home, a steady family.' But then he said, 'Mum, our home is very steady, you know. You are there, you go to work.' I said, 'But you see to me, it's hard. I'm really pushing myself. Everything I have to pay for everything.' He said, 'Mum, you don't look stressed. The way you are just doing – it's as if no one can tell we don't have a dad in this house.' I just said, 'Well, but you guys do not know how hard I am pushing myself.'

While Celeste admits being a lone mother is stressful, Samuel reassures her and defends their home as so 'steady' that no one would notice the absence of a father. When I asked Celeste if she thought ethnicity or class affected how the school treated pupils, she reflects:

> When I go to the school for parents' evening, I always go on my own. I kind of feel a bit … you know, just having to sit in front of the teacher year after year on my own. Of course, they know Samuel is from a single-parent family and I thought that it was going to affect how they treated him. But I think that Samuel has really proven that part wrong because of the way he is … some people feel just because you are a single parent, your child will be a loose cannon. But some children with two parents have not achieved half of what I have achieved with the two boys … so our greatest hope now is just his results. So I say, 'Samuel, you know what the impression is that people have about kids from single parents – please, please, please – I want you to remove that, so just do really well with your results.'

Celeste relates feeling seen and potentially judged for repeatedly attending parents' evening alone, anticipating the assumption that her children could be unstructured troublemakers. Although her children have proven this wrong, Celeste still occupies the position of surveyed subject.

Meanwhile, Emily fits Dreamfields' normative ideal as a white middle-class professional living in a Victorian detached house with her husband and son. When I ask her the same question as Celeste regarding how ethnicity or class may affect Dreamfields' discipline, she comes up with a very different answer, automatically shifting the question's focus from institutional practices to lone black mothers:

> *Emily:* I don't know, really. I will tell you what my perception, I think what I have noticed on parents' evening is that there's a lot of women, Afro-Caribbean women that attend parents' evening and no men, so I don't know whether that is affecting some of the discipline at home with the boys. I don't know, it's just a kind of – where are all the guys, where are the men?
>
> *CK:* Do you and your partner both go?
>
> *Emily:* Yeah, yeah, not all the time, but you kind of do a little scan around the room and I am thinking, oh gosh, it is always the women with their kids, but it is very rare there is a father there. And I don't know whether there's a lot of absentee dads at home. There's a lot of refugees, I think, as well, isn't there? I am not sure of the make-up of the school. So you don't know whether a lot of those boys and girls do not have any structure or discipline at home so they are coming in to the school, you know, having a little bit. As I say, I am sure most of them cannot do homework at home or there is other stuff going on, so. But I thought that was quite interesting, 'cause I always have a little scan to see, oh, that's quite interesting, where are all the guys?

Emily scans the room to find Celeste alone at parents' evening, yet Celeste's situation does not match the assumptions projected by the urban chaos discourse, and more particularly Emily, onto her. Still, Emily acts as the surveyor and arbiter of judgement; casting the gaze that Celeste anticipates receiving. Celeste comes to symbolically represent the lone black mother with an undisciplined household. Meanwhile, numerous white single mothers like Veronica or Eve remain less visible or are deemed unproblematic. Veronica never mentions the pathological hazard of single motherhood; quite the opposite, she is a valued member of the PTA. These unequal positions of surveyor and surveyed are repeated and reimagined through Dreamfields' urban chaos discourse.

'Making the adjustment'

Alexander and Franklin, black British middle-class fathers, drew on their middle-class capital to defend themselves and their families from pathological discourses. Franklin described how Culford's comments about unstructured families was 'tokenism in the sense of people quite want to put everyone into – package them as this, this, this. Yet quite often you will see endless examples of people that you cannot categorise in that way.' A media professional, Franklin recognised Culford's need to convey to the press that his job was made more difficult by having disadvantaged children, but this 'is not the whole story because there are lots of children there now who are motivated to work from well-adjusted families and all the rest of it'. Franklin was irritated at how this rhetoric overemphasised negative aspects of Urbanderry and suggested most parents were unsupportive.

Alexander references his West Indian heritage to reject Culford's claims, asserting: 'I think a little research here is needed, you know', pointing out the sweeping generalisations inherent in this discourse. He describes the disciplined churchgoing routines of many West Indian families, interjecting: 'A lot of West Indians are more English than the English.' Alexander employs his class position to defend against both raced and classed suppositions:

> So I think that comment is an easy comment to make, but when you really look into it, a lot of West Indians have come from a well-to-do background of people that's always wanted them to do well and have always encouraged them to do well and come from a strong family background. And I don't think my family is unique to that, I think they are all very similar.

Alexander asserts that his family is not an anomaly and advocates keeping an open mind. While he feels race and ethnicity are irrelevant to how parents or students are treated,[3] he defends his family against notions of urban chaos by evoking an image of the disciplined West Indian.

Franklin makes a similar point, saying: 'Am I am bucking the trend? Actually, no. My whole entire family went to university, my sisters, my brothers, my cousins. You know, this is not uncommon in my family so, and that is another thing that the media portray.' These fathers highlight how the achievements of black British people are erased *and* their lives made more difficult by narratives of black pathology reiterated by the urban chaos discourse. Franklin highlights the discourse's effects on teachers' perceptions:

> So the point I am trying to make here is that you constantly get this thing where it's, 'Oh well, if it's a black boy it's going to be a challenge to teach them, because more likely than not they are going to be from a single-parent family.'

This anticipation of pathology connects to Celeste's worries about being a single mother and the defensive, protective work that parents perform.

Both fathers commented on the necessity of asserting their middle-class credentials to receive respect. Alexander pronounced that he did not have a problem with teachers; although there might be an element of condescension at first, they soon realised 'we are on the same level' as professionals. He felt 'what all teachers need to do is have an open mind. When I go into a room, I don't make any assumptions.' For Franklin, the inherent negativity surrounding ethnic-minority students affects how he negotiates teacher relations:

> And I think that [negativity] is part of the issue ... even in my own case, I mean yes, as I sit here talking to you, you know, people sort of get that this, 'Oh yes, an intelligent person.' They even, if I am on the telephone, think that I am not even black. Okay. They think, hmm, are you black? Ah, hmm, I'm quite surprised by that.

Intelligence and middle-classness are tied to whiteness; thus a disembodied middle-class voice on the phone often leads teachers to assume Franklin is white. These raced and classed optics do not allow room for the recognition of black *and* middle-class bodies, for the ethnic-minority body is automatically marked by classed expectations. This reflects research on black middle-class educational strategies where parents were aware they did not have the same 'security of entitlement' as their white middle-class counterparts and needed to actively demonstrate their status and position to be engaged with as equals (Vincent et al., 2012).

Franklin discussed how he and his wife have developed strategies to deal with these raced and classed assumptions:

> So if I am talking to teachers ... in the past my wife would go to the school and that is even more of an anomaly for them because my wife is a doctor. So, oh hello! *(He laughs)* I'm just a journalist ... It's like, 'Oh my God!' So in a way, it's good sport ... because you just sit there being amused by this person and you can see during the course of the conversation their attitude changing. In some cases, they start off by being – in some cases – condescending, actually. *(Sarcastically)* 'Okay, so you think I can't understand what you are saying or you are trying to explain it in a way that makes it simple for me, well, guess what! Just give it to me – tell me.' Then when you start challenging them or asking them particular questions, they're like, 'Oh.' 'Cause sometimes they are just not used to it, or they are used to it, but not from the person who is sat in front of them. So that is quite fascinating, but I just see it like sport, really. It is part of life and it just amuses the hell out of me.

Franklin and his wife draw on their resources as black middle-class professionals to show teachers they are their equals. Teachers may be used to being challenged, but they do not anticipate challenges from bodies that look like this, attesting to 'the harm that racism inflicts on our ability to see, hear, feel and understand' (Back, 2009: 465). Franklin amuses himself with these situations, unveiling his position and watching teacher attitudes alter. Instead of invoking racism, these interactions become a sporting game where Franklin accepts stereotypical interpretations as an inevitable 'part of life'.

Franklin thinks Dreamfields' attitude to black boys is often very negative, particularly if they challenge authority, something his son has occasionally done. Franklin recounts talking to a teacher about Isaac's behaviour:

> Just the way they talk to me or approach me if they have not met me – those that know me already, then they have gone through that adjustment. Because again, it is easy for the teachers to sit there thinking, 'Oh well, he is not behaving or performing to the best of his ability because of some other external factor to do

with the home', because that must be reason. It can't be because he is just being awkward or being himself … it's not due to some other external factor.

Teachers must overcome the hurdle presented by blackness and make the adjustment to a more middle-class treatment where either the home or parents are not intrinsically problematic elements. This allows Isaac's misbehaviour to become a 'normal' or legitimate and innocent case of adolescent rebellion that is not rooted in pathology. Rollock and her colleagues show how the black middle class 'strategically make use of a range of resources including accent, language and comportment to signal their class status to white others to ultimately minimize the effects of racial discrimination' (2011: 1089). These resources signal respectability and middle-class belonging. Rollock points out how this 'extra work' performed by the black middle class to gain legitimacy within white society unsettles any notion of racial equality, as inclusion involves becoming palatably 'whiter'. This work and movement signal the continuing privilege of an unchallenged whiteness (2011: 1090). Black Britons must be able to access and display middle-class cultural capital in order to undo racialisation and prove their compatibility with normative white middle-class hegemony.

Meanwhile the favourable treatment conditionally available to black middle-class parents highlights how other parents are permanently excluded from accessing these concessions. Teachers must eventually take Franklin's challenges seriously as middle-class professional challenges, whereas working-class parents' challenges are responded to differently by teachers. These parents cannot easily disassociate themselves from the abject home through their accent, comportment or professional status. These 'adjustments' are unnecessary when dealing with white middle-class parents and routinely denied to working-class parents like Danese who do not have the resources to assert themselves as the teacher's equal. Unlike Franklin, they do not possess the requisite equipment to play this sport with any success.

Around the houses

Alexander concludes:

> I think if I started going around those kids' houses one by one, I would see structure … I know people are struggling to make ends meet – that goes without saying. But I would see that there's a mother and father or maybe just a father or a mother, all the combinations, whichever. And he's doing the right thing to the best of his ability and he has his child's interests at heart.

Alexander would indeed find Laila, working late nights in a restaurant to save money for a mortgage and raising two sons with her husband who works as a taxi driver. Or he would find Marie, working part-time as a teaching assistant while she completes her undergraduate degree and raises two sons. Or Esther, giving up her professional career to raise five children while her husband works in accounting. Or Bernadette, raising three sons while serving as a full-time carer for her terminally ill husband. This list goes on, but even when there was something resembling 'chaos', this was not due to a lack of love or support, but connected to financial hardship and life-changing events like marital break-up, mental health issues or a parent's sudden death. The complexity of parents' lives highlights the danger of pathological discourses and the damage they inflict along raced and classed lines on the value of parents and their children.

When numbers don't add up

> The current research is suggesting that class is a bigger impact, a bigger effector of achievement than anything else. So I have to be aware of it and acknowledge it and we have to be challenging it. But I think at this school ... when we look at children, and I take it from a data perspective, there are two types of children: those who are achieving what they should be and those who aren't. The ones that are, they are doing fine. The ones who aren't, we need to do something about. (Mr Vine, SMT)

Unsurprisingly these discourses shape Dreamfields' vision and judgements; class becomes something to be 'challenged', yet how can the existence of hierarchies be challenged while they are being simultaneously reinstated? Mr Vine adds that children are solely perceived as data, despite previous chapters showing how Dreamfields' institutional structures and the 'data' produced are not value-free, objective entities, but shaped by raced, classed and gendered norms. While Dreamfields is hardly unique in terms of how the treatment of students and parents is shaped by these value judgements, this process is accelerated by the intensification of competition and concealed by the aspirational, colour-blind doctrine epitomising its approach. This forecloses spaces for dealing with the persistent inequalities which are brought into Dreamfields and frequently perpetuated by its structures. Competition's demands make it imperative to weed out labour-intensive students or to allow them to 'fall by the wayside' while simultaneously recruiting high-achieving, external students.

The necessity of this dual process was highlighted through staff briefings and exchanges with teachers. In one February briefing, Ms Morrison announced that two 'very bright, good pupils' in the top sets would be starting Year 7. Culford asked: 'How can we say that for sure?' Ms Butler replied: 'We can promise, we have done our research this time!' Everyone laughed, noting the reference to another pupil who had arrived with similar guarantees only to be deemed difficult. One teacher described how a new student had introduced themselves as 'one of Mr Culford's specials', leading to speculation amongst staff about the 'special' nature of her admission.

Conversely, weeding troublesome students off the conveyor belt was equally important. When a long list of excluded children was read out at a briefing, Culford jested: 'Do we have any children left in this school?' Another teacher jokingly replied: 'Only good ones!' One SMT member announced in briefing that Jamal would now be escorted from lesson to lesson and was not allowed to move through the building on his own; Jamal and his mother knew this was his 'last chance' and all incidents with Jamal needed to be logged onto the SIMS to keep a comprehensive record. Later a staff member commented that Culford wanted 'to get rid of Jamal' because he took up too much time.[4] Another staff member mentioned how Terence was also 'on the way out', asserting that the SMT were trying to get him permanently excluded by making him so uncomfortable that he did something bad. When Jerome, a set one pupil who had frequently been in trouble, was considering moving schools, one teacher commented that although moving might be bad for him, it would be 'good for us, you know. Off he goes!' It did feel that once the SMT had decided to rid itself of a 'problem' pupil, this process was accelerated through increased surveillance and pressure, while evidence was carefully electronically compiled to justify this action. This mimics the 'stepping-up' of teacher surveillance described by Mr Vine in Chapter 3. Notably, all the aforementioned students were black boys.

At the non-compulsory sixth-form level, weeding students off the conveyor belt became much easier. Mr Vine describes: 'When it gets to A-level they have to meet certain criteria, and if they don't meet certain criteria, then we can say no.' Although Year 11 student Duane had achieved five good GCSEs, Mr Vine explains his departure:

> The best course of action for him would have been a B-tech or vocational course which would have led him into work or an apprenticeship, but he wanted to do A-levels. Our experience would have told us that there was a very, very high chance he would have completed badly and ended up with nothing. So we said, 'No, we will not let you take that course of action.' He then went to Urbanderry Sixth Form up the road who said, 'Oh absolutely!' and he wasted a year and got nothing out of it.

Rather than giving Duane an opportunity to study with teachers he is already familiar with, Dreamfields does not want to risk his potential failure and the harm this would inflict on their league tables. Instead Duane went to another sixth form where his failure is framed as guaranteed. One teacher thought students like Duane were some of 'the saddest cases', describing how Tyler, another Year 11 student, had also achieved the necessary grades, but was not 'strong enough' to study the A-levels he was interested in and went elsewhere. This teacher added that it was a shame because it would be too difficult and Tyler would probably fail. Several teachers thought some students with five good GCSEs were not actually 'C' students and incapable of A-level study. One teacher described how GCSE marks did not reflect the students' ability; due to Dreamfields' extensive 'hot-housing' of students they could 'get the marks without being that bright, really'. Although these students technically possess the right data, these data are subjectively interpreted and sometimes mistrusted. Mr Turner feels that Dreamfields 'generally gives students a fair start', but 'you could also say that it is forcing children to achieve in as much as it's not a true measure of the child'. Results are not seen to measure what they are supposed to because of the immense amount of teacher labour that has gone into their production. Ironically, instead of these students' aspirations being supported in line with Dreamfields' rhetoric, they are crushed beneath the pressure to guarantee predictable outcomes.

Several teachers and students were unhappy that 'spoon-feeding' continued at A-level. Sixth-former Olivia even suggested it was 'probably really immoral, because if I am not willing to put in loads of work myself perhaps I should not be getting good grades'. Florence also questioned Dreamfields' methods, saying: 'I know they need the good grades for, like, their tables and whatever, but they should not really force someone.' Alara worried that students' lack of independent study habits could prove detrimental at university, saying: 'I mean, it's almost as if they have been churning out these good grades by, um, because of the teachers – if that makes sense. Because teachers are always the ones there to push students and it never really comes from the students.' Alara questions who is ultimately responsible for producing results, suggesting that teacher labour generates grades via the student. This raises questions about what these results that schools 'live and die by', as Culford extolled in a briefing, actually end up measuring.

One teacher described how many lower-school students would not return for the sixth form by outlining how restricted offerings at A-level helped push unwanted students off the conveyor belt. He described how there were many good candidates, both internal and external, so Dreamfields could afford to 'get rid of some of the less appealing ones'. Figure 7.1 shows an increasing ratio of external students compared to Dreamfields lower-school graduates, rising from 3 externals out of 116 students in 2009 to 61 out of 187 students in 2012. Offering students courses they did not want to do effectively expedited their departure. This teacher offered Abdul as an example. Abdul 'was not a bad kid, but a bit rude … not the most appealing sort of candidate', so they could admit him to the sixth form, but tell him he could only do 'the crap courses', forcing him to go elsewhere. And 'if they multiply this scenario by thirty or forty, then they get rid of a lot of the people they don't want'. Yet where do results and intelligence intersect with the desirability of a student's personality or disposition?

Judging the 'appeal' of students is a highly subjective process where data are clearly not the only adjudicator. Unsuitable bodies are steadily dispensed with by the sixth form, undermining Dreamfields' supposed commitment to improving educational outcomes in Urbanderry. When I ask if there are rebellious students left in the sixth form, Florence replies: 'No. They've left. They've made sure that they've left.' As Angela McRobbie argues in reference to reality television's make-

Entry year	External students			Dreamfields students			
	Female	Male	Total	Female	Male	Total	Grand total
2012	34	27	61	57	69	126	187
2011	23	36	59	52	51	103	162
2010	15	7	22	39	58	97	119
2009	3	0	3	51	62	113	116

Figure 7.1 External and internal intake of Dreamfields' sixth form by year

overs: 'There is no suggestion that the victims will ever truly belong to the same social group as their improvers. This is made clear in a multiplicity of small ways such as the consoling words and concluding comments on the part of the experts who retain an ever critical and sceptical eye' (2004: 104). As with Dreamfields' makeovers, it is rare that disadvantaged students are actually able to 'catch up' and achieve parity with other students. Even if they submit to their improvement, stark hierarchies remain. This filtering-out of BME and free-school-meals students and the creation of a more white, middle-class sixth-form space is also reflected in Sumi Hollingworth's (2015: 15) research.

This filtering process has real effects on social relations. When I returned to Dreamfields to catch up with some of the Year 11 students from my sample who were now nearing the end of the sixth form, Isaac, Samuel, Joshua and Tameka all described the sixth-form atmosphere as 'segregated'. Isaac described how everyone mixed at the outset, until a group of predominantly white, middle-class students coalesced. Non-members refer to this group as 'the white group', while Joshua half-jokingly called them 'the white supremacists'. While I do not have space here to adequately explore these follow-up interviews, I want to make a key point regarding Dreamfields' structuring effects. Although Isaac says that he knows 'it sounds terribly bad', he feels integration breaks downs from Year 7 onwards and details how this process is exacerbated by the introduction of external candidates at sixth-form level. I asked him why he thought this happened:

> Because the groups form, like by the end of Year 11 you kind of have groups, but you are still united as a year group 'cause you remember what happened. You remember Years 7, 8, 9 and 10 when you've kind of been friends with everyone. However in the sixth form … you have some externals who have never been in that and they are automatically in a group, so I think by the end of sixth form it is a lot more segregated than at the beginning, definitely. So I know it's bad to say, but I think the way Dreamfields is structured almost encourages the segregation. Because, also I know they cannot help it, but because they try and take mixed ability then they get separated into classes, so like sets, so based on your ability you are put into sets. So then yes, there will be a bit of everything in the top sets – in the top sets you will have Asians and blacks and working-class and middle-class; however more towards sixth form that kind of gets undermined because Dreamfields kind of recruits a bit more of middle-class educated, you know, more A-stars, so the balance kind of gets shifted. So it is more, I know it sounds bad. I know it sounds very bad what I am saying, but without intending to they encourage segregation, definitely.

Isaac's reflection shows how structuring education systems around the marketplace and results inherently undermines racial and social parity and the development of a more egalitarian society. Dreamfields' need to recruit A-star students who are likely to produce good A-level results, coupled with the fact that many of these students are white and middle-class, is compounded by the simultaneous exclusion of 'less appealing' candidates like Abdul and results in a very different student body. The social balance shifts as a large, white and middle-class social group establishes and excludes itself from the rest of the cohort. Isaac also comments that many of these students knew each other outside school prior to arriving at Dreamfields. Out-of-school predominantly middle-class and white social networks from across Urbanderry and beyond convene in Dreamfields' sixth-form space to form a new critical mass that was not present in the lower school and which splinters off from the wider cohort. While previous research has shown how ethnic-minority children are frequently criticised by teachers for not mixing with white children (Crozier and Davies, 2008), the reverse is transpiring within Dreamfields' sixth form. Meanwhile, Tameka describes how the separations in the playground that were so readily evident in the lower school are no longer visible at sixth-form level as B-tech and A-level students have different timetables and occupy different common areas on opposite sides of the building. Similar phenomena existed in Hollingworth's (2015: 47) study, where streaming and different recreational areas evidence a black–white divide and racial segregation is naturalised through the lines of ability. These students' paths no longer crossed. Instead of the angry and indignant Tameka of Year 11, she was now resigned to these spatial and social divisions which are now less immediate and more abstract – it was just the way things were as students moved into adulthood. In Chapter 5 Tameka claimed that she would push her five good GCSEs in the face of a teacher who doubted her; however when she achieved these grades she did not insist on recognition or reparations; instead she slotted into life as a B-tech student.

Conclusion

Dreamfields cannot repair and transcend the wider social inequalities that students and their families face and bring with them to school. Although New Labour's academy programme posited that it would do just this, the actuality is a different story. Diane Reay reflects on how instead of reducing inequality, middle-class advantage has been embedded and extended under Blair's New Labour government, 'a sad record for any political leader but a travesty for a Labour one' (2008: 647). Adonis's presentation of academies as engines of social mobility is problematised by his own comments that show how this engine powers other movements, as he proudly describes how middle-class gentrifiers were opting for academies over private education and buying homes in desirable catchment areas to ensure a place for their children (2012). While some parents were encouraged to stay in Urbanderry, as Veronica mentioned, other middle-class parents with enough capital can buy a place at Dreamfields by moving house. Rather than critiquing how the education market embeds inequality, Adonis presents the mobile middle classes moving into popular academy catchment areas as a charming anecdote evidencing this model's success.

Dreamfields reinstates middle-class hegemony as white middle-class parents successfully manipulate the education market to create an 'oasis' in Urbanderry. Images of youthful professionals appeal to middle-class parents who admire Dreamfields' efficient productivity while concealing issues of teacher labour.

Meanwhile, parents' relationship to discipline is shaped through their status; while illusory for white middle-class parents, discipline carries real weight for other parents who perform extensive labour to protect their children. Ultimately the urban chaos discourse works to redraft fantasies of the 'other' by reinforcing damaging power dynamics and an optics that creates raced and classed categories. These pathological imaginings are compounded by the need to remain competitive by 'getting rid' of labour-intensive students who might jeopardise results. These subjective judgements move along raced, classed and gendered lines, making it more and more likely that certain children remain winners while others are deemed losers.

Notes

1 A neighbourhood outside Dreamfields' catchment area.
2 See Pauline Lipman's (2011) work for an excellent analysis of how the neoliberalisation of education policy in the United States and its privatisation of public, urban schools fits against the rapid gentrification and increasing stratification of cities.
3 Prior to Alexander's interview it was suggested by an administrator that he was not actually a surgeon, but a rubbish collector or 'bin man'.
4 Sadly, Jamal ended up in prison shortly thereafter, arguably taking up a lot more time (and money) ultimately.

8

Remaking inequalities in the neoliberal institution

Dreamfields Academy acts as a symbolic and material response to the supposed failures of comprehensive education and public anxieties over the loss of nationhood and prestige of empire. It responds to a perceived crisis of authority in urban areas where a racialised and classed cultural disorder is leading young people astray. Culford holds up Dreamfields' sponsor Andrew Moore and his rags-to-riches tale of the working-class boy transformed into self-made millionaire to show that anyone can become anything if they try hard enough. He also draws on Barack Obama's life story to show how individuals can beat the discriminatory effects of racism, yet these tales are notable exceptions to overall trends that show the decline of social mobility and growth of inequality across the UK. Meanwhile many of the welfare-state resources once drawn upon by working-class youth like Culford and Moore, including free university tuition and affordable social housing, no longer exist. It seems that the more mobility declines and inequality grows, the more fantastic and emphatic mythical tales of mobility become.

The mobility of the exceptional individual does not provide social justice, but only reshuffles society's winners and losers into new hierarchies. This book has shown how the aspirational rhetoric of Dreamfields and English education policy does not do what it advertises. It overlooks existing structures, while its own structuring effects play into the creation and reification of hierarchies. Rather than liberating students from their positions, Dreamfields' practices remake and reorder inequality by positioning white middle-classness as normative. This chapter draws out a few key conclusions and reflects on more equitable approaches to education.

Changing urban culture?

Although Dreamfields' 'oasis in the desert' was allegedly built to transform urban children, Dreamfields has also become a haven for Urbanderry's middle classes, changing urban culture in unanticipated ways. Besides grafting cultural capital onto students, it actively seeks out those who already have the capitals it requires to excel in the education market. Chapter 7 concluded that this reiteration of middle-class hegemony gives 'oasis in the desert' new meaning, as middle-class parents can deploy their cultural capital to secure preferential treatment and address the insecurities of class reproduction. I was surprised at parents' lack of resistance or critique of a market model of education in a left-leaning borough like Urbanderry. These movements suggest Dreamfields is remaking urban space in ways unacknowledged by the policy rhetoric surrounding academies. Instigating urban regeneration through education is framed as an obvious and neutral solution to deprivation, while serving as an effective response to the narratives of failure surrounding Urbanderry's education system explored in Chapter 1. Here invocations of a progressive-fuelled crisis melded with negotiations over inequalities and council mismanagement to pave the way for a radical educational resettlement.

As discussed in Chapter 4, Dreamfields' appeal is 'universal' and most parents embraced its opening. This is unsurprising given the turbulent educational history and low expectations previously faced by many students in Urbanderry, yet this regeneration via education carries other dimensions. Describing the redevelopment of Spitalfields in London during the early 1990s, Jane M. Jacobs discusses how

> The processes of urban transformation are part of the means by which a racialised architecture of power – material and ideological – operates. This is not simply a case of some 'imperialist' obliteration of the local by big capital. The colonial resonance of redevelopment lies in more than a convenient mirroring of imperialism's territorial expansions, frontier quests and 'foreign' invasions. Contemporary urban transformation is far more likely to engage consciously with the local character of an area than rapaciously obliterate it. (1996: 72)

Culford's gunslinging rhetoric demarcates Dreamfields from wider Urbanderry, yet his speeches also engage with the local area by referencing sponsor Moore's triumph and appealing to the rebirth of local Urbanderry pride as Dreamfields overcomes failure. Redevelopment through education becomes an effective way of reorganising urban space – what parent does not want a good local school for their child? This positive rhetoric obscures the effect of education markets both within and beyond Urbanderry. Creating 'goodness' and 'success' relies on 'failure' residing in other 'bad' schools. This reproduction of binary differences is an intrinsic feature of the market's logic; for success here there must be failure elsewhere. A transgressive 'other' must sit outside this transformative process in order for Dreamfields to possess superior qualities. Although students can be proud to attend Dreamfields, this does not address wider problems, as hierarchies persist both within the school and beyond it. Pathology moves elsewhere in this zero-sum game; demonised spaces must continually exist in order to make Dreamfields great.

While Dreamfields is positioned as a tool transforming Urbanderry's urban culture, it also provides an 'oasis' ripe for middle-class colonisation. Discipline civilises these 'unruly' spaces, making Dreamfields safe for the middle-class consumer. As Chapter 2 outlined, nineteenth-century middle-class social reformers felt urban slums could be improved by a resident gentry bringing superior culture to these areas. Dreamfields aids the re-establishment of this gentry by actively recruiting a middle-class 'buffer zone' to prevent Dreamfields from becoming a 'sink school'. Yet, as Foucault cautions us, this is not simply a return to the nine-teenth-century settlement house, but the creation of something new. First, these students are not simply desired for their superior culture, but for the expectation that they will steadily produce test results with minimal teacher labour. The demand for results both feeds off and into Dreamfields' predilection for the white middle-class student. Secondly, it is not only white middle-class bodies that can excel within this space and come to symbolise ideal pupils. As the experience of Joshua, Samuel and others exemplifies, the black (and often male) body can be valorised as an ideal cosmopolitan body if it can display white middle-class nor-mative behaviours.

Reproducing difference differently: shifting articulations of raced and classed inequality

Race and class are being lived out in various ways through neoliberal regimes like Dreamfields which (re)produces difference differently. Gayatri Spivak (1988: 296) famously highlighted the long tradition of 'white men saving brown women from brown men'; however at Dreamfields we have a mixed-raced man of working-class origins and teachers from a range of backgrounds saving both working-class and ethnic-minority students. The flexible porosity of these categories highlights their impermanence where race cannot be fixed as a transhistorical category. Instead the meaning of race alters and splinters across different contexts, manifesting in local, specific ways that connect to larger public discourses (Solomos and Back, 1996).

The treatment race and class receive as categories is therefore tied to the context of Urbanderry and the shifting significance of Goldport in the public imaginary. Although unfixed, race and class are fictions made real through the parameters of institutions and the treatment they mete out. Through the perfor-mances that institutions like Dreamfields both prefer and demand, and which in turn are noticed and negotiated by students, these categories are produced and given stability. Critiquing social constructionism's reiteration of race, Nayak asks:

> To what extent is whiteness a social construction if it is always reliant upon a white subject to enact and materialize it? ... The problematic of why whiteness as a practice is collapsed into the social category 'white people', and its implications for our understanding of race, are worthy of closer scrutiny. (2006a: 417)

This book has shown how whiteness does not exclusively rely on the white subject to be enacted and materialised. Culford comes to be perceived as white because of his embodiment of whiteness; he represents this normativity and teaches it to students. Joshua actively adopts the controlled, compact and concise modes of being exemplified by the white middle-class group of students. This shows the flexibility of race, as blackness can sometimes (and temporarily) be undone through class – at least within Dreamfields' parameters. The threat of black criminality is ameliorated by the application of a middle-class whiteness, which arguably makes these boys' blackness function as an added resource accessed through their class orientation. Within Dreamfields' confines, they can become exemplary multicultural subjects. Whiteness is therefore detachable from the white body; it can be transported to and worn by other bodies; however it is important to recognise that the valued mode of whiteness is a middle-class one. While girls like Bridget may be white, they do not adopt the 'appropriate' behaviours described in Chapter 5. Her whiteness is the wrong variety and lacks value as a racialised, filthy form of whiteness (Tyler, 2008). This shows how working-class whiteness is often regarded as a block to modernity's progress, as Haylett (2001) described, in contrast to the forward-facing ethnic-minority subject.

These shifts in who can or cannot embody valued subjecthood brings me to reflect on Stuart Hall's pronouncement that for black people in Britain 'race is the modality in which class is lived', as black people were historically understood as primarily racialised, rather than classed subjects (1996: 58). More than thirty years later, class and race are remaking each other in new ways within Dreamfields and Urbanderry as these mutually constituted categories continue to fluctuate. The racialised subject is conceptualised through the lens of class at Dreamfields. Both pathological blackness and dirty whiteness can be 'lost' through the application of middle-class behaviours and the respectability they confer, yet this shift requires labour, loss and conformity. It suggests that racism travels via the classed implications of race, and a temporary escape route from racialised pathology can be found through middle-classness. The wearing of white middle-classness presents an opening for blackness of the right kind to gain value, but only within particular spaces like Dreamfields. I would also like to emphasise that the black body remains marked and tied to historical racialisations in ways that white bodies can never be.

This becomes not only about the straightforward reinstatement of clear-cut categories, but about the formulation of a slippery new model of neoliberal privilege which depends on the reflexive, mobile self where categories are reproduced in new ways (Adkins, 2002). The flexibility Dreamfields gives to these categories while simultaneously remaking them is a testament to neoliberalism's effectiveness through ambiguity. There are openings for the inclusion of new bodies as valuable, yet closures are simultaneously occurring. This ambiguity makes it very difficult to confront and critique these methods and mechanisms as they individualise while totalising; they hold appeal, yet there are multiple conditions for their acquisition. Racism and class bias are obscured and subsumed beneath neoliberalism's focus on individual achievement and future successes.

The disavowal of the structuring force of ethnicity and socioeconomic background in a supposedly post-racial present makes it difficult for students, parents and teachers to discuss and contest how inequalities continue to be produced. To bring up raced or classed discrimination either within Dreamfields or Urbanderry is difficult and often unfathomable. As Lorna describes in Chapter 5, to mention racism is to risk being branded a racist; this problematic elision creates silences. These structuring structures have become unspeakable and there is a distinct lack of vocabulary to name inequalities that are now reframed as individualised problems. Teachers are left to solitarily grapple with how to modulate their practice and interpret the myriad black boys sitting outside teacher offices described in Chapter 5. When something does not quite feel right, most teachers and students are uncomfortable articulating their concerns and struggle to discuss them. Students, parents and teachers are meant to be happy, colour-blind subjects as difficult pasts have been transcended; to remind anyone of their persistence is to become a killjoy (Ahmed, 2010).

While discussions around migration have often revolved around the supposed inability of immigrants to assimilate into British society and the disruption of social cohesion, the segregation of the sixth form described in Chapter 7 inverts these claims. Rather than a group of unassimilable immigrants keeping themselves apart, several sixth-formers pointed out how some white middle-class students formed an exclusive group that did not integrate with other students. The possibility of fostering a vibrant multiculture that stands in opposition to postcolonial melancholia is lost, as this boundary-drawing and assertion of privilege are not broken down, but reified through the practices of a school driven by market imperatives. It is not the 'dirty white' working-class who are obstructing modernity's melting pot, but a privileged white middle-class who draw boundaries between themselves and their ethnic and classed others. Reay and her colleagues discuss how schools should try to balance the equality scales by noting a lack of social mixing, addressing class antagonisms and departing from subject setting (2011: 165–6).

Unfortunately few of these things are happening at Dreamfields; although there is a mix of pupils, social distance is often compounded by institutional structures. The belief that subject setting raises attainment levels has become an orthodoxy, despite research contradicting this notion and highlighting the social divisiveness of these practices (Lacey, 1974; Oakes, 1985; Slavin, 1987). Reay (2007: 1199) urges white middle-class parents and students to move towards an engagement with rather than avoidance of raced and classed 'others'; however this movement is not valued or encouraged by a marketised system. As Chapter 3 showed, the architect's optimistic initial plans for Dreamfields to be open and accessible to the community were quickly subverted by a focus on a securitised environment in the service of results. Yet it should also be pointed out that comprehensive education should not be regarded as a 'silver bullet' solving social inequality, as some have suggested (see Pring and Walford, 1997). Schools cannot be expected to eradicate social inequalities through better understanding and mixing alone; however they should not be actively exacerbating and reproducing them.

Good-life fantasies and the hard graft of neoliberal subjecthood

The allure of some future 'good life' acts a powerful tool of neoliberal governance motivating many parents, students and teachers to willingly accept and even embrace Dreamfields' demands. This optimistic striving in the present and hopeful duty towards tomorrow can only be expressed and realised through the narrow, officially recognised route of measurable test results. Yet this route works to close down debate in the present, as testing regimes become the only way to assess value and critical thinking becomes a distraction to progress.

Education policy and the rhetoric of the academies programme promotes the idea that freedom from local authority management instigates innovative success, yet this ignores how heads like Culford are not 'free' but inherit new parameters of obligation as their hands become tied by different imperatives. Heads might transcend having to address race, class or gender inequality, or deal with staff concerns and union demands, but quantifiable results must be consistently produced. Results become the central organising theme as education is tied to an imagined, external market looming in the distance and directing the action. These imagined futures are made real through the performance demands placed on teachers. School management remains irrevocably bound to the directives of central government and their business partners – not to the concerns of teachers, students or most parents. This pivotal shift in accountability is a hallmark of the neoliberal state.

Dreamfields' 'structure liberates' ethos and its sociological companion, the reflexive modernity thesis, both assert that modernity presents new openings for subjects to write their own biographies as our reflexive agency is freed from social structures. Yet Dreamfields' web of disciplinary structures shows that the self-regulating subject does not make itself and reflexivity is not a universally available subject position. Instead, neoliberal subjecthood is coercively produced at Dreamfields through a range of disciplinary practices. The surveillance provided by the panoptic structure and division of spaces and bodies to break collectivities combines with the punitive coercion of shouting, audit and the evangelical cultivation of good-life fantasies. This web of mechanisms works to structure the subjectivities of students and teachers, and mirrors de Certeau's argument that a range of polytheistic disciplinary practices persists beside the Panopticon (1988). Multiple forms of coercion, including disciplinary and sovereign power, are necessary to bring the neoliberal subject into being.

Berlant describes how capitalism has always generated 'destabilising scenes of productive destruction' whereby the market's whims have made and unmade lives and resources, adding that theorists like David Harvey have suggested that new forms of instability are being generated by neoliberal economic formations (2011: 192). While this movement bears some of the hallmarks of Hall's (1980) writing over thirty years ago about Britain drifting into a law-and-order society led by an authoritarian state, we have shifted towards a marketised state guiding these authoritarian movements. This brings Berlant to query what it might mean that 'a spreading precarity' spanning classes and localities is providing 'the dominant *structure* and *experience* of the present moment' (2011: 192; emphasis added). Whether an economic or political condition, a way of life, an affective atmosphere or an existential truth, this precarity indicates that 'there are no guarantees that the life one intends can or will be built' (2011: 192). As schools are parcelled out for privatisation, education becomes ever more closely tied to market demands. Dreamfields' neoliberal education shapes subjects to be more amenable and flexible to market precarity. Its structures enable students to expect, adapt and conform to 'flexible' or precarious conditions. Students learn to endlessly compete and endure difficult circumstances, and, most importantly, not to contest or question the necessity of their endurance, but to perceive it as necessary for their future happiness and survival. It is what must be done to become a self. As Mr Davis mused in Chapter 4, perhaps self-regulating, market-driven 'automatons' are needed to endure the bumpy ride ahead, as teachers both make and are made by this process. However teachers and students do not act as automatons, but as Chapters 5 and 6 showed, they continuously grapple to justify their labour and disciplinary procedures through results.

Students and teachers come to inhabit similar disciplinary spaces, undergoing monitoring and offering related justifications for enduring these parameters. In the service of imagined future gains, they meet current demands. These demands are seen to be externally produced somewhere 'out there' in the world. Dreamfields serves as a model of the workplace where its institutional demands prepare students for their future experiences as employees. Teachers exemplify the tireless worker always ready to 'go the extra mile', their work given value through a missionary-like drive to salvage urban children. Parents, students and teachers suspend their misgivings and complaints because of the pragmatic notion that Dreamfields 'works'. However, staff turnover among teachers is high; at least nine out of the nineteen teachers in my sample had left Dreamfields four years later and teachers in Chapter 4 questioned the sustainability of the enormous workload. Berlant describes how everyday living conditions 'wear out' the subject:

> The conditions of ordinary life in the contemporary world even of relative wealth, as in the United States, are conditions of the attrition or wearing out of the subject, and the irony that the labor of reproducing life in the contemporary world is also the activity of being worn out by it has specific implications for thinking about the ordinariness of suffering, the violence of normativity, and the 'technologies of patience' that enable a concept of the *later* to suspend questions about the cruelty of the *now*'. (2011: 28; emphasis added)

Teachers and students are meant to withstand the labour of the present to serve the future to come. Yet where does the cruelty of the now end, and this more forgiving later begin? Presenting this model of education as the only way to deal with children in Urbanderry and imperative to fulfilling an externalised, naturalised market conceals how education itself is part of the production, feeding and creation of this market. Dreamfields is a model neoliberal school running in sync with and constitutive of market needs. It enacts these futures to come, while the market is not regarded as a socially produced object. Dreamfields does not obliterate dreams, but encourages and inculcates an expansive belief in dreams through its training. However these future imaginaries are narrow and individualised. Dreams of a successful self who enacts normative values becomes the only dream possible or worth having. As Massey described, neoliberalism effectively alters the 'scaffolding of our imagination' by changing the way we perceive ourselves and what it is possible to do and to be. The idea that there is no alternative to this format is powerfully evidenced through the narratives of students, parents and teachers.

Neoliberalism's approach to issues through a market logic where this logic is presented as the only option fuels a cruel optimism that captures the dreams and wishes of panicking parents, striving students and saviour teachers – even if these dreams are largely illusory and come at a price. Many of Dreamfields' mobility promises go unfulfilled, as by the time students reach sixth-form college the social divisions and hierarchies experienced in the playground during lower school have become embedded. This institutionalised segregation becomes the common-sense groove people move within as future trajectories are cemented.

Although some Dreamfields students may get ahead in the employment market, there are numerous side effects to this approach. The cultivation of docility that fosters an uncritical submission to authority, a lack of imagination, and a narrow sense of agency are a few hazards. Critical thinking and critique is a messy, time-consuming and disruptive activity that only impedes the conveyor belt's progress and its production of results. Limiting any form of collective participation within Dreamfields corresponds to the academy programme's democratic vacuum, as macro policy structures and microstructures of schools mirror one another. The dictation of knowledge by capital without any democratic recourse is a problematic dynamic embedded within the longstanding tension between capitalism and democracy. This descends from the paradoxical aims of Utilitarian-led education models where popular education sought to foster obedience rather than enlightenment. This conflict has been tenuously resolved through offering a bit of voting, privacy and unfettered consumer privilege 'to prop up the sense that the good-life fantasy is available to everyone' (Berlant, 2011: 194). Yet even these paltry concessions are being eroded as parents, teachers and local people are only invited to act as consumers – not citizens – in the education marketplace. Passive consumerism cannot replace active citizenship. Meanwhile, the ability to exercise choice is tied to the possession of legitimate cultural and economic capital.

Whose knowledge? Loss, fantasy and value

While some students arrive at school with the 'right' culture intact, others must acquire particular ways of being to gain legitimacy and fit on Dreamfields' conveyor belt. Severing Dreamfields from Urbanderry both rhetorically and spatially designates many students' culture as valueless and proves alienating and detrimental. Becoming affectively attached to the 'correct' ways of being is necessary for educational success and potential future gains. Dreamfields' paradoxical values are fused together in an ambiguous, slippery package. Berlant describes how fantasy acts as both an opening and a defence where 'vague expectations of normative optimism produce small self-interruptions as the heterotopias of sovereignty amid structural inequality, political depression, and other intimate disappointments' (2011: 49). Dreamfields creates a fantasy space, presenting itself as an oasis where students and teachers can seemingly realise their sovereignty. Yet

Berlant adds: 'In scenarios of cruel optimism we are forced to suspend ordinary notions of repair and flourishing to ask whether the survival scenarios we attach to those affects weren't the problem in the first place' (2011: 49). Following Berlant's line of thought, the affects Dreamfields presents as solutions actually function as part of the problem by positioning white middle-classness as normative while other ways of being are designated illegitimate. Although Dreamfields may graft legitimate forms of capital onto its students, this added value is underwritten by sacrifice. As explored in Chapter 6, the very students occupying perilous positions that Dreamfields claims to 'save' often cannot withstand this inscription process and good-life fantasies remain out of their grasp.

The continuous marginalisation and devaluation of people who do not possess the affects of white middle-classness shows that what counts as knowledge and personhood needs to be widened beyond a racialised, classed and individualised conception of the acquisitive self in order to create more equitable futures. As Foucault remarked:

> The real political task in a society such as ours is to criticize the workings of institutions, which appear to be both neutral and independent; to criticize and attack them in such a manner that the political violence which has always exercised itself obscurely through them will be unmasked, so that one can fight against them. (Chomsky and Foucault, 2006: 41)

I hope this book has interrogated and unpacked how Dreamfields does not function in a vacuum of detached neutrality, but as part of a lengthy and contested political trajectory. Its aims – as well as many other schools like it – make certain worlds more or less possible. As Reay (2007) and Skeggs and Loveday (2012) urge, we need to move towards a position where positive meaning and value can be accorded to working-class ontologies, and I would argue, to other cultural forms worn by bodies of various colours. As Michael Keith has pointed out, there are major alterations under way in institutions socialising young people:

> The simple division between what is and what is not the state is perhaps not very helpful when the legislative changes relate much more to a transactional relationship between forms and norms of behaviour and of official sanction. (2005: 155)

This institutional socialisation process, bound to the market through the state, leaves little room for imagination. It realises working-class radicals' fears over two hundred years ago regarding the implementation of a non-democratic education system.

So where do we go from here given the rise of academies, their good-life fantasies of aspiration and the hollowing out of democratic participation? While there has been a stark absence of viable educational alternatives on offer, there are signs of an increasing scepticism over the current settlement and the wider direction of neoliberal policies accelerated by austerity measures. The Labour Party membership – if not the parliamentary party – has moved towards a more progressive politics by voting for Jeremy Corbyn as leader. However, deep divisions within the Labour Party are preventing it from providing a robust opposition, while the Conservative government is moving forward with academisation. As inequality increases across Britain and an additional £12 billion welfare cuts loom on the horizon, cracks have certainly appeared in the neoliberal dream, yet this anger and disillusionment has yet to result in a powerful progressive politics. However, this is not to say that there has not been staunch grassroots resistance to the academies and free school programme since its inception. Groups like the Anti Academies Alliance, Local Schools Network, and Parents Defending Education have monitored and critiqued the internal contradictions of these neo liberal reforms, while parents have protested against SATs testing and forced academy conversions across the country.

Instead of compounding inequities by pursuing Theresa May's proposed return to overt selection through the grammar-school system, we urgently need to move towards an education system without external or internal streaming with robust avenues for democratic participation. Instead of focusing on discipline, testing, securitisation and the demonisation of poor and ethnic-minority populations, we need to recognise how racism and poverty actively mar the fabric of our society and recognise that there can be other ways to shape our children. Education policy and practice needs to recognise that there are multiple ways of knowing and learning. Rather than teachers catering to the demands of tests and students reproducing knowledge by rote, the art of teaching should be valued and critical pedagogies promoted. Teacher training should address racism and class bias as current issues rather than tidily resolved histories. This stress-ridden, hierarchical culture of continual measurement damages and diminishes both ourselves and our children and must be addressed. We cannot continue to ignore the links between the testing regimes we put pupils through, the school cultures they create and the deteriorating mental and physical health of children and young people in the UK (Campbell and Marsh, 2016). Many children are branded educational losers through these regimes before they even reach secondary school, killing off any enjoyment of learning and self-confidence. The dead-end obsession with the production of exam results creates a landscape where individuals are left to transcend inequitable structures while disadvantage is compounded by the continuous privileging of white middle-class modes of being.

References

Abrams, F. (2012) No money in academy status these days. *Guardian* [Online] 4 June. Available at: www.theguardian.com/education/2012/jun/04/academy-status-incenti ve-cuts. [Accessed: 9 October 2013.]

Adams, R. (2016) Government drops plan to make all schools in England academies. *Guardian* [Online] 6 May. Available at: www.theguardian.com/education/2016/ may/06/government-backs-down-over-plan-to-make-all-schools-academies. [Accessed: 29 July 2016.]

Adams, R. and Perraudin, F. (2015) Education bill to close 'loopholes' blocking academies expansion. *Guardian* [Online] 3 June. Available at: www.theguardian.com/educa tion/2015/jun/03/education-bill-loopholes-academies-schools. [Accessed: 18 August 2015.]

Adkins, L. (2002) *Revisions: Gender and Sexuality in Late Modernity*. Buckingham: Open University Press.

Adonis, A. (2008) 'Academies and social mobility'. Speech to the National Academies Conference, www.standards.dfes.gov.uk/.../Andrew_Adonis_Speech_feb08.doc. [Accessed: 1 September 2009.]

Adonis, A. (2012) *Education, Education, Education: Reforming England's Schools*. London: Biteback Publishing.

Ahmed, S. (1997) 'It's Just a Sun Tan, Isn't It?' Auto-biography as an Identificatory Practice. In H. Mirza (ed.), *Black British Feminism*. London: Routledge, pp. 153–67.

Ahmed, S. (1998) *Differences That Matter: Feminist Theory and Postmodernism*. Cambridge: Cambridge University Press.

Ahmed, S. (2008) Liberal Multiculturalism is the Hegemony – It's an Empirical Fact. A response to Slavoj Žižek. *Dark Matter* [Online]. Available at: www.darkmatter101.org/ site/2008/02/19/'liberal-multiculturalism-is-the-hegemony---its-an-empirical-fact'- a-response-to-slavoj-zize. [Accessed: 18 January 2017.]

Ahmed, S. (2010) *The Promise of Happiness*. Durham, NC: Duke University Press.

Ahmed, S. (2012) A willfulness archive. *Theory and Event* 15(3).

Alexander, C. (1996) *The Art of Being Black: The Creation of Black British Youth Identities*. Oxford: Clarendon Press.

Alexander, C. (2000) *The Asian Gang: Ethnicity, Identity, Masculinity*. Oxford: Berg.

Alexander, C. (2010) Rethinking race or denying racism? *Soundings: Policy Matters for Muslims in Britain, beyond Race and Multiculturalism*. Available at: http://soundings. mcb.org.uk/?p_76. [Accessed: 19 September 2013.]

Alexander, C., Chatterji, J. and Weekes-Bernard, D. (2012) *Making British Histories: Diversity and the National Curriculum.* London: Runnymede Trust.

Archer, L. and Francis, B. (2007) *Understanding Minority Ethnic Achievement: Race, Gender, Class and 'Success'.* London: Routledge.

Archer, L. Halsall, A. and Hollingworth, S. (2007) Inner-city femininities and education: 'race', class, gender and schooling in young women's lives. *Gender and Education* 19(5): 549–68.

Archer, L. and Yamashita, H. (2003a) Theorising inner-city masculinities: 'race', class, gender and education. *Gender and Education* 15(2): 115–32.

Archer, L. and Yamashita, H. (2003b) 'Knowing their limits?' Identities, inequalities and inner-city school leavers' post-16 aspirations. *Journal of Education Policy* 18(1): 53–69.

Arday, J. (2015) Considering Mentoring among BME Learners and Issues concerning Teacher Training: The Narratives of Students and Teachers. In C. Alexander, D. Weekes-Bernard and J. Arday (eds), *The Runnymede School Report: Race, Education and Inequality in Contemporary Britain.* London: Runnymede Trust, pp. 48–50.

Aston, J. (2012) Parents fail to prevent bid to turn Downhills primary school into academy. *Independent* [Online] 15 August. Available at: www.independent.co.uk/news/educa tion/education-news/parents-fail-to-prevent-bid-to-turn-downhills-primary-school-into-academy-8049955.html. [Accessed: 21 September 2013.]

Atkinson, P. and Helms, G. (eds) (2007) *Securing an Urban Renaissance: Crime, Community, and British Urban Policy.* Bristol: Policy.

Back, L. (1996) *New Ethnicities and Urban Culture: Racisms and Multiculture in Young Lives.* London: UCL Press.

Back, L. (2007) *The Art of Listening.* Oxford: Berg.

Back, L. (2009) Whiteness in the Dramaturgy of Racism. In P. Hill Collins and J. Solomos (eds), *Handbook of Race and Ethnic Studies.* London: Sage.

Baker, W. et al. (2014) Aspirations, education and inequality in England: insights from the Effective Provision of Pre-school, Primary and Secondary Education Project. *Oxford Review of Education*, September.

Ball, S. (1990) *Education, Inequality and School Reform: Values in Crisis!* London: King's College London.

Ball, S. (2003) *Class Strategies and the Education Market: The Middle Classes and Social Advantage.* Abingdon: RoutledgeFalmer.

Ball, S. (2007) *Education Plc: Understanding Private Sector Participation in Public Sector Education.* London: Routledge.

Ball, S. (2011) Back to the 19th century with Michael Gove's education bill. *Guardian* [Online] 31 January. Available at: www.theguardian.com/commentisfree/2011/jan/31/ michael-gove-education-bill. [Accessed: 21 September 2013.]

Ball, W. and Solomos, J. (eds) (1990) *Race and Local Politics.* Basingstoke: Macmillan.

Ball, S. and Vincent, C. (2006) *Childcare, Choice and Class Practices: Middle Class Parents and their Children.* London: Routledge.

Barnes, R. (1950) *A History of the Regiments and Uniforms of the British Army.* London: Seeley Service & Co.

Baynes, C. (2013) Headteachers' 'farce' proves Harris Federation consultation is sham, claim angry Roke Primary School parents. *Croydon Guardian* [Online] 25 April. Available at: www.croydonguardian.co.uk/news/localnews/10380638.Headteacher__ farce__proves_academy_consultation_is_sham__claim_angry_parents/. [Accessed: 21 September 2013.]

Beck, U., A. Giddens and S. Lash (1994) *Reflexive Modernisation: Politics, Tradition, and Aesthetics in the Modern Social Order.* Cambridge: Polity Press.

Beckett, F. (2007) *The Great City Academy Fraud.* London: Continuum.

Beechy, V. and Donald, J. (1985) *Subjectivity and Social Relations.* Milton Keynes: Open University Press.

Benn, M. (2011) *School Wars: The Battle for Britain's Education.* London: Verso.

Benson, M. and Jackson, E. (2012) Place-making and place maintenance: performativity, place and belonging among the middle classes. *Sociology* 47(4): 1–17.

Bentham, J. (1995), ed. M. Bozovic. *The Panopticon Writings.* London: Verso.

Berkeley, R. (2013) Foreword. In C. Alexander, V. Redclift and A. Hussain (eds), *The New Muslims.* London: Runnymede Trust, p. 2.

Berlant, L. (2011) *Cruel Optimism.* Durham, NC: Duke University Press.

Bernstein, B. (1970) Education cannot compensate for society. *New Society* 15(387): 344–7.

Bhabha, H. (1994) *The Location of Culture.* London: Routledge.

Bhattacharya, G. (2008) *Dangerous Brown Men: Exploiting Sex, Violence and Feminism in the War on Terror.* London: Zed Press.

Blair, T. (2006) Speech at Specialist Schools and Academies Trust Annual Conference, 30 November. Available at: www.number10.gov.uk/Page10514. [Accessed: 1 September 2009.]

Boffey, D. (2013) Academy chain under fire following revelation of payments made to bosses. *Guardian* [Online] 20 July. Available at: www.theguardian.com/education/2013/jul/20/education-school-academies-micael-gove. [Accessed: 25 May 2016.]

Boffey, D. (2015) Youth unemployment rate is worst for 20 years, compared with overall figure. *Guardian* [Online] 22 February. Available at: www.theguardian.com/society/2015/feb/22/youth-unemployment-jobless-figure. [Accessed: 19 August 2015.]

Boffey, D. and Mansell, W. (2015) Academy chain's fees for 'consultants' put schools programme under scrutiny. *Guardian* [Online] 24 October. Available at: www.theguardian.com/education/2015/oct/24/academy-chain-fees-griffin-accountability-trustees. [Accessed: 25 May 2016.]

Boffey, D. and Mansell, W. (2016) Are England's academies becoming a cash cow for business? *Guardian*, 12 June [Online]. Available at: www.theguardian.com/education/2016/jun/12/academy-schools-cash-cow-business. [Accessed: 29 July 2016.]

Boltanski, L. and Chiapello, E. (2007) *The New Spirit of Capitalism.* London: Verso.

Bondi, L. and Laurie, N. (eds) (2005) *Working the Spaces of Neoliberalism: Activism, Professionalisation and Incorporation.* Oxford: Blackwell.

Bonilla-Silva, E. (2014) *Racism without Racists: Color-blind Racism and the Persistence of Racial Inequality in the United States* (4th ed.). Lanham, MD: Rowman & Littlefield.

Bonnett, A. (1990) Anti-racism as a radical educational ideology in London and Tyneside. *Oxford Review of Education* 16(2): 255–69.

Booth, C. (1969 [1889]), ed. A. Fried and R.M. Elman. *Charles Booth's London.* London: Hutchinson.

Bourdieu, P. (1974) The School as a Conservative Force: Scholastic and Cultural Inequalities. In J. Eggleston (ed.), *Contemporary Research in the Sociology of Education.* London: Methuen, pp. 32–46.

Bourdieu, P. (1977a) Cultural Reproduction and Social Reproduction. In J. Karabel and A.H. Hasley (eds), *Contemporary Research in the Sociology of Education.* London: Methuen, pp. 487–511.

Bourdieu, P. (1977b) Symbolic Power. In D. Gleeson (ed.), *Identity and Structure: Issues in the Sociology of Education*. Driffield: Nafferton Books (Studies in Education), pp. 112–19.

Bourdieu, P. (1984) *Distinction: A Social Critique of the Judgement of Taste*. London: Routledge.

Bourdieu, P. (1986) The Forms of Capital. In J. Richardson (ed.), *Handbook of Theory and Research for the Sociology of Education*. New York: Greenwood, pp. 241–58.

Bourdieu, P. (1987) What makes a social class? On the theoretical and practical existence of groups. *Berkeley Journal of Sociology* 32: 1–17.

Bourdieu, P. (1992) *The Logic of Practice*. Cambridge: Polity Press.

Bourdieu, P. (1999) *The Weight of the World: Social Suffering in Contemporary Society*. Cambridge: Polity Press.

Bourdieu, P. (2000) *Pascalian Meditations*. Cambridge: Polity Press.

Bourdieu, P. (2010 [1984]) *Distinction: A Social Critique of the Judgement of Taste*. London: Routledge.

Bourdieu, P. and Wacquant, L. (1992) *An Invitation to Reflexive Sociology*. Chicago: University of Chicago Press.

Burgess, S. (2015) Aspirations, Language and Poverty: Attainment and Ethnicity. In C. Alexander, D. Weekes-Bernard and J. Arday (eds), *The Runnymede School Report: Race, Education and Inequality in Contemporary Britain*. London: Runnymede Trust, pp. 17–22.

Burrows, R. (2012) Living with the h-index? Metric assemblages in the contemporary academy. *Sociological Review* 60(2): 355–72.

Butcher, H., Law, I., Leach, R. and Mullard, M. (1990) *Local Government and Thatcherism*. London: Routledge.

Butler, T. and Robson, G. (2003) *London Calling: The Middle Classes and the Remaking of Inner London*. Oxford: Berg.

Byrne, B. (2006) In search of a 'good mix': 'race', class, gender and practices of mothering. *Sociology* 40(6): 1001–17.

Cameron, D. (2012) Speech to the Scottish Conservatives, Dumfries, 19 April. Available at: www.scottishconservatives.com/2012/04/david-cameron-speech-to-scottish-conserva tive-in-dumfries/. [Accessed: 18 August 2015.]

Campbell, D. and Marsh, S. (2016) Quarter of a million children receiving mental health care in England. *Guardian* [Online] 3 October. Available at: www.theguardian.com/society/2016/oct/03/quarter-of-a-million-children-receiving-mental-health-care-in-england. [Accessed: 28 October 2016.]

Carby, H. (1982) Schooling in Babylon. In Centre for Contemporary Cultural Studies (CCCS) (ed.), *The Empire Strikes Back: Race and Racism in 70s Britain*. London: Hutchinson, pp. 181–210.

Carey, J. (1992) *The Intellectuals and the Masses: Pride and Prejudice among the Literary Intelligentsia, 1880–1939*. London: Faber & Faber.

Carter, P. (2003) 'Black' cultural capital, status positioning, and schooling conflicts for low-income African American youth. *Social Problems* 50(1): 136–5.

Causa, O. and Johansson, A. (2010) Intergenerational Social Mobility in OECD Countries. *OECD Journal: Economic Studies*. Available at: www.oecd.org/eco/growth/49849281.pdf. [Accessed: 19 September 2013.]

CCCS (Centre for Contemporary Cultural Studies) (ed.) (1981) *Unpopular Education: Schooling and Social Democracy in England since 1944*. London: Hutchinson in association with the Centre for Contemporary Cultural Studies, University of Birmingham.

CCCS (Centre for Contemporary Cultural Studies) (ed.) (1982) *The Empire Strikes Back: Race and Racism in 70s Britain*. London: Hutchinson.

Chadderton, C. (2014) The militarisation of English schools: Troops to Teaching and the implications for Initial Teacher Education and race equality. *Race Ethnicity and Education* 17(3): 407–28.

Chitty, C. (2007) Editorial: the Blair legacy. *FORUM: For Promoting 3–19 Comprehensive Education* 49(3): 203–6.

Chomsky, N. and Foucault, M. (2006) *The Chomsky–Foucault Debate on Human Nature*. New York: The New Press.

Clayton, G. (2012) The alarming democratic void at the heart of our school system. *Guardian* [Online] 26 April. Available at: www.theguardian.com/commentisfree/2012/apr/26/democratic-void-school-system. [Accessed: 21 September 2013.]

Cole, M. (2004) 'Brutal and stinking' and 'difficult to handle': the historical and contemporary manifestations of racialisation, institutional racism, and schooling in Britain. *Race Ethnicity and Education* 7(1): 35–56.

Cooper, V. (2014) Bricks and mortality: the violence of coalition housing policy. *Criminal Justice Matters* 98: 1, 8–9. DOI: 10.1080/09627251.2014.984533

Cowen, D. (2004) From the American lebensraum to the American living room: class, sexuality, and the scaled production of 'domestic' intimacy. *Environment and Planning D: Society and Space* 22: 755–71.

Cox, C.B. and Dyson, A.E., eds (1969)*The Crisis in Education*. London: Critical Quarterly Society.

Crace, J. (2015) Nicky Morgan and the plan to turn the Department of Education into Fifa. *Guardian* [Online] 15 July. Available at: www.theguardian.com/politics/2015/jun/15/nicky-morgan-education-department-failing-schools-fifa-blatter. [Accessed: 18 August 2015.]

Crozier, G. (2005) 'There's a war against our children': black educational underachievement revisited. *British Journal of Sociology of Education* 26(5): 585–98.

Crozier, G. (2015) Black and Minority Ethnic Students on the Margins: Self-segregation or Enforced Exclusion? In C. Alexander, D. Weekes-Bernard and J. Arday (eds), *The Runnymede School Report: Race, Education and Inequality in Contemporary Britain*. London: Runnymede Trust, pp. 36–40.

Crozier, G. and Davies, J. (2008) 'The trouble is they don't mix': Self-segregation or enforced exclusion? Teachers' constructions of South Asian students. *Race, Ethnicity and Education* 11(3): 285–301.

Das, V. (2010) Listening to voices: an interview with Veena Das. *Altérités* 7(1): 136–45.

Davies, B. and Bansel, P. (2007) Neoliberalism and education. *International Journal of Qualitative Studies in Education* 20(3): 247–59.

Davies, G. (2012) Harris Federation could open free school on Croydon General Hospital site. *Croydon Advertiser* [Online] 9 November. Available at: www.croydonadvertiser.co.uk/Harris-Federation-open-free-school-Croydon/story-17275122-detail/story.html. [Accessed: 19 August 2015.]

DCFS (Department for Children, Schools and Families) (2009) *What are Academies?* London: DFCS. Available at: www.standards.dfes.gov.uk/academies/what_are_academies/?version. [Accessed 30 September 2009.]

Dean, J. (2009) *Democracy and Other Neoliberal Fantasies: Communicative Capitalism and Left Politics*. Durham, NC: Duke University Press.

de Certeau, M. (1988) *The Practice of Everyday Life*. Berkeley: University of California Press.

DfE (Department for Education) (2010) *The Importance of Teaching: The Schools White Paper 2010*. London: DfE.

DfE (Department for Education) (2015a) *Protecting Children from Radicalisation: The Prevent Duty* [Online] August 2015. Available at: www.gov.uk/government/publica tions/protecting-children-from-radicalisation-the-prevent-duty. [Accessed: 29 July 2016.]

DfE (Department for Education) (2015b) *Measures to help schools instil character in pupils announced* [Online] December 2014. Available at: www.gov.uk/government/news/measures-to-help-schools-instil-character-in-pupils-announced. [Accessed: 18 August 2015.]

DfE (Department for Education) (2016) *Open Academies and Academy Projects in Development* [Online] May 2016. London: DfE. Available at: www.gov.uk/government/publications/open-academies-and-academy-projects-in-development. [Accessed: 29 July 2016.]

Diawara, M. (1998) Homeboy cosmopolitan. *October* 83: 51–70.

Dorling, D. (2014) *Inequality and the 1%*. London: Verso.

Dreyfus, H. and Rabinow, P. (1982) *Michel Foucault: Beyond Structuralism and Hermeneutics*. Brighton: Harvester.

Engels, F. (2000 [1892]) *The Condition of the Working Class in England*. London: Swan Sonnenschein.

Essed, P. and Goldberg, D. (2002) Cloning cultures: the social injustices of sameness. *Ethnic and Racial Studies* 25(6): 1066–82.

Fanon, F. (2001[1961]) *The Wretched of the Earth*. London: Penguin.

Ferguson, A. (2001) *Bad Boys: Public Schools in the Making of Black Masculinity*. Ann Arbor: University of Michigan Press.

Fordham, S. (1996) *Blacked Out: Dilemmas of Race, Identity and Success at Capital High*. Chicago: Chicago University Press.

Foucault, M. (1991a [1977]) *Discipline and Punish: The Birth of the Prison*. Harmondsworth: Penguin.

Foucault, M. (1991b [1978]) Governmentality. In G. Burchell et al. (eds), *The Foucault Effect: Studies in Governmentality*. Chicago: University of Chicago Press, pp. 87–104.

Foucault, M. (2001 [1989]) *Madness and Civilization: A History of Insanity in the Age of Reason*. London: Routledge.

Foucault, M. (2002) *The Essential Works of Michel Foucault. Volume 3: Power*, ed. J. Faubion. London: Penguin.

Foucault, M. (2008) *The Birth of Biopolitics: Lectures at the Collège de France, 1978–79*. Basingstoke: Palgrave Macmillan.

Francis, B. (1999) Lads, lasses and (New) Labour: 14–16-year-old students' responses to the laddish behavior of boys and boys' underachievement debate. *British Journal of Sociology of Education* 20(3): 355–71.

Frosh, S., Phoenix, A. and Pattman, R. (2002) *Young Masculinities*. Basingstoke: Palgrave Macmillan.

Gane, N. (2012) The governmentalities of neoliberalism: panopticism, post-panopticism and beyond. *Sociological Review* 60(4): 611–34.

Gewirtz, S. (2001) Cloning the Blairs: New Labour's programme for the re-socialization of working-class parents. *Journal of Education Policy* 16(4): 365–78.

Gewirtz, S. (2002) *The Managerial School: Post-welfarism and Social Justice in Education*. London: Routledge.

Gidley, B. (2000) *The Proletarian Other*. Occasional Paper, CUCR, London: Goldsmiths online. Available at: www.gold.ac.uk/media/migrated/media/goldsmiths/depart-ments/researchcentres/centreforurbanandcommunityresearchcucr/pdf/gidley.pdf. [Accessed: 6 February 2017.]

Gill, D., Mayor, B., and Blair, M. (eds) (1992) *Racism and Education: Structures and Strategies*. London: Sage.

Gillborn, D. (1997) Racism and reform: new ethnicities/old inequalities? *British Educational Research Journal* 23(3): 345–60.

Gillborn, D. (2005) Education policy as an act of white supremacy: whiteness, critical race theory and education reform. *Journal of Education Policy* 20(4): 485–505.

Gillborn, D. (2008) *Racism and Education: Coincidence or Conspiracy?* New York: Routledge.

Gillborn, D. (2015) The Monsterisation of Race Equality: How Hate Became Honourable. In C. Alexander, D. Weekes-Bernard and J. Arday (eds), *The Runnymede School Report: Race, Education and Inequality in Contemporary Britain*. London: Runnymede Trust, pp. 6–10.

Gillborn, D. and Mirza, H. S. (2000) *Educational Inequality: Mapping Race, Class and Gender*. London: Ofsted.

Gillborn, D. and Youdell, D. (2000) *Rationing Education: Policy, Practice, Reform, and Equity*. Buckingham: Open University Press.

Gillies, V. (2007) *Marginalised Mothers: Exploring Working Class Experiences of Parenting*. London: Routledge.

Gilroy, P. (1992) The End of Anti-Racism. In J. Donald and A. Rattansi (eds), *'Race', Culture and Difference*. London: Sage.

Gilroy, P. (2000) *Between Camps: Nations, Culture and the Allure of Race*. London: Allen Lane.

Gilroy, P. (2002 [1987]) *There Ain't No Black in the Union Jack: The Cultural Politics of Race and Nation*. London: Routledge.

Gilroy, P. (2004) *After Empire: Melancholia or Convivial Culture?* London: Routledge.

Goldberg, D. (2001) *The Racial State*. Oxford: Blackwell.

Gorard, S. (2005) Academies as the 'future of schooling': is this an evidence-based policy? *Journal of Education Policy* 20(3): 369–77.

Gorard, S. (2009) What are Academies the answer to? *Journal of Education Policy* 24(1): 101–13.

Gordon, P. (1990) A Dirty War: the New Right and Local Authority Anti-Racism. In W. Ball and J. Solomos (eds), *Race and Local Politics*. Basingstoke: Macmillan, pp. 175–90.

Gove, M. (2010) *All pupils will learn our island story* [Speech] 5 October. Available at: http://conservative-speeches.sayit.mysociety.org/speech/601441. [Accessed: 6 February 2017.]

Greany, T. and Scott, J. (2014) *Conflicts of Interest in Academy Sponsorship Arrangements: A Report for the Education Select Committee*. London: Institute of Education, University of London and London Centre for Leadership in Learning.

Green, A. (1990) *Education and State Formation: The Rise of Education Systems in England, France and the USA*. Basingstoke: Palgrave Macmillan.

Gunaratnam, Y. (2003) *Researching 'Race' and Ethnicity: Methods, Knowledge and Power*. London: Sage.

Hall, C. (2002) *Civilising Subjects: Metropole and Colony in the English Imagination, 1830–1867*. Cambridge: Polity Press.

Hall, S. (1978) Racism and Reaction. In CRE (Commission for Racial Equality) (ed.), *Five*

Views of Multi-Racial Britain: Talks on Race Relations Broadcast by BBC TV. London: CRE, pp. 23–35.

Hall, S. (1980) *Drifting into a Law and Order Society*. London: Cobden Trust.

Hall, S. (1996) Race, Articulation and Societies Structured in Dominance. In H.A. Baker, Jr. et al. (eds), *Black British Cultural Studies: A Reader*. Chicago: University of Chicago Press, pp. 16–61.

Hall, S. et al. (1978) *Policing the Crisis: Mugging, the State, and Law and Order*. Basingstoke: Palgrave Macmillan.

Haraway, D. (1991) *Simians, Cyborgs, and Women: The Reinvention of Nature*. London: Free Association Books.

Harris, R. (2009) Language and social class: a Rosen contribution. *Changing English* 16(1): 81–91.

Harris, R., Schwab, I. and Whitman, L., eds (1990) *Language and Power*. London: Harcourt Brace Jovanovich/Harper Collins.

Harrison, A. (2011) Education Bill outlines shake-up for England's schools. *British Broadcasting Corporation* [Online] 27 January. Available at: www.bbc.co.uk/news/education-12287022. [Accessed: 18 August 2015.]

Harrison, A. (2012) Michael Gove: Academy school critics 'happy with failure'. *BBC News* [Online] 4 January. Available at: www.bbc.co.uk/news/education-16409940. [Accessed: 21 September 2013.]

Haylett, C. (2001) Illegitimate subjects? Abject whites, neoliberal modernisation, and middle-class multiculturalism. *Environment and Planning D: Society and Space* 19: 351–70.

Hollingworth, S. (2015) Social Mixing in Urban Schools: Racialising the 'Good Mix'. In C. Alexander, D. Weekes-Bernard and J. Arday (eds), *The Runnymede School Report: Race, Education and Inequality in Contemporary Britain*. London: Runnymede Trust, pp. 44–7.

Hollingworth, S. and Mansaray, A. (2012) Conviviality under the cosmopolitan canopy? Social mixing and friendships in an urban secondary school. *Sociological Research Online* 17(3). Available at: www.socresonline.org.uk/17/3/2.html. [Accessed: 13 June 2013.]

Hunt, T. (2014) *Speech to Character Conference*, Demos, London, 8 December. Available at: www.demos.co.uk/files/TristramHuntspeech.pdf. [Accessed 18 August 2015.]

Hutchings, M., Francis, B. and Kirby, R. (2015) *Chain Effects: The Impact of Academy Chains on Low Income Students*. London: Sutton Trust, July.

Jacobs, J.M. (1996) *The Edge of Empire: Postcolonialism and the City*. London: Routledge.

Joseph, I. and Gunter, A. (2011) *Gangs Revisited. What's a Gang and What's Race Got to Do with It?* London: Runnymede Trust. Available at: www.runnymedetrust.org/uploads/publications/pdfs/GangsRevisited(online)-2011.pdf. [Accessed 20 January 2017.]

Kahn, J. (2001) *Modernity and Exclusion*. London: Sage.

Keith, M. (2005) *After the Cosmopolitan? Multicultural Cities and the Future of Racism*. London: Routledge.

Keith, M. and Rogers, A. (1991) *Hollow Promises? Rhetoric and Reality in the Inner City*. London and New York: Mansell.

Kulz, C. (2015) *Mapping the Exclusion Process: Inequality, Justice and the Business of Education*. Communities Empowerment Network. Available at: www.cenlive.org/#/mapping-the-exclusion-process/4588543329. [Accessed: 18 August 2015.]

Kundnani, A. (2014) *The Muslims Are Coming! Islamophobia, Extremism, and the Domestic War on Terror*. London: Verso.

Lacey, C. (1974) Destreaming in a 'pressured' academic environment. In J. Eggleston (ed.), *Contemporary Research in the Sociology of Education*. London: Methuen.

Lander, V. (2011) Race, culture and all that: an exploration of the perspectives of White secondary student teachers about race equality issues in their initial teacher education. *Race, Ethnicity and Education* 14(3): 351–64.

Lander, V. (2015) 'Racism, It's Part of My Everyday Life': Black and Minority Ethnic Pupils' Experiences in a Predominantly White School. In C. Alexander, D. Weekes-Bernard and J. Arday (eds), *The Runnymede School Report: Race, Education and Inequality in Contemporary Britain*. London: Runnymede Trust, pp. 32–5.

Langer, P. (1984) Sociology – Four Images of Organized Diversity: Bazaar, Jungle, Organism and Machine. In L. Rodwin and R.M. Hollister (eds), *Cities of the Mind: Images and Themes of the City in Social Science*. London: Plenum Press.

Lareau, A. and Horvat, E. (1999) Moments of social inclusion and exclusion: race, class and cultural capital in home school relationships. *Sociology of Education* 72(1): 37–45.

Lawler, S. (1999) Getting out and getting away: Women's narratives of class mobility. *Feminist Review* 63(1): 3–24.

Lawler, S. (2000) *Mothering the Self: Mothers, Daughters, Subjects*. New York: Routledge.

Lawler, S. (2005) Disgusted subjects: the making of middle-class identities. *Sociological Review* 53(3): 429–46.

Lawrence, E. (1982) In the Abundance of Water, the Fool is Thirsty: Sociology and Black 'Pathology'. In CCCS (Centre for Contemporary Cultural Studies) (ed.), *The Empire Strikes Back: Race and Racism in 70s Britain*. London: Routledge in association with the University of Birmingham, pp. 93–141.

Lentin, A. (2008) After anti-racism? *European Journal of Cultural Studies* 11(3): 311–31.

Leonardo, Z. (2009) *Race, Whiteness, and Education*. New York: Routledge.

Levitas, R. (1998) *The Inclusive Society? Social Exclusion and New Labour*. Basingstoke: Palgrave Macmillan.

Li, Y. (2015) Ethnic Education and Labour Market Position in Britain (1972–2013). In C. Alexander, D. Weekes-Bernard and J. Arday (eds), *The Runnymede School Report: Race, Education and Inequality in Contemporary Britain*. London: Runnymede Trust, pp. 22–7.

Lipman, P. (2011) *The New Political Economy of Urban Education: Neoliberalism, Race, and the Right to the City*. New York: Routledge.

Local Government Association. (2014) *Councils foot multi-million pound bill for academies*. [Online] December 2014. Available at: www.local.gov.uk/media-releases/-/journal_content/56/10180/6794997/NEWS. [Accessed: 14 August 2015.]

Lorde, A. (1983) There Is No Hierarchy of Oppressions. In *Homophobia and Education*. New York: Council on Interracial Books for Children.

Mac An Ghaill, M. (1988) *Young, Gifted and Black: Student–Teacher Relations in the Schooling of Black Youth*. Milton Keynes: Open University Press.

Mac an Ghaill, M. (ed.) (1996) *Understanding Masculinities: Social Relations and Cultural Arenas*. Buckingham: Open University Press.

MacLeod, J. (2009) *Ain't No Makin' It: Aspirations and Attainment in a Low Income Neighbourhood*. Boulder, CO: Westview Press.

Maguire, M. et al. (2011) The ordinary school – what is it? *British Journal of Sociology of Education* 32(1): 1–16.

Mansell, W. (2014) Regional schools commissioners – leaked report on academy 'advocates'. *Guardian* [Online] 22 April. Available at: www.theguardian.com/education/2014/apr/22/regional-schools-commissioners-leaked-report. [Accessed: 18 August 2015.]

Mansell, W. (2015) Labour's policy on academies takes a tumble in Manchester. *Guardian.* [online] 24 November. Available at: www.theguardian.com/education/2015/nov/24/labour-policy-academies-school-manchester. [Accessed: 25 May 2016.]

Massey, D. (2011) Ideology and economics in the present moment. *Soundings* 48(11): 29–39.

Mayhew, H. (2008 [1861]) *London Labour and the London Poor.* Hertfordshire: Wordsworth Editions.

Mayhew, H. (1864) *German life and manners as seen in Saxony at the present day: with an account of village life--town life--fashionable life--married life--school and university life, &c., of Germany at the present.* London: W. H. Allen.

Maylor, U. (2009) 'They do not relate to Black people like us': Black teachers as role models for Black pupils, *Journal of Education Policy* 24(1): 1–21.

Maylor, U. (2014) *Teacher Training and the Education of Black Children: Bringing Color into Difference.* New York and London: Routledge.

Maylor, U. (2015) Challenging Cultures in Initial Teacher Education. In C. Alexander, D. Weekes-Bernard and J. Arday (eds), *The Runnymede School Report: Race, Education and Inequality in Contemporary Britain.* London: Runnymede Trust, pp. 27–32.

Maylor, U., Ross, A., Rollock, N. and Williams, K. (2006) *Black Teachers in London.* London: Greater London Authority.

McClintock, A. (1995) *Imperial Leather: Race, Gender, and Sexuality in the Colonial Contest.* New York: Routledge.

McRobbie, A. (2004) Notes on 'What Not To Wear' and Post-feminist Symbolic Violence. In L. Adkins and B. Skeggs (eds), *Feminism After Bourdieu.* Oxford: Blackwell.

McRobbie, A. (2009) *The Aftermath of Feminism: Gender, Culture and Social Change.* London: Sage.

McVeigh, B. (2000) *Wearing Ideology: State, Schooling and Self-presentation in Japan.* Oxford: Berg.

Miah, S. (2012) School de-segregation and the Politics of 'Forced Integration'. *Race and Class* 54(2): 26–39.

Miah, S. (2015) *Muslims, Schooling and the Question of Self-Segregation.* Basingstoke: Palgrave Macmillan.

Mills, C.W. (2000) *The Sociological Imagination.* Oxford: Oxford University Press.

Mirza, H.S. (1992) *Young, Female and Black.* London: Routledge.

Mirza, H.S. (2005) 'The More Things Change the More They Stay the Same': Assessing Black Underachievement 35 Years On. In B. Richardson (ed.), *Telling It Like It Is: How Our Schools Fail Black Children.* London: Bookmark Publications, pp. 111–19.

Mirza, H.S. (2009) *Race, Gender and Educational Desire: Why Black Women Succeed and Fail.* London: Routledge.

Mohanty, C. (2003) *Feminism Without Borders: Decolonizing Theory, Practicing Solidarity.* Durham, NC: Duke University Press.

Morgan, M. and Bennett, D. (2006) Getting off of black women's backs: love her or leave her alone. *Du Bois Review* (3)2: 485–502.

Mortimer, C. (2016) What Justine Greening says about social mobility – and what her voting record reveals about her. *Independent* [online] 17 July. Available at: www.independent.co.uk/news/uk/politics/justine-greening-social-mobility-education-welfare-cuts-schools-spending-a7141246.html. [Accessed: 5 February 2017.]

Nandy, A. (1988) *The Intimate Enemy: Loss and Recovery of Self under Colonialism.* Oxford: Oxford University Press.

Nayak, A. (2003) Through children's eyes: childhood, place and the fear of crime. *Geoforum* 34: 303–15.

Nayak, A. (2006a) After race: ethnography, race and post-race theory. *Ethnic and Racial Studies* 29(3): 411–30.

Nayak, A. (2006b) Displaced masculinities: chavs, youth and class in the post-industrial city. *Sociology* 40(5): 813–31.

Nayak, A. and Kehily, M. (2008) *Gender, Youth and Culture: Young Masculinities and Feminities*. Basingstoke: Palgrave Macmillan.

Oakes, J. (1985) *Keeping Track: How Schools Structure Inequality*. New Haven, CT: Yale University Press.

Pearce, S. (2014) Dealing with racist incidents: what do beginning teachers learn from schools? *Race, Ethnicity and Education* 17(3): 388–406.

Phoenix, A. (1991) *Young Mothers?* Cambridge: Polity Press.

Pink, S. (2001) *Doing Visual Ethnography: Images, Media and Representation in Research*. London: Sage.

Porter, T. (1995) *Trust in Numbers: The Pursuit of Objectivity in Science and Public Life*. Princeton, NJ: Princeton University Press.

Pratt, M. (1992) *Imperial Eyes: Travel Writing and Transculturation*. London and New York: Routledge.

Pring, R. and Walford, G., eds (1997) *Affirming the Comprehensive Ideal*. London: Falmer.

Puwar, N. (2004) *Space Invaders: Race, Gender and Bodies out of Place*. Oxford: Berg.

Rabinow, P. (1984) *The Foucault Reader*. Harmondsworth: Penguin.

Rapley, T. (2007) The Art(fulness) of Open-ended Interviewing: Some Considerations on Analysing Interviews. In P. Akinson (ed.), *Handbook of Ethnography*. London: Sage.

Rattansi, A. (1992) Changing the subject? Racism, culture and education. In J. Donald and A. Rattansi (eds), *'Race', Culture and Difference*. London: Sage, pp. 11–43.

Reay, D. (1998) *Class Work: Mothers' Involvement in Their Children's Primary Schooling*. London: UCL Press.

Reay, D. (2006) The zombie stalking English schools: social class and educational inequality. *British Journal of Educational Studies* 54(3): 288–307.

Reay, D. (2007) 'Unruly places': inner-city comprehensives, middle-class imaginaries and working-class children. *Urban Studies* 44(7): 1191–201.

Reay, D. (2008) Tony Blair, the promotion of the 'active' educational citizen, and middle-class hegemony. *Oxford Review of Education* 34(6): 639–50.

Reay, D. (2013) Social mobility, a panacea for austere times: tales of emperors, frogs, and tadpoles. *British Journal of Sociology of Education* 34(5–6): 660–77.

Reay, D., Crozier, G., and James, D. (2011) *White Middle Class Identities and Urban Schooling*. Basingstoke: Palgrave Macmillan.

Reay, D. et al. (2007) 'A darker shade of pale?' Whiteness, the middle classes and multi-ethnic inner city schooling. *Sociology* 41(6): 1041–60.

Reynolds, T. (2005) *Caribbean Mothers: Identity and Experience in the U.K.* London: Tufnell Press.

Rollock, N. (2014) Race, class and the 'harmony of dispositions'. *Sociology* 48(3): 445–51.

Rollock, N. et al. (2011) The public identities of the black middle classes: managing race in public spaces. *Sociology* 45(6): 1078–93.

Rollock, N., Gillborn, D., Vincent, C. and Ball, S. (2015) *The Colour of Class: The Educational Strategies of the Black Middle Classes*. London: Routledge.

Rose, N. (1998) *Inventing Ourselves: Psychology, Power and Personhood*. Cambridge: Cambridge University Press.

Sahota, R. (2012) We dared to resist the forced academy conversion of Downhills and were fired. *Guardian* [Online] 20 March. Available at: www.theguardian.com/com mentisfree/2012/mar/20/downhills-school-forced-conversion-academy. [Accessed: 18 August 2015.]

Saul, J.R. (2009) *The Collapse of Globalism*. London: Atlantic Books.

Savage, M. (2000) *Class Analysis and Social Transformation*. Buckingham: Open University Press.

Savage, M. (2003) Review essay: a new class paradigm? *British Journal of Sociology of Education* 24(4): 535–41.

Savage, M., Bagnall, G. and Longhurst, B. (2001) Ordinary, ambivalent and defensive: class identities in the northwest of England. *Sociology* 35(4): 875–92.

Savage, M., Devine, F., Cunningham, N., Taylor, M., Li, Y., Hjelbrekke, J., Le Roux, B., Friedman, S. and Miles, A. (2013). A new model of social class? Findings from the BBC's Great British Class Survey experiment. *Sociology* 47(2): 219–50.

Sewell, T. (1997) *Black Masculinities and Schooling: How Black Boys survive Modern Schooling*. Stoke on Trent: Trentham Books.

Shain, F. (2011) *The New Folk Devils*. Stoke on Trent: Trentham Books.

Shields, R. (1991) *Places on the Margin: Alternative Geographies of Modernity*. London: Routledge.

Shore, C. and Wright, S. (2000) Coercive Accountability: The Rise of Audit Culture in Higher Education. In M. Strathern (ed.), *Audit Cultures: Anthropological Studies in Accountability, Ethics, and the Academy*. London and New York: Routledge, pp. 57–89.

Sivanandan, A. (1985) RAT and the degradation of black struggle. *Race and Class* 26(1):1–33.

Skeggs, B. (1997) *Formations of Class and Gender: Becoming Respectable*. London: Sage.

Skeggs, B. (2004) *Class, Self, Culture*. London: Routledge.

Skeggs, B. (2007) Feminist Ethnography. In P. Akinson (ed.), *Handbook of Ethnography*. London: Sage, pp. 426–42.

Skeggs, B. and Loveday, V. (2012) Struggles for value: value practices, injustice, judgment, affect and the idea of class. *British Journal of Sociology* (63)3: 473–90.

Skeggs, B., Thumin, N. and Wood, H. (2008) 'Oh goodness, I am watching reality TV': how methods make class in audience research. *European Journal of Cultural Studies* 11(5): 5–20.

Slavin, R.E. (1987) Ability grouping and student achievement in elementary schools: a best evidence synthesis. *Review of Educational Research* 57(3): 293–336.

Smith, H.J. (2013) A critique of the teaching standards in England (1984–2012): discourses of equality and maintaining the status quo. *Journal of Education Policy* 28(4): 1–22.

Solomos, J. and Back, L. (1996) *Racism and Society*. Basingstoke: Macmillan.

Spivak, G.C. (1988) Can the Subaltern Speak? In C. Nelson and L. Grossberg (eds), *Marxism and the Interpretation of Culture*. Urbana: University of Illinois Press, pp. 271–313.

Squires, P. and Stephen, D. (2005) *Rougher Justice: Anti-Social Behaviour and Young People*. Cullompton: Willan Publishing.

Stedman-Jones, G. (1971) *Outcast London: A Study in the Relationship between Classes in Victorian Society*. Oxford: Clarendon Press.

Steedman, C. (2000) Enforced Narratives: Stories of Another Self. In T. Cosslett, C. Lury and P. Summerfield (eds), *Feminism and Autobiography: Texts, Theories, Methods*. London: Routledge.

Stoler, A. (1995) *Race and the Education of Desire: Foucault's History of Sexuality and the Colonial Order of Things*. Durham, NC: Duke University Press.

Stoler, A. (2002) *Carnal Knowledge and Imperial Power: Race and the Intimate in Colonial Rule*. Berkeley: University of California Press.

Strand, S. (2011) The limits of social class in explaining ethnic gaps in educational attainment. *British Educational Research Journal* 37(2): 197–229.

Tomlinson, S. (1993) The Multicultural Task Group: The Group That Never Was. In A. King and M. Reis (eds), *The Multicultural Dimension of the National Curriculum*. London: Falmer, pp. 21–31.

Tomlinson, S. (2008) *Race and Education: Policy and Politics in Britain*. Maidenhead: Open University Press/McGraw-Hill.

Troyna, B. (1991) Underachievers or underrated? The experience of pupils of South Asian origin in a secondary school. *British Educational Research Journal* 17(4): 361–76.

Troyna, B. (1993) Underachiever or misunderstood? A reply to Roger Gomm. *British Educational Research Journal* 19(2): 167–74.

Troyna, B. (2002) Can You See the Join? An Historical Analysis of Multicultural and Antiracist Education Policies. In D. Gill, B. Mayor and M. Blair (eds), *Racism and Education: Structures and Strategies*. London: Sage.

Turner, V. (1982) *From Ritual to Theatre: The Human Seriousness of Play*. New York: Performing Arts Journal Publications.

Turner, V. (1988) *The Anthropology of Performance*. New York: PAJ Publications.

Tyler, I. (2008) Chav mum chav scum. *Feminist Media Studies* 8(1): 17–34.

Vaughan, R. and Marley, D. (2010) Reform rushed through using anti-terror rules. *Times Educational Supplement* [Online] 15 July. Available at: www.tes.com/article.aspx?story code=6050381. [Accessed: 18 August 2015.]

Vincent, C., Rollock, N., Ball, B. and Gillborn, D. (2012) Being strategic, being watchful, being determined: black middle-class parents and schooling. *British Journal of Sociology of Education* 33(3): 337–54.

Walford, G. (1991) City Technology Colleges: A Private Magnetism? In G. Walford (ed.), *Private Schooling: Tradition, Change and Diversity*. London: Paul Chapman.

Walkerdine, V. (2003) Reclassifying upward mobility: femininity and the neo-liberal subject. *Gender and Education* (15)3: 237–48.

Walkerdine, V. and Lucey, H. (1989) *Democracy in the Kitchen: Regulating Mothers and Socialising Daughters*. London: Virago.

Willis, P. (1977) *Learning to Labour: How Working Class Kids get Working Class Jobs*. Farnborough: Saxon House.

Wolfe, D. (2015) *A can of worms: David Wolfe's blog for anyone interested in academies or free schools and the law* [Online] September 2011. Available at: http://davidwolfe.org. uk/wordpress/. [Accessed: 14 August 2015.]

Wright, A. (2012) Fantasies of empowerment: mapping neoliberal discourse in the coalition government's schools policy. *Journal of Education Policy* 27(3): 279–94.

Wright, C. et al. (1998) Masculinised discourses within education and the construction of black male identities amongst African Caribbean youth. *British Journal of Sociology of Education* 19(1): 75–87.

Yosso, T. (2005) Whose culture has capital? A critical race theory discussion of community cultural wealth. *Race, Ethnicity and Education* 8(1): 69–91.

Youdell, D. (2006) *Impossible Bodies, Impossible Selves: Exclusions and Student Subjectivities*. Dordrecht: Springer.

Young, J. (1999) *The Exclusive Society: Social Exclusion, Crime and Difference in Late Modernity*. London: Sage.

Zirkel, S. et al. (2011) Isn't that what 'those kids' need? Urban schools and the master narrative of the 'tough, urban principal'. *Race Ethnicity and Education* 14(2): 137–1.

Index

individuality and individualism 62, 117, 123
inequality viii, 95, 109, 117, 166, 169–70, 175
  cultural 85
  social 164
institutional discourses 3
interviews, use of 35

Jacobs, Jane M. 21–2, 167

Labour Party 8, 16, 47, 88, 164, 174–5
Lander, Vini 31, 95, 97
Lawler, S. 28, 88
league tables viii–ix, 161
  international 15
learning support unit (LSU) 122–6, 130, 146–7
liberalism 27, 88, 117
liminal space 48, 50
'line-up' 39
local education authorities (LEAs) 6–12, 171
Lorde, Audre 31
'loud' students 98
Loveday, V. 174
Lucey, H. 150

Mac an Ghaill, Máirtín x, 17
McClintock, Anne 21
McRobbie, Angela 91–2, 162–3
management
  structure of 114, 141–2
  style of 62, 74–7
managerialism 7
market mechanisms 55, 136
marketisation 7, 15, 18, 63, 138, 141, 167, 170–3
Marxism 25
Massey, Doreen 27, 172–3
May, Theresa 14, 175
Mayhew, Henry 22
Maylor, U. 96
meritocracy vii–x, 1, 3, 70, 105–8
metrics 55
'middle-classness' 25–8, 169, 174
Mirza, Heidi Safia vii–x, 17, 23–4
mixed-race students 123, 127–8
mixing, social 101–3, 108, 170
Mohanty, C. 69
Moore, Andrew 60, 166–7
moral panics 9
Morgan, Nicky 13–15

multi-academy trusts 10–11
multiculturalism 8, 16, 31, 82, 88, 93, 99, 103–4, 108, 169–70

Nash, Lord 13–14
national curriculum 6–7
National Governors' Association 12
'naughty step' treatment 146
Nayak, Anoop 35, 91, 123, 130, 133, 168
neoliberalism ix–x, 2–3, 10, 27–8, 55–6, 88, 105, 117, 141, 168–75
'nerds' 100–1, 123
New Right ideology 8–9
'no excuses' culture 37, 109

Obama, Barack vii, 60, 166
Office for Standards in Education (Ofsted) viii, 4, 13, 44–5, 139–40
'otherness' 151, 154, 167
oversubscription 112
Oxbridge candidates 102, 112

panoptic practices 38, 44, 56, 69, 171
parent–teacher association (PTA) 135, 139–40
parental involvement 46, 62–3, 83, 137–40, 165
parenting practices 20, 28, 60, 149–50, 155
parents' evenings 154–6
performance management 51–5
permissiveness
  at home 149
  at school 90–1
la perruque 120–1
photo diaries 34
playgrounds
  enclosure of 47
  groups of students in 97–9
policing 98
poorer children 16, 19, 21, 62
'posh' people 100–1, 104, 140
power of school heads 62
preferential treatment for some students 108
'Prevent' duty 30
pride in the school
  of parents 63
  of students 65, 78, 167
  of teachers 78, 80, 150
prisons 130
private schools 71, 140